MIGRANT WORK BY ANOTHER NAME

Differential Inclusion and Precarity in Canada's International Mobility Program

Migrant Work by Another Name explores the complexities of Canada's evolving international migration and employment policy landscape. It critically examines the shift towards "mobility" programs under the recently inaugurated International Mobility Program (IMP). This shift occurs alongside the contraction of certain streams within Canada's long-standing Temporary Foreign Worker Program. The book investigates the implications of policy changes, influenced at once by public outcry over migrant worker exploitation and persistent demands for labour in the face of qualitative labour shortages in high-income countries like Canada. Grounded in a decolonial feminist political economy approach, Leah F. Vosko employs a mixed methods analysis to contrast the narrative of "mobility" with the persistent realities of precarity among transnational workers.

The book features in-depth case studies of the three largest IMP subprograms – Working Holiday, Post-graduation Work Permit, and Spousal Work Permit programs – revealing how these initiatives, despite being touted as promoting mobility, provide for temporary migrant work by another name and perpetuate precarity. This critical perspective challenges the notion of progress in contemporary migration policies, shedding light on the ongoing challenges faced by transnational workers in Canada.

LEAH F. VOSKO, FRSC, is a distinguished research professor of political economy at York University.

(Studies in Comparative Political Economy and Public Policy)

Studies in Comparative Political Economy and Public Policy

Editors: Michael Howlett, David Laycock (Simon Fraser University), and Stephen Mcbride (McMaster University)

Studies in Comparative Political Economy and Public Policy is designed to showcase innovative approaches to political economy and public policy from a comparative perspective. While originating in Canada, the series will provide attractive offerings to a wide international audience, featuring studies with local, subnational, cross-national, and international empirical bases and theoretical frameworks.

Editorial Advisory Board

For a list of books published in the series, see page 217.

Migrant Work by Another Name

Differential Inclusion and Precarity in Canada's International Mobility Program

LEAH F. VOSKO

UNIVERSITY OF TORONTO PRESS
Toronto Buffalo London

© University of Toronto Press 2025
Toronto Buffalo London
utppublishing.com
Printed in Canada

ISBN 978-1-4875-6607-4 (cloth)   ISBN 978-1-4875-6609-8 (EPUB)
ISBN 978-1-4875-6780-4 (paper)   ISBN 978-1-4875-6608-1 (PDF)

Library and Archives Canada Cataloguing in Publication

Title: Migrant work by another name : differential inclusion and precarity in Canada's International Mobility Program / Leah F. Vosko.
Names: Vosko, Leah F., author
Series: Studies in comparative political economy and public policy.
Description: Series statement: Studies in comparative political economy and public policy | Includes bibliographical references and index.
Identifiers: Canadiana (print) 20250144166 | Canadiana (ebook) 20250144247 | ISBN 9781487566074 (cloth) | ISBN 9781487567804 (paper) | ISBN 9781487566081 (PDF) | ISBN 9781487566098 (EPUB)
Subjects: LCSH: International Mobility Program (Canada) – Evaluation. | LCSH: Foreign workers – Employment – Government policy – Canada – Evaluation. | LCSH: Labor mobility – Government policy – Canada – Evaluation.
Classification: LCC HD8108.5.A2 V67 2025 | DDC 331.6/20971 – dc23

Cover design: Val Cooke
Cover image: "Doorway" by Floris Flam (©2016 Floris Flam; photo by Paul Seder)

We wish to acknowledge the land on which the University of Toronto Press operates. This land is the traditional territory of the Wendat, the Anishnaabeg, the Haudenosaunee, the Métis, and the Mississaugas of the Credit First Nation.

This book has been published with the help of a grant from the Federation for the Humanities and Social Sciences, through the Awards to Scholarly Publications Program, using funds provided by the Social Sciences and Humanities Research Council of Canada.

University of Toronto Press acknowledges the financial support of the Government of Canada, the Canada Council for the Arts, and the Ontario Arts Council, an agency of the Government of Ontario, for its publishing activities.

Canada Council   Conseil des Arts
for the Arts   du Canada

ONTARIO ARTS COUNCIL
CONSEIL DES ARTS DE L'ONTARIO
an Ontario government agency
un organisme du gouvernement de l'Ontario

Funded by the   Financé par le
Government   gouvernement
of Canada   du Canada

Canadä

In memory of Phyllis Vosko, whose advocacy for full and meaningful inclusion of all newcomers helped inspire this work, and for Morry Kernerman, in celebration of his centenary.

Contents

Tables and Figures

Tables

Appendix Tables

Figures

Acronyms

ASP	Attestation de Spécialisation Professionnelle (Certificate of Vocational Specialization)
ATIP	Access to Information and Privacy
CEEDD	Canadian Employer and Employee Dynamics Database
CEGEP	Collège d'Enseignement Général et Professionnel (General and Vocational College)
CUSMA	Canada–United States–Mexico Agreement
DEP	Diplôme d'Études Professionnelles (Vocational Study Diploma)
ESDC	Employment and Social Development Canada
GAC	Global Affairs Canada
GDP	Gross Domestic Product
IEC	International Experience Canada
IMP	International Mobility Program
IRCC	Immigration, Refugees and Citizenship Canada
IRPA	*Immigration and Refugee Protection Act*
LMIA	Labour Market Impact Assessment
NAFTA	North American Free Trade Agreement
NIEAP	Non-Immigrant Employment Authorization Program
NOC	National Occupational Classification
OECD	Organisation for Economic Co-operation and Development
OINP	Ontario Immigrant Nomination Program
SAWP	Seasonal Agricultural Worker Program
TEER	Training, Education, Experience and Responsibilities
TFW	Temporary foreign worker
TFWP	Temporary Foreign Worker Program
TRPR	Temporary Resident to Permanent Resident Pathway

Preface and Acknowledgments

This book was born out of my observation of a disjunct, in the late-2010s, between Canada's apparent efforts to reduce and overhaul its long-standing reliance on workers migrating internationally under exploitative terms and conditions via its Temporary Foreign Worker Program (TFWP) and my interactions with workers on the ground. Despite the declining number of work permitholders under the TFWP, migrant workers were seemingly coming to play an important role in a greater, rather than a lesser, number of industries and occupations. I wanted to know what was happening in practice – whether the decline of the TFWP was fact or fiction – and to learn more about dynamics of continuity and change at a policy level. At the time, the International Mobility Program (IMP) was a little-known moniker, coming into more widespread use around 2014. In the decade to follow, however, programs under its auspices grew markedly and came to encompass more temporary work permitholders than under the TFWP. As such, the IMP now represents the dominant program through which transnational workers migrate to Canada.

I arrived at this conclusion by taking a series of untrodden paths. In the process, in recruiting subjects, analysing unexamined administrative data, and searching for and piecing together underexplored policies, guidelines, and protocols, I benefited from the support of five exceptional student research assistants, several of whom have moved on to major projects and posts of their own: Cynthia Spring and Keelin Griffin, who enthusiastically supported this endeavour from the get-go and helped me see this book through to publication; Shreya Ghimire and Sanjana Rahman, whose help was vital in transcribing and coding interviews; and Seulsam Lee, whose deft and careful work with data updates in the final leg of the process was immensely valuable. I count myself extremely lucky to play a small part in the careers of these exemplary trainees.

I also owe my thanks to collaborators on related subjects for giving me the space to pursue this project and for offering constructive comments when I needed them most. For our engaging discussions and exchanges, I am grateful to Eric Tucker and Sarah Marsden, with whom I have learned a great deal about the dearth of effective mechanisms for enforcing migrant workers' paper rights, Andrea Noack for her incisive insights about data analysis, Tanya Basok, who has taught me so much about interviewing migrant workers, and Christina Gabriel and Valerie Preston, both of whom offered feedback on the proposal for the project from which this book emerged.

At York University, I am extremely fortunate to have close colleagues that consistently support me in my research – thank you to Amar Bhatia, Tania Das Gupta, Luin Goldring, Adrian Smith, Mark Thomas, Ethel Tungohan, and Sanober Umar for asking great questions at critical moments. I am similarly privileged to work and have worked with fantastic doctoral and postdoctoral trainees who keep me on my toes by raising issues emerging from their work even though their topics differ from my own – thanks especially to Nicole Bernhardt, Tyler Chartrand, Tka Pinnock, Rajdeep Sidhu, and Marion Werner.

I also owe a debt to colleagues from afar, especially to Shannon Gleeson, Beth Lyon, and Kate Griffith from Cornell's School of Industrial and Labor Relations and Law School, who hosted me at key moments in the writing process, as well as to my Ithaca College colleague Leigh Ann Vaughn for actively listening to me rehearse many of the arguments in these pages, to Dalia Gesualdi for engaging me in stimulating conversations, to members of the International Labor Organization's Expert Working Group on Temporary Labour Migration, especially Christiane Kuptsch and Fabiola Mieres, who gathered together scholars and analysts who helped me see the significance of Canada's IMP in global context, and to all the researchers involved in the Social Sciences and Humanities Research Council of Canada (SSHRC) "Liberating Migrant Labour?" Research Partnership, for encouraging me to transform aspects of the exploration in this book into a comparative project attentive to not only external but settler-colonial dynamics at the crux of the rise of international mobility programs within and beyond Canada.

Transnational workers – including those participating in the study informing this book – are a consistent source of inspiration for me. So too are organizations, and individuals that represent them, with whom I have long engaged – most centrally, the Workers' Action Centre, Justicia for Migrant Workers, the Immigrant Workers' Centre and the United Food and Commercial Workers Union, four organizations at the forefront of raising awareness of the myriad workplace and residency problems confronting transnational workers.

From government, I am also grateful to Immigration Refugees and Citizenship Canada (IRCC) and Statistics Canada, particularly to the policy and data analysts whose recognition of the value of independent in-depth empirical study of the IMP enabled me to obtain access to administrative data vital to creating a portrait of its core subprograms.

Thanks too to three anonymous reviewers and the guidance of Daniel Quinlan, acquisitions editor extraordinaire, along with the staff at University of Toronto Press, Linda Bucay Harari, and the SSHRC for its critical financial support via an Insight Grant.

And then there are my friends and family, who never fail to show their interest in my scholarship – special thanks to my dear friends May, Dan, Kathy, Elise, Renuka, Jacky, Barbara, Brenda, Deborah, Dorothea, Alicia, and Peter – and to my extended family – especially, my sister Judith and her family (David, Bram, and Simon), and the Kernerman crew, particularly Morry Kernerman, whose centenary I wish to honour through the publication of this book.

As always, the loves of my life (big and getting bigger), Gerald and Sydney, cheered me on at every stage of the research and writing process, always took a keen interest in the stories I told about my research, and consistently reminded me not to lose sight of the end game.

This book honours the life of my mother Phyllis, who devoted her career, as an English as a second language teacher for adults, to advocating for newcomers and taught me the value of hospitality and full and meaningful inclusion.

MIGRANT WORK BY ANOTHER NAME

Chapter One

Introduction

Workers migrating for employment internationally are an important source of labour in high-income receiving states. In Canada, historically, many have entered via the long-standing Temporary Foreign Worker Program (TFWP) and its precursors, filling jobs unattractive to citizens and permanent residents, whose exploitive conditions are well-documented. Yet, despite the vital role of workers enrolled in the TFWP in addressing qualitative labour shortages (i.e., demands for workers to fill precarious jobs in occupations and industries undesirable to citizen-workers), their presence is routinely met by protectionism (i.e., measures emphasizing the need to preserve so-called Canadian jobs for Canadians) (Marsden, Tucker, & Vosko 2021a). In a move reflecting this protectionist impulse and formally recognizing the need to limit exploitation, starting in 2014 the Government of Canada began to reduce and more strictly regulate temporary *migrant* work programs (cast typically as economically *necessary* migration often characterized by heightened forms of exploitation and employer control) under the TFWP.[1] At the same time, it expanded avenues for *mobility* (cast typically as economically *beneficial* migration assumed to foster a greater degree of agency and more favourable conditions) under the International Mobility Program (IMP).[2] This dual strategy continues to inform Canada's approach to temporary labour migration.

Challenging the migration/mobility distinction, this book explores and critiques new directions and continuities in international migration for employment on a temporary basis to Canada in the twenty-first century through a study of the IMP. From a policy perspective, the TFWP is assumed to involve *migrant* workers compelled to take up employment abroad on an ostensibly temporary basis (Rajkumar et al. 2012), an increasingly large proportion of whom labour under exploitative conditions in industries such as agriculture.[3] The IMP, in contrast, is said to encompass *mobile* workers, such as specialized knowledge workers and recent post-secondary graduates, who, on account of their socially recognized skills and qualifications, opt to take advantage of less temporally fixed employment opportunities overseas fostered by conditions established in international agreements promoting reciprocity and competitiveness (ESDC 2014, 1). In light of the IMP's rapid expansion, I explore how opportunities for mobility under its auspices operate and their effects, probing the degree to which the program's inauguration marks a departure from conditions long associated with migrant work in Canada. I pursue this investigation by way of case studies of the three largest free-standing IMP subprograms, collectively comprising more than 60 per cent of work permitholders under the IMP umbrella in 2023[4] – the Working Holiday program, representing the largest component of International Experience Canada (IEC); the Post-Graduation Work Permit program; and the Spousal Work Permit program. As products of an (im)migration policy framework that sorts participants in a manner contributing to different degrees of inclusion, I argue that these fast-growing "mobility programs" provide for temporary migrant work by another name and perpetuate precarity – or the simultaneous experience of labour market insecurity and insecurity of presence – among work permitholders in the process. By facilitating access to temporary residency and employment on "non-work" bases in the face of qualitative labour shortages, the youth mobility-oriented Working Holiday program; the Post-graduation Work Permit program, targeting educational migrants' application of newly attained credentials; and the Spousal Work Permit program, supporting family reunification, contribute to cultural-exchange, probationary, and relational precarity respectively. These forms of precarity are experienced acutely by those from countries of origin subject historically to racialized barriers to entry erected via nationality, and to women confronting gender norms, heightening racialized gendered labour market insecurity.

1. Canada's Two Programs Facilitating Employment among International Migrants on a Temporary Basis: Addressing Qualitative Labour Shortages?

Canada's approach to facilitating employment among transnational workers evolved considerably in the late 1990s and early 2000s.[5] Whereas in the latter half of the twentieth century bilateral arrangements and state brokerage dominated under the TFWP, around the turn of the twenty-first century immigration and trade policy enabled employers to draw increasingly upon transnational workers under novel arrangements informed by "free trade principles," such as "reciprocity," and "competitiveness" (Pellerin 2008). With the creation of the World Trade Organization and, closer to home, the North American Free Trade Agreement (NAFTA), the actors and logics involved in recruiting, placing, and employing transnational workers changed profoundly such that employers (including transnational corporations seeking to transfer employees seamlessly) were empowered in selection processes (see Chapter 2).

It is in this context that Canada's TFWP took its current form. Enabled by the *Immigration and Refugee Protection Act* (IRPA) (2001) and its associated regulations, the TFWP permits host state employers to hire migrants on a temporary basis to fill positions that they demonstrate cannot be filled domestically. Such positions include vacancies that reflect qualitative labour shortages, a term used herein to convey the constructed nature of many such gaps, building upon Sassen's (1981) formative conception of scarcities of structurally disempowered workers. Sharma (2006, 19; see also 2007) also uses this term in an analysis of Canada's Non-Immigrant Employment Authorization Program (NIEAP), the earliest precursor to the TFWP; she demonstrates that the NIEAP marked a major shift in Canadian immigration policy such that more "(im)migrants recruited for the Canadian labour market came to enter as 'migrant workers' rather than as 'landed immigrants' with permanent residency rights," justified on the basis of addressing "employer-identified" labour shortages. Expanding upon the insights of such scholars, I utilize qualitative labour shortages herein to encompass positions in industries and occupations in which precarious jobs are common, that is, to include 3-D (i.e., dirty, dangerous, and degrading – as well as poorly paid) positions undesirable to citizen- and permanent resident-workers.

Large TFWP subprograms operate via agreements that Canada negotiates with specific sending states and use a restrictive work permit (i.e., often employer-specific and time-limited) and a Labour Market Impact Assessment (LMIA) overseen by Canada's national labour ministry (Employment and Social Development Canada, or ESDC). Distinctly, the embrace of trade principles led to the birth of the IMP, designed officially to facilitate entry under international agreements promoting national competitiveness and/or reciprocity; with approximately ninety subprograms "whose primary objective is to advance Canada's broad economic and cultural national interest," professionals and skilled workers are the IMP's official targets (ESDC 2014, 1). Many subprograms of the IMP, such as those geared to educational migrants prefiguring the Post-graduation Work Permit program, were once distinguished only as subprograms of the TFWP exempt from labour market tests due to their association with reciprocity (Boyd, Taylor, & Delaney 1986, 931). Other IMP subprograms, of more recent origin and tied to national competitiveness, such as those devoted to intercompany transferees, emerged from the implementation of agreements, such as NAFTA (1994) (now known as the Canada–United States–Mexico Agreement, or CUSMA), and expanded with the General Agreement on Trade in Services of 1995. In 2014, such LMIA-exempt categories, associated with permits of longer duration, were grouped together under a separate umbrella program – the IMP – aiming "to advance Canada's broad economic and cultural national interest, rather than filling particular jobs" (ESDC 2014, 1). Thus, the IMP represents a retroactive reclassification and consolidation of a particular subset of pre-existing TFWP subprograms, supplemented by a subset of new subprograms, reinforcing Canada's iteration of the mobility side of the global mobility / migration policy construct.

As this dualistic policy construction cohered, from the early 2000s to the late 2010s, Canada experienced considerable growth in international migration for employment on a temporary basis. Taken together, permitholders under both the IMP and the TFWP grew from a total of 132,215 in 2002 to 945,650 in 2023 (Figure 1.1). This growth was driven by the expansion of the IMP, which began to outpace the TFWP in 2009. Thereafter, permitholders under the IMP continued to grow while their numbers under the TFWP contracted and then plateaued before experiencing an uptick in 2022/3, post-pandemic. Consequently, by 2023 four times as many transnational workers held new work permits under the IMP than under the TFWP. Whereas Canada issued 69,275 permits under programs subsequently reclassified to fall under the IMP in 2002, it issued fully 764,770 in 2023, representing an elevenfold increase (Figure 1.1). Meanwhile, it issued 64,025 and 183,885 under the TFWP in these years (Figure 1.1; Table 1.1). The constrained growth of TFWP subprograms, widely recognized as highly exploitative, and the expansion of IMP subprograms, presumed to be less so, marked this period.

The appreciable drop in work permitholders under the TFWP between 2013 and 2015 took place alongside the introduction of a series of regulatory and administrative changes – responding to negative media reports and public outcry – designed to restrict employer access and to reduce worker mistreatment under its auspices (Marsden, Tucker, & Vosko 2021a). These changes included increases in application fees, restrictions on which employers can apply based on local employment conditions and on occupation/sector (ESDC 2014), and the introduction of an inspection system to enforce workplace laws applicable to

Figure 1.1 Work Permitholders, Annual Numbers, 2002–23: Temporary Foreign Worker Program and International Mobility Program

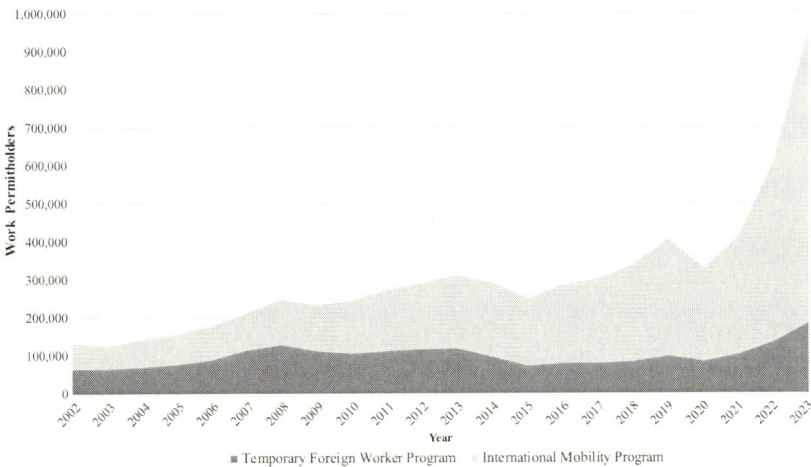

Sources: IRCC (2021a, 2023a, 2024a).

Note: Values between 0 and 5 are suppressed, all values are rounded to the nearest 5 to maintain anonymity.

participants in programs holding closed work permits (Marsden, Tucker, & Vosko 2021b).

The degree to which these changes, especially the introduction of a new federal inspection system to enforce such workplace laws applicable to closed work permit holders, has yielded less exploitative terms and conditions of employment across the assumed migration/mobility divide is, however, questionable (Marsden, Tucker, & Vosko 2021b). So too is whether or not the rebranding and expansion of IMP subprograms – including those that offer time-limited open work permits – is meaningful given especially evidence of continuing worker mistreatment in certain sectors above and beyond that emanating from employer tied permits (e.g., on food services, see Hari 2018; Fudge & Tham 2017). *Mobility* for employment increased inside North America and globally in the first quarter of the twenty-first century, as imperatives to attract "economically desirable" workers took on greater importance.[6] Yet, in Canada, as elsewhere, categorization practices contributing to a national "pecking order" (Portes 1997, 799) perpetuating various "social divisions" remained (for a discussion of divisions on the basis of "foreignness," see Castles 2006, 743–4). And there is mounting evidence that such practices, carried out via the immigration system, exhibit continuities with age-old racialized and gendered practices as discussed in greater detail below.

Table 1.1 Work Permitholders under the Temporary Foreign Worker Program, by Subcategory and Year in Which the Permit(s) Became Effective, 2014–23

Subcategory	2014	2015	2016	2017	2018	2019	2020	2021	2022	2023
Agricultural Workers	39,425	40,080	45,140	48,040	53,080	56,650	52,040	60,565	69,530	73,260
Seasonal Agricultural Worker Program	29,795	30,735	34,130	35,175	35,815	36,820	31,470	34,145	37,100	37,040
Agricultural Stream	9,565	9,305	10,915	12,875	17,310	19,875	20,710	26,520	32,590	36,456
Other Agricultural Workers	90	55	110	15	0	0	0	0	0	0
Other Workers with LMIA	43,365	25,450	25,035	24,145	24,705	34,600	29,275	38,165	63,490	107,640
Live-in Caregivers	12,010	7,250	6,465	3,585	3,030	3,460	2,645	4,245	2,950	3,090
TFWP Total (work permitholders)	94,680	72,965	78,450	78,470	84,005	98,060	84,610	103,205	136,020	183,885

Sources: IRCC (2021a, 2023a, 2024a).
Notes:
1. Values between 0 and 5 are suppressed, all values are rounded to the nearest 5 to maintain anonymity.
2. Totals may not be equal to the sum of permit holders in each program as an individual may hold more than one type of permit over a given period.
3. The size of "Other Workers with LMIA" in 2023 corresponds to the decision to raise the cap on low wage workers up to 20% from 10% of workforces and 30% in some sectors (IRCC 2024x).

Looking inside the TFWP, while numbers of permitholders plateaued in the 2010s, the period after Canada's 2014 program overhaul saw the consolidation and growth of agricultural subprograms. As such, the TFWP was reshaped. The Low-Skilled Pilot Programs for Agriculture and other workers with LMIAs, constituting a quarter of new work permitholders in 2012, were eliminated. The Caregiver subprogram (and its successors), through which there was a pathway to permanent residency, was terminated (in 2019) after the federal government announced that it was launching two new pilot programs, the Home Child Care Provider Pilot and Home Support Workers Pilot, to replace the previous caregiving programs that had been reformed in 2014 (IRCC 2019b).[7] At the same time, permits issued to Other High-skilled Workers with an LMIA declined; after peaking in 2013, so too did permits issued to Other Low-skilled Workers with an LMIA (Auditor General 2017, 13). As these changes occurred, Canada issued nearly four times more new work permits under agricultural subprograms of the TFWP in 2023 than in 2002 (IRCC 2024a). Consequently, nearly 40 per cent of new permitholders under the TFWP were in agriculture in 2023 (73,260 of 183,885). There were also significant reductions in the admission of TFWP permitholders destined for positions designated as "high"- and "low"-skilled outside agriculture. Collectively, these developments magnified historical patterns of recruitment by country of origin such that by 2023 the three top sending countries for TFWP subprograms in agriculture were from Latin America and the Caribbean: Mexico, Guatemala, and Jamaica.

Meanwhile, as Table 1.2 suggests, in depicting broad distinctions between IMP subprograms, although the number of work permitholders under the IMP grew nearly every year from 2014 to 2023, there was variation in the degree of growth.[8] For example, the number of new work permits issued to those under trade-related IMP subprograms – extended in significant proportions to citizens of states with longer-established trade agreements with Canada (i.e., former colonial powers such as the US) – remained steady, whereas those issued under subprograms with "non-work" purposes (e.g., Working Holiday, Post-graduation, and Spousal Work Permit programs) – drawing increasingly on citizens of states whose nationals have been subject historically to discriminatory treatment via immigration policy (e.g., China and India, as illustrated below) – saw significant growth. Furthermore, while some permitholders under the IMP hold closed work permits (e.g., all of the trade agreement streams) and are thus covered by the protective regime introduced in 2015 under the regulations issued pursuant to the *Immigration and Refugee Protection Act* (2002), the remaining two-thirds

Table 1.2 Work Permitholders under the International Mobility Program, by Subcategory and Year in Which the Permit(s) Became Effective, 2014–23

Subcategory	2014	2015	2016	2017	2018	2019	2020	2021	2022	2023
Agreements	32,830	30,745	29,240	26,625	27,215	28,235	19,005	21,765	24,865	16,430
Canada-International	21,545	19,660	18,325	17,665	17,205	17,115	8,665	9,685	13,010	5,290
Provincial/ Territorial International	615	510	325	170	125	115	50	55	60	5
Canada-Provincial/Territorial	10,520	10,565	10,615	8,810	9,900	11,015	10,300	12,030	11,800	11,135
Other Agreements	190	45	0	0	0	0	0	0	0	0
Canadian Interests	164,210	145,835	178,760	196,345	226,500	277,540	222,760	260,075	343,875	545,320
Significant Benefit	34,300	24,025	21,030	23,540	26,265	34,575	18,850	25,370	31,390	43,165
Reciprocal Employment	57,360	53,365	58,765	70,115	71,645	72,045	22,395	23,275	60,275	78,545
Research, Education, Training	175	395	445	405	265	240	125	100	85	135
Competitiveness and Public Policy	70,205	64,990	95,110	99,810	126,140	168,390	179,885	209,505	250,215	421,380
Charitable or Religious Work	2,860	3,530	3,695	2,735	2,460	2,625	1,720	2,010	2,215	2,725
Vulnerable Workers	–	–	–	–	–	–	–	880	1,080	2,055
Other IMP	10	145	95	50	105	400	715	28,885	101,705	206,245
IMP Total (work permitholders)	196,510	176,280	207,565	222,720	253,455	305,805	242,130	310,475	470,680	764,770

Sources: IRCC (2021a, 2023a, 2024a).

Notes:

1. Values between 0 and 5 are suppressed, all values are rounded to the nearest 5 to maintain anonymity.
2. Totals may not be equal to the sum of permit holders in each program as an individual may hold more than one type of permit over a given period.
3. The growth of the "Competitiveness and Public Policy" subcategory from 2022 to 2023 is driven by the number of postgraduate work permitholders.
4. The size of the "Other" subcategory in the IMP in 2023 is closely related to the Canada-Ukraine Authorization for Emergency Travel, under which open work permits were issued to individuals as a result of the conflict in Ukraine.

are excluded from such protection as they hold open work permits. Fast-growing subprograms of the IMP thereby merit greater scrutiny as to the nature and effects of their conditionalities and, accordingly, the degree to which they resemble long-standing migrant work programs responding to qualitative labour shortages and often characterized by considerable potential for exploitation.

2. Differentiation under the International Mobility Program

In studying IMPs and IMP participants' experience, I engage the notion of *differential inclusion* to describe "how incorporation in a sphere, society, or realm can involve various degrees of subordination, rule, discrimination, racism, disenfranchisement, exploitation, and segmentation" (Casas-Cortes et al. 2015, 156; see also Hall 1986; Crenshaw 1990; McCall 2005). Differential inclusion reveals inclusion and exclusion to be continuous, rather than oppositional, processes. It registers how borders neither exclusively nor necessarily represent the edges of the "national" political community but lie at its centre (Sharma 2006, 145; De Genova 2013; Nyers 2019).[9] Thus conceived, differential inclusion offers both a means of conceptualizing and a lens for analysing connections between (im)migration and labour control regimes that together produce different modes and degrees of precarity (i.e., in employment and residency status) among transnational workers by providing for certain (albeit often highly circumscribed) rights and entitlements while denying others.

Looking through this lens, some studies of the Canadian case focus on degrees of inclusion of specific occupational groups of TFWs (e.g., agricultural, domestic, and construction workers) (see, for e.g., Satzewich 1991; Basok 2002; Bakan & Stasiulis 2012; Barnetson 2015), though few address participants in IMP subprograms and their forerunners (for exceptions, including studies exploring tourism workers, see Smith & Staveley 2014; Yoon 2014a, 2014b; Helleiner 2017). Other studies examine the relationship between different entry categories, ranging from permanent residents to undocumented workers, and security of presence, access to spousal accompaniment, and eligibility for settlement services; this stream of research reveals variegated access to social insurance programs, such that certain benefits are inaccessible to transnational workers under the TFWP altogether, whereas others are technically available but difficult to access (on employment insurance, see Nakache & Kinoshita 2010; Vosko 2012; on language training, see Haque 2014). A subset also illustrates how, coupled with the provision of closed work permits, institutionalized deportability (De Genova 2002) – or threats and acts of deportation – circumscribes the exercise of voice over workplace grievances and/or demands for fair and safe working conditions – both individual and collective – among transnational workers under the TFWP, even where they work in a narrow band of industries and occupations in a common geographical location (Basok, Bélanger, & Rivas-Sanchez 2014; Vosko 2018, 2019). Challenging the assumption that recognition by the settler-colonial state is a great equalizer (Coulthard 2014), still other studies of differential inclusion explore axes of social difference affecting the experiences of transnational workers in Canada's settler-colonial context. Helping to correct a noted disregard for legacies of colonialism within migration studies (Walters 2015, 11), one branch of this scholarship brings gender, as it intersects with social relations of race, to the fore. Here, studies investigating the experiences of migrant domestic workers (Atanackovic & Bourgeault 2014; Tungohan et al. 2015; Bakan & Stasiulis 2012) reveal links between differential inclusion of racialized (im)migrant women domestic workers and the state's interest in reproducing white settler colonialism historically (Daenzer 1993; Calliste 1991) and contemporaneously (Arat-Koç 2006, 2018; Stasiulis & Bakan 1997; Hanley, Larios, & Koo 2017). Attending to the unequal exchange occurring between Canada and lead sending countries for its TFWP, another branch of scholarly inquiry exposes the significance of country of citizenship/origin, linking differential inclusion on this basis to settler colonial (Smith 2019) and imperial dynamics (André 1990; Smith 2015), and thereby to processes of racialization – or the delineation of racial difference and allocation of individuals into groupings through historically and geographically specific practices of classification, representation, and signification (Miles & Brown 2003, 100–1; see also Mirchandani & Chan 2007) – long integral to immigration systems (e.g., Satzewich 1991; see also Chartrand & Vosko 2021).

Centring such dynamics, I explore how axes of differentiation, such as gender, age, and country of citizenship/origin, operate within IMP subprograms. While mobility programs are often assumed to transcend ongoing colonial dynamics and (often gendered) processes of racialization, this inquiry queries this supposition by analysing differential inclusion *among* differently located participants in IMP subprograms with "non-work purposes." Reflecting an understanding of inclusion and exclusion as continuous rather than distinct processes, in disclosing differential inclusion, I build upon Anderson's (2019, 8) attempt to demigrantize migration studies by linking "who sheds and who retains their migrancy" to racialized processes upholding nation states' legitimacy. Anderson (2019) roots this effort in the larger project of moving beyond "methodological nationalism"[10] or methodological de-nationalism, which we also hold in common (Vosko 2011, 2012), that is, the commitment to denaturalize the nation state as the container of social processes such as migration (Wimmer & Glick Schiller 2002). Methodological de-nationalism, as I pursue it in this book, involves challenging the idea that categories such as "migrant" or "mobile" workers, engaged by nation-states such as Canada, in exercising national sovereignty, are natural and static and, instead, examining their operation and effects on social groups. But, while Anderson (2019, 8) connects experiences of differential inclusion among migrants to Britain to those of "minority ethnic citizens" located in that national context, and focuses on processes "migrantizing" the latter, my approach here is assessing whether or not the policy construction of the *mobile* worker that IMP subprograms project is apt – both across and within specific subprograms. Does this policy construction transcend Working Holiday, Post-graduation, and Spousal permitholders' temporary migration status (i.e., de-migrantize), reinforce (i.e., migrantize) this status such that their conditions of work and residency closely resemble those facing permitholders under TFWPs long associated with exploitation, or some combination of the two (i.e., migrantize some permitholders while liberating others)? If the latter, to what degree is migrantization a polarizing force? For example, does it impede expressions of agency (individual and collective) among workers from different countries of origin enrolled in the same subprogram, some who may identify more as "mobility" program participants and others who may identify as "migrant" workers?

In exploring migrantization and differential inclusion, I engage a decolonial feminist political economy of labour migration framework to probe the nature and extent to which capital interests, and states located in a stratified global hierarchy of production and social reproduction[11] shaped by these interests, benefit from temporary migrant labour (see, for example, Gabriel 2008, 2011; Plewa & Miller 2005; Castles 2006). This framework helps reveal an often obscured but fundamental link between "domestic labour shortages" and persistent employer demands for low-cost and tightly controlled labour that can be met by maintaining low wages, high levels of uncertainty, deportability, and limited access to regulatory protection – conditions made possible by temporary residency status. Critically, adopting a political economy of labour migration framework, whose orientation is decolonial and feminist, also underscores how long-standing TFWPs, in providing cost savings for employers in receiving states, such as Canada, misallocate resources necessary for sustainable processes of social reproduction.

Facilitated by an international division of labour that marginalizes certain countries (typically in the Global South), particularly those subject historically and contemporaneously to (neo)colonial and racializing dynamics, and designates particular workers as a labour reserve to be recruited via migration programs, whose rise coincides with ongoing processes of land, resource, and labour expropriation placing pressure on workers to join the global labour force,[12] this misallocation (Sassen 1981) flows from the fact that transnational workers' (intergenerational) reproduction occurs in the sending state while their (daily) maintenance takes place only partially in the receiving state. Fostering differential inclusion, historically and to the present, subprograms falling under Canada's TFWP have generated short-term cost savings in the receiving state partly through enforced limitations on the duration of stay and partly through excluding or partially excluding migrantized participants from access to social and statutory benefits and entitlements. Meanwhile, they engender long-term labour cost-savings by "exempting" the receiving state "from the need to build the kinds of infrastructure and service organizations that would be required by an equal number of national workers" (Sassen 1981, 71) – social reproductive costs that continue to be borne by transnational workers' households and communities abroad (on the case of migrant farm workers, see, for example, Vosko & Spring 2021).

In examining how differential inclusion among IMP participants is shaped by axes of social difference, this book explores whether and, if so, in what ways and to what degree, mobility programs likewise allow for analogous labour cost savings. In pursuit of this aim, I lend attention to the top "countries of origin" (i.e., countries of citizenship) for subprograms through which IMP participants are migrantized to bring into view linkages between histories and ongoing dynamics of colonialism and/or processes of racialization through nationality, and differentiation not only between *migrant* workers under the TFWP and *mobile* workers under the IMP but among the latter. Across the programs under investigation, I am concerned with whether the involvement of workers from countries of origin whose mobility has long been constrained in certain IMP subprograms is liberating or whether this "inclusion" contributes to perpetuating racialized patterns of exploitation (Latham et al. 2014).

Here, the unequal exchange occurring between Canada and the lead countries of origin for the IMP overall – particularly India (the top country of origin of Post-graduation and Spousal permitholders) but also China (especially retrospectively) is a vital backdrop. These two countries of origin have the highest and second-highest levels of participation

in global chains of labour and value in which transnational corporations "take advantage of differential unit [labour] costs," evinced partly
through immigration systems of major receiving countries like Canada
(Suwandi 2019, 51). That is, as Suwandi (2019) illustrates, transnational
corporations achieve this high level of participation not only by engaging nationals of India and China as workers inside these countries but
by using immigration systems to employ such nationals externally. As
a result, the global commodity chains within which such nationals are
employed are not only favourable to settler states such as Canada, but
to the modern immigration system upon which they depend, limiting
(permanent but also certain categories of temporary) (im)migrants from
certain countries writ large.

Migrantizing processes enacted through immigration systems are
also, of course, by no means new but, rather, deeply rooted historically.
Indeed, Canada adopted explicitly racist immigration policies restricting Chinese immigrants from settling permanently as early as the mid-
1880s. For example, in an era in which it otherwise took a laissez-faire
approach to immigration policy, it implemented the *Chinese Immigration
Act* (1885) to restrict and regulate Chinese immigration by instituting a
head tax, which effectively denied entry to many and subjected others
to relations of indebtedness with employers. As Cho (2002, 3) suggests,
"the problem ... was not finding cheap labour but doing so without
appearing to do so." In this sense, the early treatment of Chinese immigrants coming to Canada to engage, paradoxically, in projects in the
national interest, represented an effort to moderate public anxiety, especially the expression of xenophobic sentiments, and employers' demand
for cheap labour – a tension that continues to shape the parameters of
IMP subprograms for which China serves as a leading source (IRCC
2021a, 2023a). Distinctively, yet working towards similar ends, the early
treatment of Indian immigrants to Canada illustrates how racialized
processes of migrantization often come hand in hand with "post-colonial"
state sovereignty. As Mongia (1999) shows in her study of the history
of the passport, early requirements for this form of identification effectively authorized racialized difference on the basis of nation. In this
era, from an immigration policy standpoint, nationals of India were
transformed from British subjects into Indian immigrants. Analogous
to the tenor of the earliest head tax applied to Chinese immigrants, this
sleight of hand enabled Canada to limit the number of immigrants from
India without "drafting restrictive immigration legislation specifically
targeted towards Indians since this would have exposed, in an indubi-
table way, that notwithstanding citizenship of Empire, different "British
subjects" were endowed with differential access to mobility" (Mongia

1999, 536). Even as the focus in Canadian immigration policy post-1960 shifted to emphasize skill-based migration, regulations continued to restrict the family sponsorship of non-Europeans and maintained quotas on immigration from India, Pakistan, and Ceylon (Kelley & Trebilcock 2014, 320).

Setting the stage for different "nationalities" to have differential access to "mobility," common to the historical cases of Chinese and Indian immigration to Canada was the desire, on the part of government, to formally extend equal treatment to immigrants from different countries of origin while allowing differential inclusion to infuse this supposed equivalence. Accordingly, in this book, while recognizing that country of citizenship (the unit of analysis of administrative data labelled country of origin) is correlated imperfectly with transnational workers' self-identified homes or places of origin, I join scholars analysing country of origin/citizenship in administrative data in an attempt to disclose, at a high level of abstraction, colonial and racializing dynamics (Boyd, Taylor, & Delaney 1986; Trumper & Wong 2007; see also Chartrand & Vosko 2021). Along these lines, and as I conceive of racialization as a process of ascribing "racial meanings to objects, people, and processes … *Not a synonym for non-White*" (Ray, Herd, & Moynihan 2023, 140, emphasis added),[13] I use terms such as "racialized non-white" and "racialized-white" in exploring country of origin dynamics.

Ways in which racialized processes take shape in the early twenty-first century do not fit easily into the nation-state container utilized in immigration data collection. Nevertheless, receiving countries, such as Canada, differentiate between, and regulate the inclusion of, (im)migrants on the basis of "where they come from," or the country that sponsors their travel documents (Mongia 1999, 2018). Indeed, until the elimination of explicitly discriminatory immigration policies in the 1960s and the ostensible embrace of non-discrimination through the adoption of a points system, much-criticized subsequently for perpetuating long-standing exclusions, in Canada this differentiation by citizenship was tied explicitly to racial categories (Satzewich 1989, 1991).[14]

Contemporaneously, processes of racialization, often linked to the "post-colonial" order of national states, which, as Castles (2006, 743–4) illustrates, still retains colonial distinctions between who is "native" to a place and who is a "foreigner" (e.g., a migrant), and the devaluation of activities (paid and unpaid) vital to sustainable processes of social reproduction, continue to operate, albeit often in and through rationales of differentiated mobility within "free" trade areas, security perimeters, and global labour markets (see, for example, Trumper & Wong 2007;

Chartrand & Vosko 2021). Building on prevailing analyses and the historical and contemporary patterns and tendencies they reveal, in forwarding a decolonial feminist political economy of labour migration approach in these pages, I thus draw distinctions between top countries of origin, which remain salient despite the repudiation of policies, such as Canada's point system, demonstrated to be discriminatory on the grounds of race and gender,[15] and growing global interconnectedness – distinctions evident in the doors through which differentially located TFWP and IMP participants enter the country.[16]

3. Doors of Entry: Front, Side, and Back

Modes of entry are a central mechanism of differential inclusion among migrants for employment. In exploring their contours, the notion of entering the receiving state through metaphorical doors – front, side, and/or back – is apt (Zolberg 1989). Scholars commonly use the notion of "front door" to refer to "official *imm*igration policy (i.e., directed at permanent settlement), predicated on prioritizing "skilled" transnational workers channelled through a fortified regime" (Wright & Clibborn 2017, 166, emphasis added). Yet with the expansion of different forms of international migration for employment, not only on permanent but also temporary and temporary-to-permanent bases, to fulfil varying objectives, the moniker "front door" refers increasingly to official channels that do not require a labour agreement before the receiving state grants visas to workers. "Side-door" entry is assumed to involve migration for employment, often on a permanently temporary basis (which may involve circularity) (Rajkumar et al. 2012), via official channels often requiring labour agreements, whose terms typically require employers to demonstrate labour shortages in order to secure visas for workers (Howe et al. 2020, 217). State-sanctioned "back-door" entry entails the provision of visas that permit employment but assume other activities to be primary (Howe et al. 2020, 221).

Qualitatively, front-door entry is presumed to accord relatively stable residency status and pathways to permanent residency. Provided that workers entering in this manner are "economically desirable," it also entails freedom of movement in the labour market (via the provision of open work permits) and family accompaniment – that is, security of presence, spousal work permits, and access to the full range of settlement services (Rajkumar et al. 2012). Side-door entry, in contrast, often involves "vexed and contingent" pathways (Howe et al. 2020, 216) for those recruited by specific employers or industry associations (often via the provision of closed work permits) to fill essential jobs undesirable to locals in occupation and sectors, such as in agriculture; as such, entering through "side doors" is correlated with high rates of exploitation in which workers are "at best, wanted as unwanted" (Hage 2000, 121). There is a paucity of scholarship investigating state-sanctioned back-door entry to Canada and other settler states. To the extent that researchers probe its associated conditions, however, prevailing studies focus on "cultural exchange" programs and often reveal "a regulatory construction of work as primarily cultural, as opposed to economic, activity," fostering precariousness in employment and insecurity of presence among participants (Bowman & Bair 2017, 8). They also illustrate how back-door programs, such as those recruiting au pairs, working holidaymakers, and certain groups of educational migrants, like their side-door counterparts, permit, and may even incentivize, participation in jobs cast as essential yet undesirable to locals.[17]

Applying the foregoing definitions to the Canadian context, the largest subprogram of the TFWP (the Seasonal Agricultural Worker Program or SAWP) is best described as "side door" as it involves labour agreements and provides for closed work permits. Driven by what Marsden, Tucker, & Vosko (2021a) label protectionist and protectivist rationales (i.e., applied to standards and enforcement systems permitting the investigation and sanctioning of employers), the SAWP and most other TFWP subprograms also require employers to demonstrate a "labour shortage" via an LMIA in order to hire transnational workers. In contrast, IMP subprograms are assumed to involve "front-door" entry as most provide for open work permits; moreover, as permitholders under the IMP typically secure employment in-land (i.e., upon entry to Canada), their employers are subject neither to labour agreements nor to labour market tests. Yet assuming such a sharp divide, premised on a presumed migration/mobility distinction, between side-door subprograms under the TFWP and ostensibly front-door subprograms under the IMP, is misleading given the variegated nature of IMP subprograms. It also risks obscuring state-sanctioned back-door entry under the IMP and misguidedly implies that participants in IMP subprograms follow linear pathways when they may traverse multiple doors – and jump between different programs, even from one back-door program, otherwise designed to allow for one-time entry of fixed duration, to another – in pursuit of greater security of presence (or permanency) and high-quality employment. The three largest IMP subprograms serving as case studies in this book – the Working Holiday, Post-graduation Work Permit, and Spousal Work Permit programs – are rationalized on the basis of "non-work purposes" associated with state-sanctioned back-door entry. Falling under International Experience Canada, the Working Holiday program is structured around bilateral reciprocal youth mobility agreements negotiated between Canada and over thirty countries. On its own, the Working Holiday program covered about 80 per cent of International Experience Canada participants between 2012 and 2023 cumulatively (IRCC 2023b; IRCC 2024a, 2024b). Young people (typically aged 18–35) participating in the Working Holiday program are assumed to be motivated by the desire for foreign travel. They are therefore expected to be open to the possibility of working for more than one employer while in Canada. As entrants through prototypical back doors, Working Holiday participants typically do not have job offers prior to arrival and are expected to work in more than one location as they travel domestically. Accordingly, Canada issues open work permits of fixed duration under the Working Holiday program, although their length varies by country of origin (IRCC 2019a). Consequently, although these entrants' open work permits enable them to work for virtually any employer, they lack direct routes to greater security of presence. Permitholders' entry via front doors is not contemplated under the Working Holiday program, whose design reflects blockages rather than pathways to permanent residency, though permitholders themselves may wish ultimately to settle in Canada.

Distinct from the Working Holiday program, as Canada's premier off-shoot of educational migration program, representing the largest IMP,[18] the Post-graduation Work Permit program aims to attract (select) highly trained workers with high levels of socially recognized skills who are seeking ultimately to settle permanently. It is fuelled, on the one hand, by Canadian universities' need to increase revenue in the face of restricted budgets by attracting international students[19] – who are subject to high fees – and by students' larger contributions to the country's economy. On the other hand, federal and provincial/territorial governments' desires to attract and retain transnational workers with high levels of socially recognized skills motivate the program. While the Post-graduation Work Permit program offers open work permits and can lead ultimately to front-door entry, this possibility is conditional upon having navigated successfully through multiple doors; in order to participate in the Post-graduation Work Permit program, applicants must first fulfil qualifying criteria as former students migrating for non-work purposes, then engage in eligible employment for sufficient duration over a specified period to gain access to pathways to permanent residency, and, finally, to find and apply successfully under a suitable immigration scheme. Like Working Holiday permitholders, Post-graduation permitholders enter initially through the back door, although there are possibilities for those that qualify to pass through hierarchically organized passages such that they ultimately reach front doors.

Akin to the Working Holiday and Post-graduation Work Permit programs, Canada's IMP targeting spouses, the Spousal Work Permit program, also involves back-door entry on account of the non-work purposes that it aims to serve. This IMP subprogram takes shape through LMIA exemptions – providing effectively for adjoining doors of entry – applied to partners of transnational workers seeking to reside in Canada to engage in employment on a temporary basis. Such exemptions are available for spouses demonstrated to be in a genuine union (i.e., either a marital relationship or common-law partnership) with a "principal foreign national" (or principal) denoting "the first foreign national of the couple" as a means of supporting the retention and integration of principal migrants deemed desirable for long-term residence in Canada (IRCC 2024d). Accordingly, until new restrictions on Spousal permits, limiting access to spouses of international students enrolled in graduate-level or select professional degree (e.g., medicine, law, nursing) programs, and expanding access to low-skilled migrant workers labouring in a sector characterized by labour shortages or a government priority, such as the natural and applied sciences, construction, health care, natural resources, education, sports, and military sectors, were introduced in early 2025 (IRCC 2025), the principal had to be either a full-time post-secondary student or a "skilled" worker coming to Canada to work (under either an open or closed permit or pursuing permanent residency through the Atlantic Immigration Program or Provincial Nominee Programs).[20]

Spousal work permitholders may accept any employment available in the general labour force. Like their counterparts in the Working Holiday and Post-graduation Work Permit programs, spouses receive open work permits. As the exemptions applicable to this group fall under the Canadian Interest – Public Policy, Competitiveness and Economy stream of the IMP, policies facilitate the entry of spouses as a means of attracting principal applicants acquiring or holding high levels of socially recognized skills. This rationale resembles that motivating the Post-graduation Work Permit program with a twist: Spousal permitholders' access to Canada and its labour market is secondary, conditional upon traversing doors of entry contiguous with principal permitholders.

4. Studying Precarity under IMPs: Cultural Exchange, Probationary, and Relational

Utilizing the heuristic of doors, this book pursues a multi-method approach centring and bridging three modes of inquiry. The first is critical public policy analysis, approaching policy design, implementation, enforcement, and the like as an "exercise of economic and political power" (Graefe 2007), of immigration laws, legislation, regulations, policies, and guidelines/protocols for their implementation drawing on publicly available primary sources as well as internal memoranda, departmental records, and publications permissible for viewing under Canadian laws governing freedom of information obtained via access to information and privacy requests (ATIPs).[21] Second, to discern patterns and trends in the entry and labour force conditions of Working Holiday, Post-graduation and Spousal permitholders, I analyse administrative data on entry obtained via custom runs from Immigration, Refugees and Citizenship Canada (IRCC) principally for the 2002–23 period and on permitholders' demographic characteristics and the jobs they hold, as well as, where applicable, their pursuit of permanent residency, from the Canadian Employer and Employment Dynamics Database (CEEDD) for the 2002–1 period for Post-graduation and Spousal permitholders, to encompass the most recent year available at the time of publication, and the 2002–18 or 2019 period for Working Holiday permitholders, as 2018 and 2019 represent the most recent reliable years available given border closures to this group during the COVID-19 pandemic.[22] One of the few vehicles tracking the labour force experiences of temporary work permitholders,[23] the CEEDD is a unique, underexplored administrative database to which I gained access via a research agreement with IRCC and Statistics Canada. Accordingly, in the chapters to follow, summary and descriptive data examining the types of jobs obtained by work permitholders enrolled in the IMP, the industries in which they are employed, and their working conditions (e.g., income level, job tenure), with attention to social location (gender, country of citizenship, province of residence, age, language, etc.), draw on the CEEDD data. So too do the ensuing explorations of the three subprograms of focus; in studying the Working Holiday, Post-graduation, and Spousal Work Permit programs with attention to permitholders' experience, cross-tabulations from the CEEDD generate individual profiles of the selected programs, providing greater information about permitholders' employment and residency status, particularly their conditions of work and transitions to permanency, with attention to social location (e.g., gender age, country of origin) and context (e.g., industry). Third, and finally, to give texture to the experiences of permitholders under the Working Holiday, Post-graduation Work Permit, and Spousal Work Permit programs, I draw on in-depth interviews with 35 current and former work permithold-ers, recruited through word of mouth as well as via posting to relevant social media groups, website pages, and forums (e.g., Facebook groups and forums such as Reddit).[24] Using accounts created solely for the pur-pose of this inquiry, recruitment via social media focused on groups and pages most relevant to Working Holiday, Post-graduation and Spousal permitholders' experiences, such as "Working Holiday Canada & now what?! From IEC to PR" and college and university-specific interna-tional student forums.

Participants answered questions about how they negotiate parame-ters for gaining entry and securing employment, working conditions as temporary work permitholders, and transitions to permanent residency. That is, interviews sought to explore policies and their effects in action, as well as to supplement and assist in the interpretation of statistical data analysis, as appropriate. Interviews were transcribed and coded[25] for both descriptive characteristics of interviewees' work and residency experiences (e.g., types of employment contracts, wages earned, hours of work, length of permit) and emergent themes identified in interview-ees' reflections, themes such as those related to what I conceptualize ultimately, via the multi-method approach adopted herein, as "cultural exchange precarity," "probationary precarity," and "relational precar-ity."[26] To balance "the need for confidentiality and the need for context," in the chapters to follow, I assign each interviewee a pseudonym, utiliz-ing the first letter of their name while adopting a name common in the country of origin with which they identify, in attempt to preserve as much of interviewees' lived experience as possible (Allen & Wiles 2016, 153) (see also Appendix 1: Interviewees).[27]

Informed by each of these methods and the strategy of active "mix-ing" of methods (Mirchandani et al. 2018; Leckenby & Hesse-Biber 2007), chapters devoted to exploring the contours and effects of the three largest IMP subprograms are best described as case studies aimed at in-depth inquiry of the Working Holiday, Post-graduation Work Per-mit, and Spousal Work Permit programs. Case studies shed light on social phenomena from multiple angles and, in particular, identifying ways in which political and economic conditions interact with social location (e.g., processes of gendering and racialization via country of citizenship) and context (e.g., occupation and geography) to shape the experiences of work permitholders (Yin 2006). They also aid in the iden-tification and consideration of strategies for change. But, while the case studies of the three programs of focus aim to be thorough, they are by no means representative. The goal, rather, is to use in-depth inquiry into Working Holiday, Post-graduation and Spousal programs to develop a textured understanding.

Structure of the Book

The remainder of the book unfolds in five chapters. Chapter 2 begins with an overview of the IMP probing the origins, evolution, and contemporary contours of its core domains via a survey of laws, policies, and administrative practices, and a profile attending, on the one hand, to the composition of IMP categories, streams, and subprograms, and, on the other hand, dimensions of labour market (in)security shaping permitholders' experience. The chapter focuses on the IMP's largest umbrella categories, Agreements and Canadian Interests (and their core streams) – with an emphasis on the latter as the Canadian Interests category encompasses a majority of permitholders. It launches the inquiry by evaluating the validity of the migration/mobility policy construct on the basis of whether the dual rationale for the IMP (i.e., fostering reciprocity and competitiveness) – and the associated assumption that major subprograms recruit permitholders poised to hold jobs characterized by security and durability – is sound. Calling into question the chief categories and streams of the IMP, the chapter substantiates a central contention of this book – that many subprograms housed in the IMP's foremost streams are not "new" but, rather, have deep roots that may emanate from the TFWP and its precursors or reciprocal intergovernmental agreements of various sorts. As such, their raison d'être is complex and varied. Equally important, large IMP streams do not necessarily deliver the degree of labour market security that policies promise. As it is risky to assume IMPs provide for high-quality employment across-the-board, conditions associated with the three top IMP subprograms to be investigated in this book – the back-door Working Holiday, Post-graduation Work Permit, and Spousal Work Permit programs – merit greater examination.

Moving to the case studies, Chapters 3 to 5 inquire into the pathways through which Working Holiday, Post-graduation, and Spousal permitholders navigate as entrants whose presence is rationalized on "nonwork" bases. These case studies reveal three distinct types of precarity among groups of permitholders entering initially through the back-door – cultural-exchange precarity among working holiday makers, probationary precarity among postgraduates, and relational precarity among spouses – who subsequently encounter blocked, multiple hierarchically ordered, and adjoining doors of entry respectively. Tracing its origins to 1951, when Canada first promoted and facilitated travel and work exchange opportunities for Canadian and non-Canadian youth,[28] Chapter 3 explores how Canada's cultural exchange-oriented Working Holiday program operates among the participants it targets – namely, "youth," an expansive category defined to encompass those aged 18–35. The Working Holiday program assumes that participants conform with the image of the "cultural sojourner" – the prototypical adventure-driven unencumbered young person who seeks to combine extensive international travel with wage-earning to support this adventuresome time-limited objective. Yet beginning in the 2010s, evidence of the growing participation of Working Holiday permitholders in industries and occupations characterized by qualitative labour shortages began to accumulate, including in a policy evaluation conducted by IRCC in 2019. Building from this evaluation, Chapter 3's investigation finds that while some Working Holiday permitholders reflect the ideal typical "cultural sojourner," a considerable subset offers a "flexible" labour supply for employers in industries such as accommodation and food services, as well as retail and arts, recreation, and culture – key sites of precarious jobs. Despite the difficulty of isolating Working Holiday permitholders historically, administrative data analysis using the CEEDD makes possible previously unprecedented analyses highlighting patterns of stratification within this group.

Together with policy analysis and open-ended interviews of work permitholders, such analyses of the character of Working Holiday participants' labour force experience illustrate that the distinction between *mobility*-oriented "cultural exchange" and *migrant* work-oriented programs is porous – much less watertight than the policy imaginary suggests. They also reveal "cultural exchange precarity" among permitholders overall – that is, the corrosive conditions that many experience in the essential and/or frontline industries in which they are most concentrated. At the same time, a profile of permitholders shows that, given their, on average, longer work permits, those from affluent countries of origin with the largest quotas for participation in the Working Holiday program more closely approximate the figure of the "cultural sojourner" with greater (albeit still constrained) access to permanent residency via immigration streams valuing the accrual of "skilled" Canadian work experience. In contrast, the experiences of permitholders with shorter work permits, hailing from relatively less affluent countries with access to generally smaller quotas, whose nationals are often racialized as non-white, deviate from this archetype. The sum of these trends: the migrantization of the latter vis-à-vis the former. Still, while the Working Holiday program is conceived and organized on the basis that permitholders across the board (i.e., the wide spectrum of countries of origin) spend a finite period time in Canada, via the provision of non-renewable work permits, and limited access to repeat participation, designed to compel such back-door entrants to return to their countries of origin (i.e., to block or inhibit front-door entry), those seeking greater security of presence, especially in the long run, engage in creative individual-level strategies. Such strategies can involve "program jumping," in pursuit of permanent residency in the absence of direct pathways, via the subprogram in which they are enrolled.

From a different angle, applying the "doors of entry" analytic to Post-graduation permitholders and exploring factors conditioning their residency status and labour force participation in Canada, Chapter 4 reveals that permitholders confront "probationary precarity" – a staged process beginning with permitholders pursuing degrees at Canadian post-secondary institutions, while engaging in paid work, followed by applying for time-limited work permits pegged to the length of potential permitholders' previous degree/certification programs that offer potential, and conditional, pathways to permanency.[29] Applying such insights, this chapter illustrates the institutionalized pressures that Post-graduation permitholders face to take on precarious employment in order to achieve security of presence. Former international students who demonstrate that they hold valid temporary status in Canada, or have left the country, and have recently completed a qualifying academic, vocational, or professional training degree program full-time at an eligible learning institution in Canada may obtain an open work permit. Yet Post-graduation permitholders who wish to apply for permanent residency must accrue the necessary employment experience, which may not relate to their educational credentials, skills, experience, or interests. Throughout this multi-staged trial period, during which time their residency status is tenuous, Post-graduation permitholders must demonstrate their value to the Canadian labour force, leaving a large proportion to endure multiple dimensions of labour market insecurity on the often precarious pathways – requiring navigation through multiple hierarchically ordered doors – to permanent residency. At the same time, while administrative data analysis and open-ended interviews reveal that permitholders experience high degrees of precariousness overall, tied to the disconnect between the jobs they hold and their educational and skills profiles and correlated with the sectors in which they are most concentrated, which are defined by qualitative labour shortages. This pattern of precariousness is evident especially among permitholders from countries of origin whose nationals are racialized as non-white.

Arguably, the intensity of precarity among the latter takes shape in the context of a Canadian labour market context characterized, more broadly, by a racialized gendering of jobs wherein the availability of certain types of jobs may be linked to not only geographical location but also discrimination in the labour force (Block & Galabuzi 2018; see also Cranford & Vosko 2006; on Ontario, see Vosko et al. 2020, Chapter 1).

Against this backdrop, Chapter 5, considering the case of Spousal permitholders, discloses patterns of dependence perpetuated by policies pegging spouses' criteria for admission, labour force participation, and access to permanent residency to ties and conditions applicable to "principal" permitholders, specifically students and "skilled workers," via an immigration policy framework that sorts entrants in a manner contributing to gradations of inclusion. Such policies promote conceptions of "the family" reflecting racialized gender norms (i.e., nuclear families cohabitating in a national state) while simultaneously supporting receiving-country employers' persistent demands for *migrant* workers to fill precarious jobs in occupations and industries undesirable to citizen-workers. Partly on account of the dualistic policy emphasis responding, on the one hand, to employer demand (without heightening public concern over exploitation) while acknowledging, on the other hand, that socio-economic considerations are central to all adult permitholders regardless of marital/ family status, Spousal permitholders confront unique vulnerabilities as they negotiate doors adjoined to their common law/marital partners; on account of their relationally determined permit conditions, they are positioned to accept and retain precarious employment. The chapter thus develops the notion of "relational precarity" to capture the nature and effects of policies governing permitholders' employment and residency status in ways that both uphold certain (i.e., nuclear) family forms and satisfy employers' demands for labour to address qualitative labour shortages – policies that foster dependency akin to the closed work permit, albeit on a principal (married or common-law spouse) rather than an employer, without providing for analogous protections. Despite changes in 2024 limiting spousal accompaniment to international students enrolled in MA and PhD programs, Canada is also extending opportunities for spousal sponsorship to a wider array of principal work permitholders possessing lower levels of socially recognized skills than those targeted originally (i.e., full-time post-secondary students and skilled workers), many of whom are enrolled in programs inhibiting access to permanent residency drawing mainly on migrants from Mexico and Latin America; in this context, such insecurities are poised to intensify.

The book concludes with Chapter 6, "Contesting Differential Inclusion and Precarity under Canada's International Mobility Program," underscoring the ways in which the migration/mobility policy construct animating Canada's IMP is misleading, and the consequences for transnational workers engaged under its auspices. While Canada's IMP aims to attract well-educated *mobile* workers with high levels of socially recognized skills and qualifications, the case studies pursued in Chapters 3 to 5 reveal that this umbrella program does not entail a meaningful departure from conditions long associated with the country's *migrant* work programs. As a product of an (im)migration policy framework fostering differential inclusion, the programs investigated in-depth provide for legalized yet tenuous residency status, often coupled with precariousness in employment. By rationalizing access to temporary work permits on "non-work" bases, in the face of qualitative labour shortages, the Working Holiday, Post-graduation Work Permit, and Spousal Work Permit programs contribute to cultural-exchange, probationary, and relational precarity respectively. Under their auspices, all three groups of permitholders initially enter Canada and join its labour force through the back door. Yet, should they wish to extend their time in the country and/or pursue permanent residency, they encounter blocked, multiple hierarchically ordered, and/or adjoining doors of entry. Furthermore, although permitholders' precarity takes expression in different ways tied to features of the IMP in which they are enrolled, indicative of migrantization and its polarizing effects, each case study reveals that those from countries of origin subject historically to racialized barriers to entry erected via nationality and/or subject to legacies of external colonialism, as well as women, experience cultural-exchange, probationary, and relational variants acutely.

With these findings, Chapter 6 then draws interview data together with a survey of organizing campaigns and initiatives to chart efforts among groups of Working Holiday, Post-graduation, and Spousal permitholders and their allies to redesign policy and rethink practice. Informed by the voices of permitholders and aimed at rejecting central tenets of methodological nationalism in the design and implementation of laws, regulations, and policies governing IMPs, the chapter elevates policy options and political strategies, including greater pathways to permanent residency and meaningful access to labour and social protection. While not a panacea, taken together, the strategies examined in the conclusion point the way to incremental changes directed at gaining momentum sufficient to forge meaningful inclusion.

Chapter Two

Querying the Migration/Mobility Program Policy Construct: Labour Market Insecurity under Canada's "New" International Mobility Program

This chapter traces the origins, evolution, and contemporary contours of the IMP vis-à-vis the TFWP through a survey of laws, policies, and administrative practices shaping the emergence and governance of its core domains, and offers a statistical profile attending to the nature of work permitholders' labour force participation. Querying the validity of the migration/mobility distinction, with attention to the "mobility program" policy construct, it validates the contention that many IMPs are by no means new. Key IMP subprograms have deep roots, emanating from exemptions to LMIAs required of employers under the TFWP and its precursors or under reciprocal intergovernmental agreements. Tracing the varied origins of IMPs further illustrates their wide-ranging policy rationales, and that those underpinning major program categories, streams, and subprograms deviate from the raison d'être for the umbrella program (i.e., the IMP overall); accordingly, IMPs may not provide for the labour market security that its associated policies promise and may, in fact, contribute to differential inclusion among permitholders. As it is risky to assume that all permitholders under the IMP are mobile workers accessing high-quality jobs, conditions associated with two streams housing the three largest IMP subprograms of focus in this book – Reciprocal Employment and Competitiveness and Public Policy – merit close scrutiny.

In pursuit of this investigation, the ensuing analysis unfolds in three parts, beginning in Section 1 by exploring the origins and evolution of categories, streams, and subprograms falling under the IMP umbrella. This examination shows that some IMPs emanate from reciprocal arrangements and/or trade agreements while others arise from pilot programs (provincial or federal). What unites IMPs, in contrast to programs falling historically under the TFWP, is their exemption from LMIAs. This feature, coupled with the rapid growth of the IMPs at a time when the federal government overhauled and dramatically reduced the scope of the TFWP with the stated aims of remedying exploitation while continuing to respond to qualitative labour shortages, cultivates the assumption that IMP participants, especially open work permitholders, are less in need of labour and social protections than their TFWP counterparts. Having set this backdrop, attending to dynamics related to country of origin, Section 2 sketches the contours of key IMP streams and subprograms. Next, Section 3 explores the two largest IMP categories – Agreements and Canadian Interests – before focusing on streams within the Canadian Interest category, within which the Working Holiday, Post-graduation and Spousal subprograms fall. Together, Sections 2 and 3 test the assumption that the foremost *mobility* programs under the largest IMP category (Canadian Interests) and its major streams (i.e., Reciprocal Employment and Competitiveness and Public Policy) foster the acquisition of high-quality jobs among permitholders. In interrogating this assumption, the analysis shows that permitholders under the IMP do not necessarily experience labour market security. There is, rather, significant variation in the character of permitholders' employment by stream, suggesting that subprograms under certain streams can foster precariousness. Furthermore, even though "non-work" purposes rationalize the largest subprograms of the Reciprocal Employment and Competitiveness and Public Policy streams of Canadian Interests, a majority of permitholders falling under their auspices are employed, a significant proportion of whom hold precarious jobs and work in industries associated with qualitative labour shortages.

1. The IMP: Background

1.1 Origins

The IMP facilitates employment of limited duration among workers migrating internationally, often under conditions which may be established by international agreements or that promote reciprocity, on the one hand, and competitiveness in the global economy, on the other hand; these two drivers, which are not mutually exclusive, overarch the IMP's main categories, streams, and subprograms.

Under contemporary trade law, "reciprocity" means that "any advantage that is granted to one state has to be reciprocated by the beneficiary state" (Pellerin 2008, 41). Yet governments in settler-colonial contexts have long embraced the reciprocity principle in selecting parties to intergovernmental agreements providing for various forms of movement, including among youth seeking to gain work experience abroad, deemed culturally compatible (see, for example, Helleiner 2017). Since the turn of the twentieth century, "competitiveness" has, in turn, been equated with the process of "opening up" via "free trade." But while some subprograms of the IMP find analogues in the early post–World War II era, others emerged out of the implementation of modern trade agreements, such as those geared to professionals from Canada's major trading partners or intra-company transferees. For example, subprograms for intra-company transferees grew with the expansion of the traditional nexus of actors and logics involved in migrant worker programs in the 1990s, a process advanced considerably with the adoption of NAFTA and the creation of the World Trade Organization.

In this context, core drivers of free trade, including both reciprocity and competitiveness, increasingly came to influence both the rationale for and design of programs aimed at attracting transnational workers (Pellerin 2008). For example, Annex 1603 of NAFTA (1994) prohibited the use of labour market tests to authorize temporary entry for employment, creating a powerful exemption from processes designed to tightly control which occupational groups could enter and engage in employment temporarily. Accordingly, in the era of "free trade," the embrace of global competitiveness through reciprocity heightened employer power in migrant selection processes (including that of transnational corporations seeking to transfer employees seamlessly across countries).

The prohibition of mandating labour market tests for certain forms of entry, while by no means "new" insofar as certain groups were long exempt from such requirements (e.g., reciprocal employees, participants in exchange programs) (Citizenship and Immigration Canada 2004), expanded considerably under trade agreements such as NAFTA. Significantly, NAFTA discharged certain employers (e.g., those in highly competitive industries critical to trade) from providing proof of domestic labour shortages in order to gain access to transnational workers, that is, from obtaining LMIAs crafted to preserve jobs for workers in Canada and to protect migrant workers from abuse by, among other things, providing basic labour protections and decent compensation (e.g., paying a prevailing wage as required under the TFWP in the early 2000s) (Marsden, Tucker, & Vosko 2021b). Consistent with the global race to recruit talent, the prohibition reflected the Government of Canada's mounting effort, together with its provincial counterparts, to align the mobility of professionals with its goal of pursuing "competitiveness" through trade. Consequently, within the bi- and multilateral trade agreements that Canada maintains with various countries, common types of work permitholders associated with particular IMP subprograms include traders, investors, professionals, and intra-company transferees (Pellerin 2017, 359). The legitimization of such subprograms thus utilizes the mobility of transnational workers to advance negotiations on trade and investment liberalization (OECD 2014), casting the receiving state, in response to employer/industrial demand, as a recruiter with wide-ranging discretionary powers, a dynamic accelerating in the early 2000s.[1]

Since that time, the absence of a requirement for an LMIA has come to unify the diverse subprograms of the IMP: on the one hand, groups of workers, such as intra-company transferees, migrating under trade-related categories empowering employers (including transnational corporations seeking to transfer employees seamlessly between countries) in the selection process, such that they are no longer required to demonstrate domestic labour shortages and, on the other hand, participants in youth mobility programs, spouses, and other groups long exempt from LMIAs, retroactively reclassified for reasons unrelated to trade. Under the IMP, a large subset of workers participating in these varied subprograms receive open work permits, some of which provide opportunities for renewal and/or pathways to permanency, a feature effectively rationalizing the lack coverage under the suite of labour protections extended to closed work permitholders in the mid-2010s, whose parameters are explored below.

The expansion of IMP subprograms took place in this context. Starting in 2009, the number of transnational workers holding work permits under the IMP came to exceed that under the TFWP. From 2017 to 2023, the IMP encompassed approximately three times as many permitholders as the TFWP. Furthermore, while ESDC has long played a central role in administering the TFWP, IRCC and Canadian Border Services Agency administer the IMP. Consequently, program administration is directed at regulating *mobility* across national borders even though dynamics particular to the Canadian labour market, such as employer demands, may function as a central motivator with the contraction of TFWP subprograms targeting industries characterized by qualitative labour shortages (Chartrand & Vosko 2021, 95).

Given especially the central drivers shaping Canada's IMP, policy mirroring in other settler-colonial countries also bears mention here. As Canada's IMP rose to prominence, so too did programs motivated by competitiveness and rooted in trade-related principles, such as reciprocity, in countries such as Australia, Aotearoa New Zealand, and the United States. Given their long history of shared entry categories across the migration/mobility policy construction,[2] such countries saw the proliferation of subprograms associated historically with entry categories cast as "nontypical," insofar as they do not require labour market testing, providing for a greater degree of free movement in the labour market (often facilitated by open work permits) and, in some instances, greater routes to permanent residency. One way of classifying such subprograms, as depicted in Appendix Table A.1, is by dividing them into those geared to benefiting the "national" labour market, those facilitating nation-to-nation reciprocity (i.e., internationally oriented), and those viewed to benefit the global labour market (i.e., transnationally oriented). Subprograms of benefit to national labour markets seek to attract valuable future immigrants; as such, the adjudication of admission rests typically on processes distinct from labour market testing (e.g., admittance to an educational program). A subset of educational migrants ranging from students to postgraduates, as well as spouses, permitted to engage in work represented two such subsets. In contrast, "international" subprograms facilitate reciprocal benefits from one national labour market to another, with rules varying by agreement; such subprograms encompass youth mobility schemes, including working holiday programs. Finally, "transnational" subprograms foster capital mobility and typically do not offer routes to permanent settlement; they emanate largely from international trade agreements, and are often advocated by not only nation-states but a variety of non-state actors. This last subset includes, but is not limited to, categories related to trade agreement business entry (e.g., those facilitating the entry of intra-company transferees, traders, and investors), supporting the entry of spouses of skilled workers, short-term secondees, and "global talent." While the proliferation of such "nontypical" work permits within and across settler-colonial countries is seemingly paradoxical insofar as they seek to address such key concerns (i.e., to strengthen national labour markets, improve international relations, and augment global competitiveness), as they are adopted in such contexts, these "new" national, international, and transnational IMP subprograms reflect prevailing global hierarchies of nation-states and the relations of inequality they perpetuate.

1.2 Evolution

At one level, the IMP and the TFWP respond to the same policy goal – the recruitment of transnational workers for employment in Canada. However, the roots of the TFWP lie in the Non-Immigrant Employment Authorization Program (NIEAP) of 1973. Representing the earliest overarching program governing migrant work providing mainly for closed work permits, as Sharma (2007, 163) illustrates, the NIEAP served to "categoriz[e]... certain (im)migrants as migrant workers ... legally through [a] regulatory framework ... entrenched within successive Canadian Immigration Acts." This framework defined a migrant worker as a "'foreign worker' who upon arrival ...[has] with her or him an official *temporary employment authorization* from the Canadian state," a precursor to the contemporary LMIA (Sharma 2007, 163, emphasis added). From the inception of the NIEAP, migrant workers falling under its auspices were subject to a labour market test. In contrast, the IRPA (2002), replacing the *Immigration Act* in place since the 1970s (albeit amended continually) and permitting the minister of immigration to pass regulations governing the issuance of temporary work permits to foreign nationals, allowed for the creation of categories of LMIA-exempt migration streams (*Immigration and Refugee Protection Regulations*, SOR/2002–227, ss. 204–8). Accordingly, after 2004, when the government issued its consolidated "Foreign Worker Manual," exempt streams and permits, whose subprograms expanded through to 2013, have included those tied to international agreements; subprograms deemed of "significant benefit" to Canada; the Reciprocal Employment stream; the designated by the minister stream, initially comprising subprograms tied to research, educational, and training programs; the competitiveness and public policy stream (e.g., aimed at spouses of students and skilled workers, post-graduates, postdoctoral fellows and grantees); and permits for asylum seekers/refugees and applicants for permanent residency, among others (for a full list of LMIA exemptions in 2024 charting their evolution by decade and classifying them in accordance with their varied purposes (i.e., fulfilling national labour market objectives, fostering nation-to-nation reciprocity, or facilitating globalization), see Appendix Table A.1: List of Exemptions from Labour Market Impact Assessment, 2024.)

In the early 2000s, the expansion of these LMIA-exempt subprograms, prefiguring sizable contemporary IMPs, took place alongside the accelerated growth of a variety of TFWP subprograms, not only those in agriculture and domestic work, the two domains in which Canada's migrant worker programs are most long-standing and in which exploitative conditions are common, but in wide-ranging industries from accommodation and food services to mining and construction. Yet in the 2010s, as workplace problems among TFWP participants – especially those holding closed work permits, such as wage theft, excessive overtime, and unjust dismissal (often triggering premature repatriation) – came under greater scrutiny (Marsden, Tucker, & Vosko 2021a), awareness of the adverse conditions of work and residency facing migrants enrolled in TFWP subprograms mounted. This awareness sparked public outcry, prompting the Conservative government of Canada at that time, despite having overseen a massive expansion of such subprograms, to initiate an "overhaul" effectively scaling back the TFWP in 2014 in the face of a federal election (Marsden, Tucker, & Vosko 2021a, 73).[3] As a consequence, the TFWP maintained its form yet came to be limited to a few long-standing subprograms, initially reduced to agriculture and domestic work plus a handful of "high-skilled" subprograms and subsequently to agriculture and a small number of "high-skilled" subprograms (Vosko et al. 2023). Meanwhile, in 2014, many LMIA-exempt categories, permitted under IRPA (2002) and its associated regulations, initially distinguished only as subprograms of the TFWP that did not require labour market tests, were reclassified as falling under a separate umbrella program known as the IMP.[4] Thus, while the IMP was billed as a new-era umbrella program, introduced in the mid-2010s, it more genuinely represents a rebranding of existing subprograms – calling into question the extent to which it offers opportunities for meaningful inclusion and/or for shedding the "migrancy" long associated with the TFWP (i.e., for de-migrantization). Additionally, in 2015, alongside this recalibration and/or redistribution of subprograms between the TFWP and the IMP and a reclassification of programs falling under the latter, in the transition in leadership between the Conservative and Liberal Parties, the federal government implemented a new protective regime (Marsden, Tucker, & Vosko 2021a). Albeit characterized by key design flaws, including the compliance orientation it bestows on federal labour standards officers who are charged with supporting the enforcement of (often highly deficient) provincial labour laws and policies through cooperative measures, the goal of this regime is laudable – namely, the enforcement of workplace rights among migrant workers. But because its terms apply exclusively to those holding closed work permits, a majority of whom fall under the TFWP, relatively few IMP participants, including those participating in its largest subprograms, benefit from its terms. Yet, despite holding open work permits, some IMP participants face de facto restrictions on their employer, type of work or occupation, location, and duration of work, which may flow, for example, from requirements for accessing pathways to permanency (e.g., among Post-graduation permitholders) or work permit conditions applied to the so-called principal to whom Spousal permitholders are attached.

Given such exclusions, together with barriers or partial barriers to entry facing work permitholders in internationally and transnationally oriented IMP subprograms in particular, distinctions between the countries of origin from which major subprograms of the TFWP versus

Table 2.1 Weight of Total Temporary Work Permitholders under the Temporary Foreign Worker Program vs. the International Mobility Program, by Select Country of Origin (Top Fifteen, including both programs) (Permitholders, Cumulative Totals, 2013–23)

Country of Origin	% TFWP	% IMP	TFWP Total	IMP Total	Both Programs Total
India	10	90	106,615	910,240	1,016,855
Mexico	85	15	328,030	56,265	384,295
USA	12	88	36,040	265,935	301,975
France	7	93	18,160	239,915	258,075
Philippines	58	42	158,070	113,160	271,230
China	6	94	14,050	226,540	240,590
UK and Territories	14	86	17,505	110,580	128,085
Jamaica	87	13	108,375	15,955	124,330
Guatemala	99	1	119,950	890	120,840
Ukraine	3	97	6,080	195,525	201,605
Republic of Korea	19	81	20,475	87,970	108,445
Australia	4	96	3,360	85,500	88,860
Japan	8	92	5,820	70,685	76,505
Brazil	9	91	7,145	72,770	79,915
Ireland	7	93	4,530	64,365	68,895
Program Totals	27	73	954,205	2,516,295	3,470,500

Sources: IRCC (2021a, 2023a, 2024a).
Notes:
1. Values between 0 and 5 are suppressed, all values are rounded to the nearest 5 to maintain anonymity.
2. Totals may not be equal to the sum of permitholders in each program as an individual may hold more than one type of permit over a given period.
3. The prominence of Ukraine in the IMP is closely related to the Canada-Ukraine Authorization for Emergency Travel, under which open work permits were issued to individuals as a result of the conflict in Ukraine. As a result of these measures, the number of permitholders from Ukraine under the IMP more than doubled between 2022 and 2023.

the IMP, as well as within the IMP, recruit workers also merit scrutiny. Overall, the IMP draws heavily upon permitholders emanating from a greater diversity of countries of origin, with the notable exception of countries in Latin America and the Caribbean, comprising the chief countries of origin of workers under the TFWP. As Table 2.1 shows, a majority of workers from India – the largest country of origin for the TFWP and IMP combined – enter Canada under an IMP work permit. So too do a majority of those from other top countries of citizenship of the TFWP and IMP, such as Australia, China, France, Japan, Brazil, Ireland, and Ukraine, well over 90 per cent of whom were IMP work permitholders between 2013 and 2023 (Table 2.1).

Table 2.2 Top Fifteen Countries of Origin for the Temporary
Foreign Worker and the International Mobility Program
(Permitholders, Cumulative Totals, 2013–23)

Country of Origin	% of TFWP total	% of IMP total
India	9.4	21.3
Mexico	29.0	1.3
USA	3.1	6.2
France	1.6	5.6
Philippines	14.0	2.6
China	1.2	5.6
UK and Territories	1.5	2.6
Jamaica	9.6	0.4
Guatemala	10.6	0.0
Ukraine	0.5	4.6
Republic of Korea	1.8	2.1
Australia	0.3	2.0
Japan	0.5	1.7
Brazil	0.6	1.7
Ireland	0.4	1.5
Program Totals	84.1	59.2

Sources: IRCC (2021a, 2023a, 2024a).
Note: Percentage based on data within which values between
0 and 5 are suppressed, and all values are rounded to the
nearest 5 to ensure anonymity.

Considering the decade between 2013 and 2023, the top 10 countries
of origin of the IMP included a mix of wealthier and powerful countries
in Europe, East, Southeast and South Asia, as well as the United States
and Australia, and lack any representation from Latin America and the
Caribbean (Table 2.1). Six such countries of origin are signatories to a
trade agreement with Canada (the United States, France, United Kingdom, Australia, Korea, Japan) (Table 2.2). In these years, at least 80 per
cent (in many cases over 90 per cent) of all permitholders from each of
these countries came under IMP rather than the TFWP (Table 2.1).

2. Contours of the IMP: Structure, Permit Conditions, and Pathways to Permanent Residency

As an umbrella program, Canada's IMP – so-named with the overhaul
of the TFWP in 2014 – encompasses seven categories organized by LMIA
exemption code, comprising streams divided further by subprogram.
The largest overarching category is Canadian Interests (comprising
71 per cent of all IMP permitholders in 2023) (Table 2.3).[5]

Table 2.3 Select International Mobility Program Categories, Streams and Subprograms, Permitholders, Canada, 2010–23

Group	Categories			2010	2011	2012	2013	2014	2015	2016	2017	2018	2019	2020	2021	2022	2023
Agreements (total)	Streams	Substreams		27,625 20%	32,000 20%	33,805 19%	35,530 18%	32,830 17%	30,745 17%	29,240 14%	26,625 12%	27,215 11%	28,235 9%	19,005 8%	21,765 7%	24,865 5%	16,430 2%
	Canada-International			19,555 14%	20,625 13%	22,045 13%	22,140 11%	21,545 11%	19,660 11%	18,325 9%	17,665 8%	17,205 7%	17,115 6%	8,665 4%	9,685 3%	13,010 3%	5,290 0.7%
	Provincial/Territorial – International			335 0.20%	490 0.30%	520 0.30%	565 0.30%	615 0.30%	510 0.30%	325 0.20%	170 0.10%	125 0.05%	115 0.04%	50 0.02%	55 0.02%	60 0.01%	5 0.001%
	Canada – Provincial/Territorial			6,860 5%	10,370 6%	10,955 6%	12,660 7%	10,520 5%	10,565 6%	10,615 5%	8,610 4%	9,000 4%	9,830 3%	9,140 4%	12,030 4%	11,800 3%	11,135 1.5%
	Other Agreements			910 1%	575 0.40%	325 0.20%	215 0.10%	190 0.10%	45 0.03%	–	–	–	–	–	–	–	–
				111,155 80%	128,900 80%	141,010 81%	159,245 82%	164,210 84%	145,835 83%	178,760 86%	196,345 88%	226,500 89%	277,540 91%	222,760 92%	260,075 84%	343,875 73%	545,320 71%
Canadian Interests (total)	Significant Benefit			16,070 12%	18,820 12%	20,425 12%	30,355 16%	34,300 0	24,025 14%	21,030 10%	23,540 11%	26,265 10%	34,575 11%	18,850 8%	25,370 8%	31,390 7%	43,165 6%
	Reciprocal Employment	Subprograms		54,105 39%	59,000 37%	62,910 36%	60,460 31%	57,360 29%	53,365 30%	58,765 28%	70,115 31%	71,645 28%	72,045 24%	22,395 9%	23,275 7%	60,275 13%	78,545 10%
		IEC		49,085 35%	54,200 34%	57,950 33%	55,160 28%	51,955 26%	48,180 27%	52,620 25%	62,290 28%	62,410 25%	61,640 20%	18,725 8%	17,775 6%	50,480 11%	67,785 9%
			Working Holiday			42,850 25%	42,910 22%	41,580 21%	39,105 22%	43,950 21%	52,450 24%	51,770 20%	51,055 17%	14,695 6%	12,695 4%	40,700 9%	56,850 7%
	Competitiveness and Public Policy	Subprograms		38,965 28%	48,860 30%	55,370 32%	66,635 34%	70,205 36%	64,990 37%	95,110 46%	99,810 45%	126,140 50%	168,390 55%	179,885 74%	209,505 67%	250,215 53%	421,380 55%
		Post-Graduate Worker Program		16,895 12%	22,200 14%	26,735 15%	33,340 17%	36,785 19%	33,570 19%	54,940 26%	56,220 25%	74,560 30%	97,935 32%	121,890 50%	129,005 42%	132,780 28%	241,815 32%
		Spouses of Skilled Workers		14,170 10%	16,750 10%	18,825 11%	21,955 11%	20,940 11%	18,780 11%	23,505 11%	25,365 11%	29,085 11%	40,730 13%	37,620 16%	49,295 16%	61,175 13%	93,285 12%

(Continued)

Table 2.3 (Continued)

Categories		2010	2011	2012	2013	2014	2015	2016	2017	2018	2019	2020	2021	2022	2023
	Spouses of Students	3,180 2%	3,360 2%	3,230 2%	4,370 2%	5,615 3%	6,505 4%	10,515 5%	11,645 5%	16,000 6%	23,365 8%	15,915 7%	25,725 8%	50,865 11%	72,315 9%
	Other Canadian Interests	2,185 2%	2,405 1%	2,605 1%	2,570 1%	3,035 2%	3,925 2%	4,140 2%	3,140 1%	2,725 1%	2,865 1%	1,845 1%	2,110 1%	2,300 0.50%	2,230 0.30%
Other IMP permitholders		65 0.05%	15 0.01%	20 0.01%	20 0.01%	10 0.01%	145 0.08%	95 0.05%	50 0.02%	105 0.04%	400 0.13%	715 0.30%	29,765 10%	102,785 22%	206,254 27%
Mobility Programs Total (work permitholders)		138,510	160,510	174,405	194,165	196,510	176,280	207,565	222,720	253,455	305,805	242,130	310,475	470,680	764,770

Sources: IRCC (2021a, 2023a, 2023b, 2024a).

Notes:

1. Values between 0 and 5 are suppressed; all values are rounded to the nearest 5 to maintain anonymity.

2. The label "Other Canadian Interests" includes "charitable or religious work" and "research, educational, or training programs." The "Other IMP Permitholders" classification includes those falling under LMIA exemptions for "vulnerable workers," "public policies," "no other means of support," "PR applicants to Canada," and "humanitarian reasons," categories rationalized on bases distinct from those rationalizing the IMP as a whole (i.e., distinct from "reciprocity" and "competitiveness").

2.1 Structure and Permit Conditions

IMPs offer a mix of closed and open work permits[6] ranging from one month to seven years in duration (sometimes with the possibility of extension), although open work permits predominate, and the most common length of participants' first work permit is one year. Issuing mostly closed work permits, the Agreements category encompasses streams pursuant to largely trade-related reciprocal international agreements, such as CUSMA, formerly NAFTA, and the Canada-Europe Trade Agreement. Its major subprograms, defined as Canada-international, provincial/territorial-international, and Canada-provincial/territorial (e.g., the Atlantic Immigration Program), facilitate entry for business visitors pursuant to these agreements, typically traders, investors, professionals, technicians, intercompany transferees of varying kinds, and, in certain cases, spouses of work permitholders entering under one of the agreements. Reflecting Canada's trade obligations, the top three countries of origin of entrants under these agreements in 2023 were Mexico, the United States, and Colombia, with which Canada also has a trade agreement but does not fall within the top 15 sources for the TFWP and IMP.

Involving the issuance of both closed and open work permits, the largest umbrella category within the IMP, Canadian Interests, comprises a variety of streams related to advancing Canada's economic, social, and cultural interests, including Significant Benefit, Reciprocal Employment, Designated by the Minister, and Charitable and Religious Work. The Significant Benefit stream provides government with the flexibility to respond to situations in which the employment activities of a "foreign national would create or maintain significant social, cultural or economic benefits or opportunities for Canada" (e.g., unique work situations, non–free trade agreement intercompany transferees, bridging open work permits) (IRCC 2023d). Reciprocal Employment enables "foreign nationals to take up employment in Canada when Canadians have similar reciprocal opportunities abroad … [that] result in a neutral labour market impact" (e.g., academic exchanges and youth mobility programs) (IRCC 2023e). The Designated by the Minister stream is subdivided into two components: Research (e.g., educational co-ops) and Competitiveness and Public Policy, categories determined to be "necessary for public policy reasons related to the competitiveness of Canada's academic institutions or economy" (e.g., medical residents) (IRCC 2023f). Finally, the fourth stream falling within Canadian Interests is Charitable and Religious Work (IRCC 2024e).

Under the Significant Benefit stream, the top three countries of origin for which are India, the United States, and France, Canada issues closed work permits with a few exceptions (e.g., open work permits are issued to live-in caregivers and their spouses with permanent residency applications submitted and applicants holding Bridging Open Work Permits). Under the Reciprocal Employment stream, for which the top three countries of origin are France, the United Kingdom, and Australia, it also mainly issues closed work permits. However, under the Working Holiday subset of International Experience Canada, participants receive open work permits of up to 24 months, depending upon the country of origin. Distinctly, while Canada issues a mixture of open work permits and closed work permits under the Competitiveness and Public Policy stream, whose three top countries of origin are India, China, and the Philippines, participants in its two largest subprograms also receive open work permits: spouses (and dependants) of high-skilled workers[7] and full-time students,[8] whose work permit duration is pegged to that of the "principal applicant," and Post-graduation permitholders, whose work permit duration is up to three years maximum (IRCC 2021a, 2023a, 2024a).

2.2 Access to Permanent Residency

On account of the finite nature of the work permits provided under the IMP, many of its major categories, program streams, substreams, and subprograms, including those serving as case studies in Chapters 3 to 5, are not designed to foster permanent residency. At the same time, whether or not work permits under the IMP's auspices are relatively short and non-renewable or longer and potentially extendable in some way, despite the lack of administrative data concerning the proportion that wish to transition, qualitative interviews undertaken for this book demonstrate that some work permitholders desire, and may pursue, permanent residency as a means of attaining security of presence either as their permits are winding down or shortly thereafter. This tendency reflects the findings of a growing body of research documenting how the legal status trajectories of many migrants fail to adhere to policy design facilitating or, for that matter, impeding permanent residency such that temporary entry categories leading to permanent residency have multiplied (Rajkumar et al. 2012; McLaughlin & Hennebry 2013; Tungohan et al. 2015). For example, Goldring, Landolt, and Pritchard's (2022, 184) research exploring the experiences of migrants holding what they term "precarious legal status" illustrates that "migrants crisscross state programs, submit simultaneous and repeat applications for different types of authorized legal status ... or exit and enter the country to renew or alter their legal status" (see also Goldring 2014; Goldring & Landolt 2021). Regardless of their trajectory, however, IMP permitholders' pursuit of continued security of presence is typically conditional on the ability to demonstrate sustained value to the Canadian labour force, a criterion compelling some to accept jobs, in anticipation of transitioning to permanent residency, incommensurate with their skills and experiences. These jobs are often in industries characterized by qualitative labour shortages, in which precarious employment is the norm, including those long reliant on workers migrating via the TFWP (e.g., accommodation and food services).

The IMP permitholders surveyed in this book who seek permanent residency typically utilize four immigration pathways: the Canadian Experience Class, the Federal Skilled Worker Program, the Federal Skilled Trades Program, and Provincial/Territorial Nominee Programs.[9] Among these pathways, those of the Canadian Experience Class, Federal Skilled Worker Program, and Federal Skilled Trades Program share the most features in common as they each fall under the federal Express Entry program, organized to meet the needs of provinces/territories and especially employers, by, particularly in the case of the Canadian Experience Class, foregrounding (or "expansive[ly] 'branding'" (Dobrowolsky 2017, 203)) "Canadian experience" more than the federal human capital model orienting its point-system precursor (Kaushal 2019). Figure 2.1 summarizes the steps involved in applying under these three pathways. However, it must be emphasized that the Federal Skilled Worker Program has more rigorous requirements than the Canadian Experience Class and Federal Skilled Trades Program, as applicants under this stream must pass through an additional initial screening stage (see Figure 2.1, Step 1.5).[10] In addition to this screening, they must fulfil the same set of requirements applicable to those applying under the Canadian Experience Class. In its present iteration, most notably, entry under Canadian Experience Class requires applicants to demonstrate at least the equivalent of one year of full-time (i.e., 1,560 hours) skilled work experience in Canada in the three years prior to applying, experience that cannot be gained from the performance of work for remuneration as a student visa holder. In practice, the hours requirement amounts to full-time work of 30 hours/week for 12 months or an equal amount of part-time work over 24 months maximum. However, weekly hours exceeding 30 are not permitted such that applicants cannot qualify without performing eligible work for at least a year. "Skilled work" is, in turn, defined as work experience in one or more occupations classified as managerial, professional, or technical/

Figure 2.1 Criteria for Accessing Permanent Residency under Three Major Federal Immigration Schemes**** (as of 2024*)

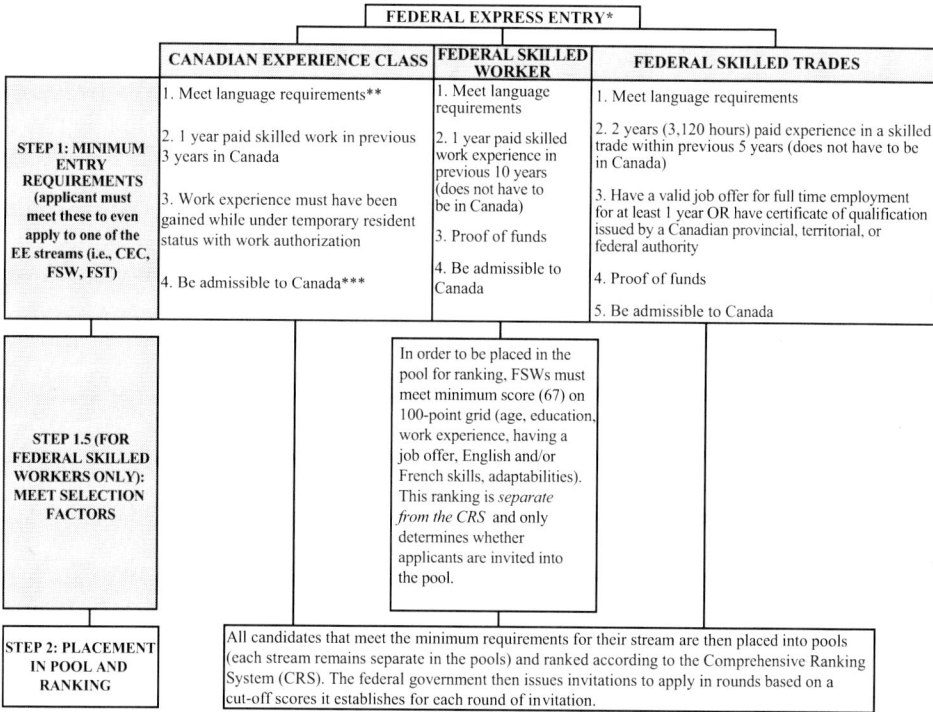

	FEDERAL EXPRESS ENTRY*		
	CANADIAN EXPERIENCE CLASS	**FEDERAL SKILLED WORKER**	**FEDERAL SKILLED TRADES**
STEP 1: MINIMUM ENTRY REQUIREMENTS (applicant must meet these to even apply to one of the EE streams (i.e., CEC, FSW, FST)	1. Meet language requirements** 2. 1 year paid skilled work in previous 3 years in Canada 3. Work experience must have been gained while under temporary resident status with work authorization 4. Be admissible to Canada***	1. Meet language requirements 2. 1 year paid skilled work experience in previous 10 years (does not have to be in Canada) 3. Proof of funds 4. Be admissible to Canada	1. Meet language requirements 2. 2 years (3,120 hours) paid experience in a skilled trade within previous 5 years (does not have to be in Canada) 3. Have a valid job offer for full time employment for at least 1 year OR have certificate of qualification issued by a Canadian provincial, territorial, or federal authority 4. Proof of funds 5. Be admissible to Canada
STEP 1.5 (FOR FEDERAL SKILLED WORKERS ONLY): MEET SELECTION FACTORS		In order to be placed in the pool for ranking, FSWs must meet minimum score (67) on 100-point grid (age, education, work experience, having a job offer, English and/or French skills, adaptabilities). This ranking is *separate from the CRS* and only determines whether applicants are invited into the pool.	
STEP 2: PLACEMENT IN POOL AND RANKING	All candidates that meet the minimum requirements for their stream are then placed into pools (each stream remains separate in the pools) and ranked according to the Comprehensive Ranking System (CRS). The federal government then issues invitations to apply in rounds based on a cut-off scores it establishes for each round of invitation.		

Source: IRCC (2024i).

Notes:

*   Information is current to 2024.

**   Applicants under Express Entry must prove their English or French language ability via an approved language test evaluating writing, reading, listening, and speaking abilities (the Canadian Language Benchmarks (CLB) for English and the Niveaux de competence linguistique canadien (NCLC) for French). The minimum results required vary by program. The Federal Skilled Worker Program requires minimum scores of 7 on either the CLB or the NCLC. CEC requires a CLB or NCLC of 7 for those applying with TEER 0 or 1 work experience, or CLB or NCLC 5 for those applying with TEER 2 or 3 experience. The Federal Skilled Trades Program requires CLB or NCLC scores of 5 on speaking and listening language abilities, and 4 on CLB/NCLC on reading and writing (IRCC 2024f).

***   Applicants who are inadmissible under Canada's immigration laws cannot apply for PR. Applicants can be inadmissible for a number of reasons, including security reasons (e.g., espionage, terrorism), human or international rights violations (e.g., war crimes, crimes against humanity), criminality, medical reasons (e.g., conditions dangerous to public health or safety, potential to cause excessive demand on health or social services), financial reasons, misrepresentation/false documents, failure to comply with any provision of IRPA, and/or having an inadmissible family member (IRCC 2024j).

**** PNPs are an increasingly common route by which former work permitholders transition to permanent residency. However, they are not included in this table as each province maintains distinct streams according to provincial priorities. For example, Ontario has nine distinct PNPs.

skilled trades (i.e., TEERs 0, 1, 2, or 3 of Canada's National Occupational Classification (NOC) scheme respectively).[11] As such, applicants must demonstrate that they have performed duties set out in the lead statement of the occupational description in the NOC, including all essential duties and most of the main duties listed in the relevant description. Requirements for Federal Skilled Trades Program applicants vary from those applicable to Canadian Experience Class and Federal Skilled Worker Program applicants in two principal ways: applicants must have two years of paid experience in a skilled trade within the previous five years, although this experience does not have to be in Canada, and have a valid job offer for full-time employment for at least one year, or a certificate of qualification issued by a Canadian provincial, territorial, or federal authority. Both Federal Skilled Trades and Federal Skilled Worker Program applicants must also demonstrate proof of funds.[12]

Applicants under the Federal Skilled Worker Program, Federal Skilled Trades Program, and the Canadian Experience Class that fulfil these requirements are then ranked via the Comprehensive Ranking System administered federally. This system is the contemporary iteration of Canada's points-based immigration system (inaugurated with the introduction of the Express Entry category), dating to 1967, which serves as the basis for issuing invitations to apply for permanent residency to those with the highest scores. Under the Comprehensive Ranking System, a maximum of 1,200 points are allocated across several categories, including not only core human capital (e.g., age, education level, official language proficiency) and skill transferability (e.g., foreign work experience) factors but also spousal factors.

Provincial/territorial nominees applying under an Express Entry stream are also awarded 600 points under the Comprehensive Ranking System. In this way, this fourth most prevalent immigration stream is desirable to many IMP participants, especially those with high levels of socially recognized skills, education, and work experience as Provincial and Territorial Nominee Programs typically apply stringent criteria in these areas. First established in the mid-1990s by the federal government and a few provinces, Provincial and Territorial Nominee Programs are maintained by each province/territory (except for Quebec and Nunavut) and are designed to attract applicants to fill jobs deemed critical at a provincial/territorial level with applicants who wish to live in the province/territory in question. However, despite the fact that each nominee program has different targets, limiting their suitability to particular applicants, the categories of investors, skilled- and semi-skilled workers, and international students have been common historically (Dobrowolsky

2017, 203). Under Provincial and Territorial Nominee Programs, there are two general processes for obtaining entry: one is paper-based entry, the route through which applicants apply for nomination under a non–Express Entry stream and submit an application for permanent residency to IRCC once they have been nominated by an employer provincially. The other is via Express Entry (described above), wherein provinces work with and through this federally administered system to nominate candidates for provincial settlement who meet the threshold for one of the three aforementioned federal streams (the Canadian Experience Class, the Federal Skilled Worker Program, and the Federal Skilled Trades Program).

Bringing the largest number of provincial/territorial nominees to Canada, Ontario's provincial nominee program (the Ontario Immigrant Nomination Program, OINP) is a model of how this immigration entry category functions (Government of Ontario 2024). Under its auspices, there are three overarching categories (the expression of interest, MA or PhD graduates, and express entry), two of which may be accessible to students and skilled workers – the expression of interest and express entry categories. Applicants with a job offer may fall under the "foreign worker" (skilled positions), the "in-demand skills" ("in-demand" occupations), or the "international student" (i.e., recent graduate) substreams – and they must be invited to apply and have a full-time permanent job offer from an Ontario employer. The Master's or PhD stream requires graduates of Ontario-based Master's or PhD programs to register an expression of interest and receive an invitation to apply. Ontario's express entry streams operate through the federal Express Entry program, and comprise streams for skilled workers, French-speaking skilled workers, and skilled trades. Candidates in the express entry streams that receive a provincial nomination receive fully 600 additional points, "which is usually sufficient to trigger an invitation to apply [...] at the next round of invitations" for permanent residency from the federal government (IRCC 2024k). Illustrative of the shared responsibility over Provincial and Territorial Nominee Programs, Ontario Express Entry candidates are vetted by the province, which nominates them before the federal government gives final approval (IRCC 2022a). Given this chapter's concern with querying the migration/mobility policy construction, a key area of interest, to which the analysis now turns, is how various permit conditions and their fulfilment, typically a prerequisite for accessing pathways to permanent residency surveyed above, interact with and shape permitholders' labour force experiences under different umbrella categories and streams of the IMP.

3. Labour Market (In)security among Permitholders in the Largest IMP Categories and Streams

Analysing differential inclusion among IMP permitholders, and determining whether the subprograms in which they enrol allow for cost savings long associated with those of the TFWP, Chapters 3 to 5 examine labour market (in)security among Working Holiday, Post-graduation, and Spousal permitholders – participants in the IMP's three largest subprograms – while they hold work permits of finite duration. A useful starting point for this exercise entails exploring such dynamics across major IMP categories and streams, specifically the broader Agreements and Canadian Interests categories.

Indicators utilized by researchers, individually and cumulatively, to establish degrees of labour market (in)security or precariousness in a given job are helpful in discerning the quality of employment among permitholders, for example, in terms of degree of control over the labour process, income level, access to regulatory protection (see, for example, Vosko 2006, 2010; Vosko et al. 2020). To this end, the CEEDD facilitates analysis of four useful indicators: rates of unionization/professionalization (a good proxy for degrees of control over the labour process);[13] firm size, an indicator of (in)access to minimum terms and conditions of employment (as evidence suggests that workers in firms of twenty employees or more are more likely to see their labour standards enforced than those employed by smaller firms); income from employment[14] (a central means of attaining resources required for individual and household subsistence); and, multiple jobholding (another measure relevant to income adequacy in a main job as its presence highlights a strong motivation to secure income from employment). In addition, by revealing key domains in which permitholders are employed, and whether or not they are characterized by qualitative labour shortages, in which precarious jobs are the norm, industry of employment, another variable available, offers supplementary insight into labour market (in)securities confronting permitholders.

Neither the presence of one indicator of labour market insecurity nor being employed in an industry in which precarious jobs are common necessarily denote a high degree of insecurity among work permitholders. Arguably, however, experiencing more than one indicator of labour market insecurity entails precariousness (Vosko 2006, 2010). For this reason, in analysing employment outcomes among IMP participants in this book, I attend to the presence or absence of multiple indicators with a view to the nature of the subprogram in question. As a means of sketching patterns across large IMP categories, in this chapter I utilize an index that stipulates that if two or three of the foregoing indicators (i.e., no union/professional association, small firm, multiple jobs) are common among work permitholders under a given stream or subprogram, their job is deemed to be precarious.[15] Income from employment is not included in the index because it is reported on an annual basis, and no data are available on number of hours worked per year, making it impossible to discern hourly wages. But, because annual income helps reveal workers' degree of dependence on paid employment, I use this indicator to add texture to the index and offer further context to permitholders' experiences as *temporary* work permitholders. While some studies show that former IMP participants transitioning to permanent residency tend to fare better in the labour force with respect to their employment earnings than direct-entry economic immigrants (see, for example, Banerjee & Lam 2024, who compare exclusively IMP participants transitioning through Provincial and Territorial Nominee Programs and the Federal Skilled Worker Program and "1-step" immigrants, or direct-entry economic immigrants), permitholders' experiences when they hold finite work permits (i.e., prior to and/or in transition) are less well-documented (see also Hou & Picot 2023).

Focusing in on these dimensions of labour market (in)security in examining the Canadian Interests and Agreements categories reveals that a greater proportion of work permitholders under Agreements have high annual employment incomes compared to the proportion of permitholders under Canadian Interests, who are overrepresented in lower income categories. Likewise, a larger proportion of permitholders enrolled in streams falling under Canadian Interest than those under Agreements hold more than one job. Proportions working in small firms and non-unionized/non-professionalized jobs are similar under both categories. Where industry is concerned, permitholders under Agreements are overrepresented in scientific, technical, and professional services, whereas those under Canadian Interests are overrepresented in retail and administrative services. Without exploring dynamics by stream, however, it is difficult to discern whether, and, if so, in what ways and to what degree, trends by industry, such as the presence or absence of qualitative labour shortages, shape labour market (in)security among permitholders.

Considering indicators of precariousness cumulatively, distinctions between permitholders' experience of labour market (in)security gain greater clarity. Indeed, fully 50 per cent of work permitholders under Canadian Interests hold precarious jobs, compared with 37 per cent of those falling under Agreements, when an index is applied to these two umbrella categories. While neither percentage is negligible, the magnitude of precariously employed permitholders under Canadian Interests (i.e., whose conditions of work and employment resemble those long associated with permitholders enrolled in subprograms of the TFWP associated with exploitation) is noteworthy (Statistics Canada 2023).

3.1 Canadian Interests

As it represents the foremost IMP category, breaking down Canadian Interests by its Significant Benefit, Reciprocal Employment (encompassing all International Experience Canada subprograms, including the Working Holiday program), Competitiveness and Public Policy (including the Spousal and Post-graduation IMP subprograms), and other streams (including "research, educational, or training programs" and "charitable or religious work") reveals differences in employment outcomes among their respective permitholders. The rates of non-unionization/professionalization are higher for Significant Benefit (86 per cent)[16] and the Competitiveness and Public Policy (80 per cent) permitholders compared to Reciprocal Employment (68 per cent)permitholders.[17] In contrast, employment at a small firm is more common among Reciprocal Employment (27 per cent) and Competitive and Public Policy permitholders (24 per cent) than for Significant Benefit permitholders (18 per cent), and permitholders under Competitiveness and Public Policy and Reciprocal Employment also have higher rates of multiple jobholding (54 per cent and 31 per cent, respectively) compared with those under the Significant Benefit stream (22 per cent of whom hold multiple jobs). In turn, considerably more permitholders under Significant Benefit (fully 46 per cent) report high annual employment income ($70,000+) compared to their counterparts under Reciprocal Employment and Competitiveness and Public Policy, 17 per cent and 9 per cent of whom report earnings at this level respectively.

One potential explanation for such differences in income level relates to industry: as Appendix Table A.2, depicting the Industrial Distribution of Permitholders, Select International Mobility Program Categories and Streams, 2021, illustrates, Significant Benefit permitholders are overrepresented in professional, scientific, and technical services, and underrepresented in retail trade, administrative services, and accommodation and food services, whereas those under the Reciprocal Employment stream are overrepresented in accommodation and food services and those falling under the Competitiveness and Public Policy stream are overrepresented in retail, as well as administrative and

Table 2.4 Employment Outcomes among Permitholders under Canadian Interests by Stream, 2021

Streams	Annual Income					Indicators of Precariousness			
	Less than $30,000	$30–$50,000	$50–$70,000	$70–$90,000	$90,000+	Non-unionized/ non-professionalized	More than 1 job	Small firm	Precarious
Significant Benefit	20%	18%	15%	15%	31%	86%	22%	18%	31%
Reciprocal Employment	47%	22%	13%	7%	10%	68%	31%	27%	36%
Competitiveness and Public Policy	42%	35%	14%	5%	4%	80%	54%	24%	54%

Source: Statistics Canada (2023).

support services, industries associated with high levels of precarious-ness in Canada and its largest provinces (Vosko 2006; Vosko et al. 2020). The Significant Benefit stream also provides for higher annual income from employment at a single large firm, whereas a larger proportion of permitholders under Competitiveness and Public Policy hold multiple jobs yielding low annual income from employment. Viewed alongside dynamics by industry, the prevalence of both multiple jobholding and low annual employment income among Reciprocal Employment and Competitiveness and Public Policy permitholders highlights a disjunc-ture between such permitholders' employment situations and the for-mal aims of these streams and the *mobility* program policy construct underpinning the IMP, which associates mobility programs with labour market security. This disjuncture underscores the risk of upholding a regime enforcing workplace and social rights among closed work permitholders exclusively, on account of an analogous assumption that *migration* program participants represent the principal group in need of protection, given well-documented exploitation under the TFWP. Attesting to the danger of overlooking transnational workers in need of protection, the precariousness index reveals that 31 per cent of permit-holders under the Significant Benefit stream, 36 per cent of permithold-ers under the Reciprocal Employment stream, and fully 54 per cent of permitholders under the Competitiveness and Public Policy stream experience two of the three indicators of labour market insecurity in their main jobs. Thus, although many permitholders under the Recip-rocal Employment and Competitiveness and Public Policy streams are assumed to enter for "non-work purposes," they clearly face pressure to engage in employment, including in precarious jobs, as many experi-ence exceedingly high degrees of labour market insecurity.

4. Conclusion

Taking into account the magnitude of the largest streams of Canadian Interests (i.e., Reciprocal Employment and Competitiveness and Public Policy), these findings highlight the importance of exploring the degree to which indicators of labour market insecurity are present individually, multiply, or, as appropriate, cumulatively by IMP subprograms in tan-dem with in-depth analysis of subprogram parameters and open-ended interviews investigating permitholders' experience in the labour force and as temporary residents. Adopting a strategy of active mixing of methods (Mirchandani et al. 2017), the chapters that follow pursue this investigation through case studies of the three largest subprograms of the IMP. Collectively, the Working Holiday component of International

Experience Canada and the Post-graduation and Spousal IMP subprograms comprised over 60 per cent of all IMP work permitholders in 2023. That year, entries under the Post-graduation program, the case study at the centre of Chapter 4, accounted for the largest number of permitholders arriving under the auspices of the IMP (fully 32 per cent). In turn, spouses of skilled workers and students, the focus in Chapter 5, represented the second largest group of entries (22 per cent of total IMP arrivals). Finally, Working Holiday program entrants, the group dominating the International Experience Canada subset of Reciprocal Employment (representing 9 per cent of total IMP arrivals), the case study at the centre of Chapter 3, stood in third place, accounting for about 7 per cent of IMP entrants. This next chapter explores the experience of permitholders under this youth mobility scheme.

Chapter Three

Cultural Exchange Precarity: Working Holiday Permitholders

One of the most profound shifts in Canada's (im)migration policy architecture is the expansion of programs devoted to "cultural-exchange" – namely, Co-operative, Young Professionals, and especially Working Holiday components of the International Experience Canada subprogram of the IMP. Starting in the late 1990s, the Working Holiday program grew dramatically in scope and magnitude (Figure 3.1).[1] Targeting "youth" – an elastic category defined to encompass those aged 18–35 travelling abroad who may require resources for their excursions – the Working Holiday program aims to fulfil non-work objectives partly through the provision of work permits via reciprocal interstate agreements. Yet despite the proliferation of such agreements, little is known about Working Holiday permitholders' experience in Canada.

To address this knowledge gap, this chapter explores the nature of these permitholders' labour force participation attending to whether and, if so, how and in what ways, they fulfil demands for labour in particular contexts (e.g., geographical, industrial, occupational). The analysis illustrates that program parameters take Working Holiday permitholders to be "cultural sojourners" – or adventure-driven, unencumbered young people seeking to combine international travel with access to supports to realize this objective. Beginning in the 2010s, however, evidence pointing to Working Holiday permitholders' increasing participation in industries and occupations characterized by qualitative labour shortages, including that drawn from a policy evaluation by IRCC in 2019, began to accumulate. Policy and administrative data analysis, together with open-ended interviews with Working Holiday permitholders, suggests that while some conform to the image of the ideal-typical "cultural sojourner," others, more accurately cast as *migrant* workers, comprise a sizable group, entering through state-sanctioned back doors, who offer a "flexible" labour supply for employers in industries, such as accommodation and food services, in which precarious jobs are the norm. Furthermore, while policies seek to ensure that Working Holiday permitholders' time in Canada is finite via the provision of non-renewable work permits designed to compel these back-door entrants to return to their countries of origin such that they are "permanently temporary" (Rajkumar et al. 2012), permitholders' sustained attempts to secure pathways to greater security of presence in Canada, especially those from relatively lower-income countries of origin, suggest that a significant subset is misfit with, and indeed, is struggling against, the categorization of cultural sojourner.

The foregoing dynamics, apparent at the intersection of Working Holiday permitholders' employment and residency status, produce "cultural exchange precarity" for many such workers. While Canada's Working Holiday program reflects a distinction, at a policy level, between *mobility*-oriented "cultural exchange" and *migrant* "work-oriented" programs, this distinction is not watertight. On the one hand, Canada extends Working Holiday permits of sufficient length to facilitate greater access to permanent residency via parallel immigration streams valuing the accrual of "skilled" Canadian work experience to permitholders closely approximating "cultural sojourners," many of whom hail from a few affluent countries of origin identified with whiteness,[2] several of which have close ties to the British Commonwealth. Yet, on the other hand, the tendency to cast Working Holiday permitholders as "cultural sojourners" at a policy level can also function to justify insecurity long confronting migrant workers; many permitholders, particularly those devoid of lengthier work permits and prospects for repeat participation from outside the foregoing group of affluent countries of origin, are subject to corrosive conditions in the essential and/or frontline industries in which they are most concentrated.

The following three-part analysis develops these contentions. Section 1 introduces the notion of "cultural exchange precarity" emerging from the case study of Canada's Working Holiday program, situating it alongside similar programs operating in high-income countries, such as Australia, Aotearoa New Zealand, and the United States, with reference to the small body of literature on the subject. Section 2 describes and analyses criteria for admission, work permit conditions, and pathways to permanent residency among Working Holiday permitholders falling under the International Experience Canada subprogram of the IMP in the first two decades of the 2000s. Exploring how the Working Holiday program's cultural exchange orientation shapes program design, it reveals that, despite providing for open work permits, a move aimed at facilitating permitholders' mobility whose limited efficacy Chapter 2 established, tight constraints on duration of stay, repeat participation, and the absence of direct pathways to permanent residency characterize the program overall. At the same time, interstate agreements between Canada and certain countries of origin, and their distinct terms, are poised to contribute to divisions among Working Holiday permithold-ers on the basis of country of origin: specifically, polarization between Working Holiday permitholders from relatively less affluent countries, those with which Canada has either no interstate agreement or an agree-ment providing for smaller quotas and shorter durations of stay, and those from more affluent countries with which Canada has agreements providing for larger quotas and longer durations of stay (three of which belong or previously belonged to the British Commonwealth). Against this backdrop, Section 3 examines the effects of such provisions, as well as the design of the Working Holiday program as a whole, on permit-holders via an analysis of administrative data and open-ended inter-views with permitholders across a wide spectrum of countries of origin, revealing cultural exchange precarity among permitholders overall, and especially among those from countries of origin whose nationals are often racialized as non-white.

1. "Cultural Exchange Precarity": Locating Canada's Working Holiday Program

The literature on cultural exchange programs in high-income receiving countries, such as Canada, reveals that "a discursive and regulatory construction of work as primarily cultural, as opposed to economic, activity" underpins the back-door programs falling within this cat-egory, programs which provide visas that permit employment but take other activities to be primary and do not offer direct pathways to per-manent residency (Bowman & Bair 2017, 8). It illustrates how programs envisioned as fulfilling non-work purposes, such as those geared to au pairs, working holidaymakers, co-operative students, and young pro-fessionals, tend to allow, and may incentivize, participation in jobs cast as essential yet undesirable to locals, thus contributing to precarious-ness among work permitholders. For example, several inquiries into the operation of cultural exchange programs common in Australia reveal Working Holiday permitholders' precariousness in employment, particularly in low-wage sectors such as agriculture and tourism, long identified with migrant work programs (Meldrum-Hanna et al. 2015; Vosko 2022). Consistent with US-based studies demonstrating how Working Holiday permitholders are "suspended between the rhetoric of cultural exchange and the reality of temporary work" (Bowman &

Bair 2017, 3), Australia- and Aotearoa New Zealand-based inquiries also link permitholders' labour market insecurity to their ambiguous status as overseas travellers seeking extended cultural experiences, on the one hand, and workers fulfilling qualitative labour shortages, on the other hand (Reilly 2015; Robertson 2014; Stringer & Michailova 2019; Tham & Fudge 2019).

Investigations probing the experiences of permitholders enrolled in cultural exchange programs falling under International Experience Canada likewise point to the precariousness of their jobs (e.g., Coderre & Nakache 2021). Still, few studies investigate in depth how "cultural exchange" programs designed to fulfil non-work objectives, specifically Working Holiday programs, shape permitholders' conditions of work and residency. Fewer still examine such programs with attention to dynamics surrounding permitholders' country of origin as they relate to processes of racialization informing (im)migration policy in settler-colonial contexts. Notable exceptions attentive to such dynamics include Helleiner's (2017, 299) historically grounded policy analysis of Irish Working Holiday permitholders, which reveals how Canadian immigration policy discourses "position … Irish migrants as … 'culturally compatible'" and, thus, economically desirable workers and future immigrants, despite the temporary nature of the Working Holiday program, as they are easily incorporated into "white settler Canadianness." In this study of a dominant and long-standing group of Working Holiday permitholders, Helleiner (2017) makes visible how such "cultural exchange" programs relate to racialized (im)migration policies and nation-making. From a distinct yet compatible angle, works by Yoon (2014a, 2014b, 2015) also illustrate how processes of racialization tied to country of origin affect the labour force experiences of Korean Working Holiday permitholders in Canada. Supplementing Helleiner's emphasis on how policies oriented to a particular conception of white Canadian nationhood contribute to the prioritization of Irish citizens, who, as Hari & Ahmed (2023, 1) contend, represent a "stand-in for the infinite variability of whiteness in Canadian nationhood," under the Working Holiday program, Yoon's (2014a) qualitative research finds that, compared with those from anglophone and francophone countries, Working Holiday permitholders that are Korean nationals experience lower levels of job mobility than anticipated. Despite holding open work permits, Yoon's respondents report working in racially segmented settings in service and hospitality industries, often in Korean-owned businesses (principally restaurants), resulting in exploitation hidden within "diasporic bubbles."[3]

Confounding the dominant conception of the "cultural sojourner," cast as a young traveller, typically from a relatively high-income country of origin seeking to earn money to fund their long-term tourism, the foregoing studies offer windows into Working Holiday permitholders' experience in Canada and beyond. They point to ways in which these back-door permitholders' conditions of work and employment closely resemble those of migrant workers, who, despite facing heightened forms of exploitation and no direct pathways to permanent residence, are often motivated to seek repeat participation or to find other routes to greater security of presence and ongoing access to the labour force that avoid blockages flowing from program design. But, while some underline the significance of racialized processes oft tied to nation-building (Helleiner 2017) in shaping dominant conceptions of "cultural exchange," a further objective of this chapter is to discern patterns fostering stratification, in particular migrantization, among Working Holiday permitholders. As interview data illustrate, some permitholders choose the Working Holiday permit because of the freedom it affords them as "travellers." As Freya, who came to Canada from Germany on a one-year Working Holiday permit, during which time she first worked full-time in the hospitality sector as a housekeeper, then in the service sector as a restaurant worker (both seasonal positions), and then in high tech as a software developer, notes, "it gives you a great opportunity to travel around, see the country, see so many different cultures in places, while you're able to work wherever you want." In contrast, other permitholders, wanting to live and work in Canada, perceive the Working Holiday permit as the only feasible pathway to earn sufficient funds; for example, Reiko, a permitholder from Japan, who was unemployed and actively looking for work at the time of interview, shares that she could not afford to study in Canada and, as such, emphasized that "my only option was to get … their Working Holiday permit." Meanwhile, So-hyun, a permitholder from South Korea who worked part-time as a cashier in a fast food chain and then full-time as a cashier in a local bakery,[4] indicates that without this permit "it is not feasible to make a living by myself."

In describing Working Holiday permitholders' experience, I develop the notion of "cultural exchange precarity" to refer to the nature and effects of policies governing their labour force participation and residency status in ways that uphold a conception of youth mobility, one that assumes a lust for international travel among people aged 18–35 after and/or in between completing secondary school and/or post-secondary degree programs while satisfying employer demands for labour to address qualitative labour shortages in the receiving country.

In applying this concept, I seek to discern which Working Holiday permitholders confront the fewest obstacles to shedding their temporary status (i.e., migrancy) to move as truly mobile cultural sojourners and which permitholders are positioned to retain it (i.e., akin to migrant workers). Cultural exchange precarity's dual emphasis – on culturally oriented travel and engagement in (often precarious) employment – reflects the tone and substance of policies constructing typical Working Holiday participants as adventure-seeking free agents aiming to reside in Canada on a short-term basis, who are permitted to hold jobs across the country in sectors of their choice, with the aim of financing travel, that simultaneously exempt them, as open work permitholders, from protections accorded to closed work permitholders (see Chapter 2). After a deeper look at program design and its evolution, Section 2 operationalizes this notion.

2. Canada's Premier Cultural Exchange Work Permit Program: Admission Criteria, Permit Conditions, and Blocked Pathways to Permanent Residency among Working Holiday Permitholders

The Government of Canada facilitates cultural exchange opportunities for Canadian and foreign youth through International Experience Canada, the IMP subprogram which came to encompass the Working Holiday program in the early 2000s as the federal government moved to overhaul the TFWP and recalibrate the balance between *migrant* work programs under its auspices and a diversity of so-called *mobility* programs under the IMP.

2.1 International Experience Canada

Since its formal inception at the turn of the twenty-first century, International Experience Canada has evolved and grown considerably. Work permitholders under its auspices increased more than fourfold (from 15,890 to 67,785) between 2002 and 2023 – such that IEC represented Canada's third-largest IMP overall (assuming spouses of students and skilled workers represent one group) (Figure 3.1). Considering the years 2002–23 cumulatively, there was gender parity among International Experience Canada permitholders (IRCC 2023g). With respect to age, more than 50 per cent of International Experience Canada permitholders in Canada were over the age of 25 in this period (IRCC 2023h; IRCC 2024l). Constituting 27.1 per cent, 11.2 per cent, 9.3 per cent, 8.7 per cent, and 7.9 per cent respectively in 2023, a group of relatively

Figure 3.1 Proportion of International Experience Canada and Working Holiday Permitholders in the International Mobility Program by Year in Which the Permit(s) Became Effective, 2002–23

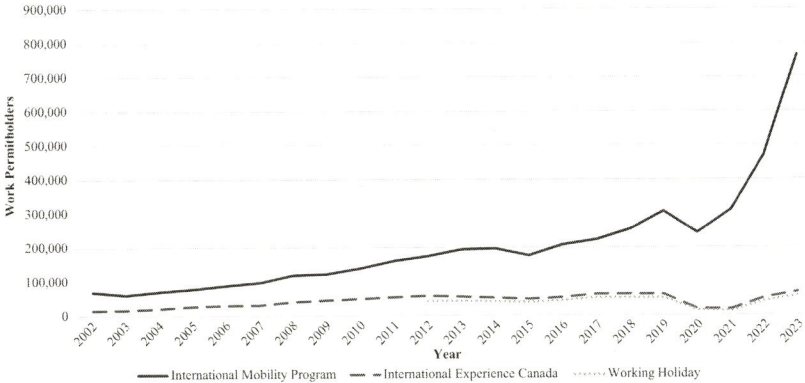

Sources: IRCC (2021a, 2023a, 2023b, 2024a).
Notes:
1. Values between 0 and 5 are suppressed, all values are rounded to the nearest 5 to maintain anonymity.
2. International Experience Canada and Working Holiday permitholders included in International Mobility Program; Working Holiday permitholders included in International Experience Canada total; shown as dashed and dotted lines respectively to demonstrate contribution to overall program size.

affluent countries, three of which share a tight connection to Commonwealth citizenship and four of which share a particular conception of "whiteness" (i.e., tied to Western European lineage), form the top five countries of citizenship of International Experience Canada permitholders – namely, France, the United Kingdom, Japan, Australia, and Ireland (Table 3.1).

The growth of International Experience Canada in these decades is especially notable given Canada's practice of limiting participation through country-specific quotas under each of its subprograms. Structured around bilateral reciprocal youth mobility agreements and arrangements negotiated between Canada and thirty-eight other countries, agreements under International Experience Canada typically include one or more of the program's three categories.

Table 3.1 International Experience Canada Permitholders by Top Ten Countries of Origin (%), 2013–23

	2013	2014	2015	2016	2017	2018	2019	2020	2021	2022	2023
1	France (24.2%)	France (21.9%)	France (21.5%)	France (20.0%)	France (23.3%)	France (24.1%)	France (24.7%)	France (34.8%)	France (32.2%)	France (27.0%)	France (27.1%)
2	Australia (14.9%)	Australia (17.1%)	Australia (16.5%)	Australia (16.7%)	Australia (12.8%)	Ireland (12.3%)	Ireland (11.7%)	United Kingdom (11.7%)	United Kingdom (13.8%)	United Kingdom (11.7%)	United Kingdom (11.2%)
3	Japan (9.9%)	Japan (11.6%)	Japan (11.2%)	Japan (10.8%)	Japan (9.9%)	Australia (11.4%)	United Kingdom (10.8%)	Ireland (7.9%)	Ireland (9.3%)	Ireland (9.7%)	Japan (9.3%)
4	Ireland (8.7%)	Ireland (8.4%)	Ireland (8.8%)	United Kingdom (9.3%)	Germany (8.9%)	United Kingdom (11.4%)	Australia (10.7%)	Germany (7.8%)	Japan (5.0%)	Australia (9.2%)	Australia (8.7%)
5	United Kingdom (7.9%)	United Kingdom (7.9%)	United Kingdom (8.0%)	Germany (9.3%)	Ireland (8.5%)	United Kingdom (9.8%)	Japan (9.7%)	Australia (6.4%)	Australia (4.7%)	Japan (8.2%)	Ireland (7.9%)
6	Germany (7.4%)	Germany (7.4%)	South Korea (7.9%)	Ireland (8.1%)	United Kingdom (8.3%)	Germany (8.2%)	Germany (8.1%)	Japan (5.7%)	Germany (4.6%)	Germany (6.8%)	South Korea (6.9%)
7	South Korea (5.3%)	South Korea (5.1%)	Germany (7.5%)	South Korea (7.9%)	South Korea (7.5%)	South Korea (4.1%)	South Korea (5.4%)	South Korea (4.6%)	Chile (4.3%)	South Korea (5.5%)	Germany (5.9%)
8	Aotearoa New Zealand (2.6%)	Aotearoa New Zealand (3.0%)	Aotearoa New Zealand (2.9%)	Aotearoa New Zealand (5.9%)	Aotearoa New Zealand (3.1%)	Aotearoa New Zealand (3.4%)	Aotearoa New Zealand (2.9%)	Czech Republic (2.1%)	South Korea (4.3%)	Aotearoa New Zealand (2.4%)	Aotearoa New Zealand (2.7%)
9	Czech Republic (2.0%)	Czech Republic (1.7%)	Czech Republic (1.6%)	New Zealand (3.2%)	Czech Republic (1.8%)	Czech Republic (1.8%)	Taiwan (1.5%)	Belgium (1.6%)	Czech Republic (3.4%)	Spain (2.1%)	Chile (2.5%)
10	Spain (1.6%)	Chile (1.3%)	Taiwan (1.5%)	Taiwan (1.7%)	Taiwan (1.6%)	Italy (1.4%)	Czech Republic (1.3%)	Spain (1.6%)	Spain (2.1%)	Chile (1.9%)	Spain (2.1%)

Sources: IRCC (2021a, 2023a, 2024a).

Note: Percentage based on data within which values between 0 and 5 are suppressed and all values are rounded to the nearest 5 to ensure anonymity.

Formal agreements under the Working Holiday program, and its less institutionalized forerunners, are nevertheless the most long-standing. While the Government of Canada created the International Experience Canada umbrella under the IMP at the turn of the twenty-first century, precursors to the Working Holiday program originated formally in 1951, before which time official immigration policy barred non-immigrant (i.e., temporary) visitors from working while in Canada (unless they were in-demand workers approved by the National Employment Service) (IRCC 2019b, 10). Resonating with scholarship probing distinctions among groups of Working Holiday permitholders, Canadian government archives reveal key antecedents: they show that between at least 1959 and 1970, there were frequent inquiries and policy changes facilitating the admittance of Australian and Aotearoa New Zealand citizens taking "working holidays" in Canada, although these decisions and practices were spread across various institutions, including high commissions, consulates, immigration bureaus, and foreign offices.[5] Across these records, government representatives imply that, regardless of official policy, there were movements of young people on "working holidays" among at least the three countries and that local officials exercised discretion in authorizing them on a case-by-case basis rather than under any overarching program. Generally, correspondences indicate that participants' common British Commonwealth citizenship granted these people "on holiday" preferential treatment over those also "on holiday" yet lacking such commonalities with Canadians.

Contemporaneously, the Working Holiday program is also host to, by far, the largest number of permitholders under the International Experience Canada triumvirate. Considering the 2012–23 period, fully 81 per cent of foreign youth enrolled in International Experience Canada are Working Holiday permitholders, such that Canada's Working Holiday program represents the fourth-largest such program in the OECD (behind only Australia, the US, and Aotearoa New Zealand) (IRCC 2023b; IRCC 2024b; OECD 2019, 27).

2.2 Entry

Allowing for work with virtually any employer in any industry across the country, Canada issues open work permits to youth participating in the Working Holiday program (IRCC 2019b). While ages of prospective permitholders range from 18 to 35 years depending upon country of origin, most reciprocal agreements cover persons aged 18–25. As of August 2023, Canada had agreements with 38 countries. With the exception of the reciprocal agreement between Canada and Australia,

Table 3.2 Working Holiday Work Permit Quotas and Durations by Top Ten Countries of Origin, 2023

Top Countries of Origin (2023)	Quota – All IEC Streams (2023)	Working Holiday Quota (2023)	Duration of Working Holiday Permit
1. France	13,450	7,000	24 months
2. United Kingdom	10,000	10,000	24 months
3. Japan	6,500	6,500	12 months
4. Australia	Unlimited	Unlimited	24 months
5. Ireland	10,700	10,500	24 months
6. Korea	6,500	6,500	12 months
7. Germany	5,000	4,490	12 months
8. Aotearoa New Zealand	2,500	2,500	23 months
9. Chile	1,750	1,618	12 months
10. Spain	2,000	1,845	12 months

Sources: IRCC (2023i, 2023j).

which is not capped, all agreements include quotas. Canada's Working Holiday agreements with affluent countries, such as the United Kingdom, Ireland, and France, capped at between 7,000 and 13,000+ in 2023, contain the largest annual quotas versus those with countries such as Japan and Korea, both of which had annual quotas of 6,500 that year (Table 3.2). Reflecting such differentials, Working Holiday permitholders from affluent countries with the highest quotas tend to conceptualize themselves more as sojourners and to place greater value on cultural exchange than on the quality of employment available. Accordingly, Sophia, an interviewee from Europe, emphasizes how working holidays are normalized among young people, noting, "what I always found very interesting … coming from a European country … was that the Working Holiday is very well-known … when I turned 18, [the question was] 'do you want to do a gap year?' … that's a working holiday." Freya, also from Europe, expresses a similar sentiment while recognizing that with a Working Holiday permit, "while you're able to work, it's not going to be the most professional or challenging job … it just gives you a different perspective on life."

Strengthening the Working Holiday program's construction as cultural exchange, outside these agreements, Recognized Organizations – a small group of universities and various non-profit organizations subject to limited regulations and permitted to assist prospective Working Holiday participants, both from countries with and without reciprocal agreements with Canada, in securing permits and employment, typically for a fee – are also granted modest annual quotas under the Working Holiday program. Pointing to some of the inequities fostered by country-specific quotas and entry requirements, permitholders from countries without reciprocal agreements with Canada, such as Davi,[6] coming to Canada from Brazil to work in veterinary services, highlight that the requirement to apply to the Working Holiday program through a recognized organization means "spend[ing] a lot of money before coming here [to Canada]," putting them at an immediate disadvantage upon their arrival, that is, undermining their ability to sojourn, thus setting the stage for differential inclusion.

2.3 Work Permit Conditions

The standard length of work permits issued under the Working Holiday program varies by permitholders' country of origin. Canada's agreements with a majority of countries set out a 12-month maximum. Yet those with Australia, France, Ireland, Aotearoa New Zealand, and the United Kingdom have long included terms of 24 months.[7] These longer permits make it more feasible for permitholders from such "culturally compatible" source countries, to quote Canada's former minister of immigration Jason Kenney (as cited in Helleiner 2017, 300), typically imagined to be cultural sojourners, to transition to permanent residency.[8] The more generous duration of permits issued to nationals from these countries is notable as these countries are also among the top eight countries of citizenship of young people admitted under the International Experience Canada program, constituting fully 58 per cent of participants in 2023 (Table 3.1). This country of origin dynamic is likewise linked to the fact that, as stated above, France and Ireland have the two highest quotas, standing at 13,450 and 10,500 in 2023 respectively, while Australia's quota is unlimited (IRCC 2023k; IRCC, 2023l; IRCC 2023m). The one-year work permits provided to Working Holiday permitholders from remaining countries of origin have another drawback. Their short duration can be a major hurdle for permitholders seeking to redress problems they are experiencing at work. Moreover, the fact that longer-term permits (i.e., of 24 months), though still highly restricted, are provided to permitholders from a few affluent countries, those identified with whiteness and which have relatively large quotas, threatens to undermine collective action by exacerbating divisions among Working Holiday permitholders.

The ability to participate more than once under Canada's Working Holiday program is also highly restricted. A few reciprocal agreements allow for additional participation within or across any International

Experience Canada category (e.g., those between Canada and Croatia, Italy, Chile, and San Marino), and a few allow for more than one participation but only under different subsets of International Experience Canada (i.e., more than one Working Holiday participation is not permitted) (e.g., as set out in agreements between Canada and Austria, Estonia, and Germany). Only Canada's agreements with Australia and the United Kingdom permit additional participation within a single International Experience Canada category (including the Working Holiday program), although this possibility is only available to applicants that came initially as Working Holiday permitholders before 2015. Recognized organizations are also granted limited annual quotas through which permitholders from countries with reciprocal agreements with Canada can access additional participation even where they have exhausted the annual quotas provided for by agreement (IRCC, 2024m). Akin to permits granted across the Working Holiday program, the award of these additional participations is independent of where the permitholder intends to work – that is, the region, industry, and occupation.[9] This restrictive architecture around extension under the Working Holiday program, which is mainly permitted in situations in which an intermediary organization is involved (otherwise under reciprocal agreements with small quotas), reflects the *mobility*-oriented goal of targeting adventure-seeking young sojourners. Yet Working Holiday permitholders' considerable labour force participation in Canada, alongside the contraction of subprograms of the TFWP outside agriculture and the moratorium on the hiring of migrant workers in food services and retail trade under its auspices in 2014 (CIC News 2014), industries in which many Working Holiday permitholders are employed, suggests that this characterization – and its attendant comparison – is not straightforward. Rather, a closer look at the Working Holiday program and profile of Working Holiday program participants' labour force participation reveals cultural exchange precarity.

2.4 (In)access to Permanent Residency

Working Holiday permitholders' prospects for transitioning to permanent residency, coupled with their desire, in certain instances, to utilize the program as a means of attaining greater security of presence (see below), also confound the assumption that their employment in Canada is ancillary to its cultural exchange emphasis. Under the Working Holiday program, there is no direct pathway to permanent residency – that is, permitholders face blocked doors. At the same time, there are no barriers to Working Holiday permitholders or former permitholders (or those entering via other International Experience Canada programs) seeking to apply for permanent residency through avenues unconnected to the Working Holiday program. That is, consistent with the growing body of literature documenting the complex and multiple legal status trajectories among temporary work permitholders, noted in Chapter 2, they may apply independently through general channels, such as those associated with the major streams of Canada's Express Entry program – namely, the Canadian Experience Class, the Federal Skilled Worker Program, and the Federal Skilled Trades Program immigration entry categories – as well as the Provincial and Territorial Nominee Programs (see Chapter 2 for a review of these immigration entry categories).[10] Still, each of Canada's federally administered express entry streams have requirements that Working Holiday permitholders are unlikely to fulfil based on their experience under the Working Holiday program alone – especially the vast majority of those from countries of origin outside the handful of countries with which Canada has interstate agreements providing for work permits of 24 months' duration (i.e., France, Australia, Ireland, Aotearoa New Zealand, Portugal, and the United Kingdom) (Table 3.2). Still, following the expiration of her Working Holiday permit, participant So-hyun obtained a visitor visa and then applied for and received a student visa to pursue graduate studies in Canada. She states that while "there's no clear … pathway from Working Holiday to PR … there are other pathways." Specifically, permitholders can attempt to "program jump" – in this instance, move between the Working Holiday, Young Professionals, and Co-op programs comprising International Experience Canada – in which case they may experience "staggered inclusion" (Bélanger et al. 2023). For example, the Canadian Experience Class requires applicants to have at least one year of the equivalent of full-time employment (1,560 hours) working in a managerial, professional, or technical/skilled trade occupation in Canada in the three years before applying. Yet, for many Working Holiday permitholders, the duration of their permits militates against attaining the requisite number of hours in a "skilled" job, especially because few have jobs lined up before arriving in Canada. Paradoxically, closed work permitholders under the Young Professionals program of International Experience Canada may have an easier time fulfilling this criterion as they must have a job deemed to be skilled (and falling in the same skilled NOC upon which Canadian Experience Class is built) prior to arriving in Canada.[11]

As the Federal Skilled Worker Program has corresponding hours and occupational requirements, and requires proof of funds and a minimum score of 67 points for other immigration selection factors under the federally administered Comprehensive Ranking System, it is similarly difficult for Working Holiday permitholders to attain permanent residency under this immigration stream. Working Holiday permitholders may apply under the Federal Skilled Worker Program. Yet entry barriers are formidable: the short duration of most work permits under the Working Holiday program and permitholders' limited access to repeat participation, two features that also inhibit the attainment of "skilled" employment, as well as limits on provisions for study (i.e., permitholders can only register in programs of six months or less), make it difficult to achieve the points threshold solely on the basis of work experience under the Working Holiday program. A parallel dynamic is at work under the Federal Skilled Trades Program, although certain program requirements exceed those under Canadian Experience Class and the Federal Skilled Worker Program, such as the requirement for at least two years of full-time work experience in a skilled trade within a narrow list of trades within five years prior to application, and having a valid job offer. In such cases as well, while it is virtually impossible for Co-op participants to access these streams utilizing their program-specific experiences, permitholders under the Young Professionals subset of International Experience Canada stand the greatest chance of attaining permanent residency under the Federal Skilled Worker and Federal Skilled Trades Programs as well. Working Holiday permitholders have the additional option of applying for permanent residency through Provincial and Territorial Nominee Programs maintained by each province/territory (except for Quebec and Nunavut) and designed to attract applicants to fill jobs deemed critical at a provincial/territorial level who wish to live in the province/territory in question. In general, as Chapter 2 illustrates, Provincial and Territorial Nominee Programs require applicants to have high levels of socially recognized skills, education, and work experience. However, as each provincial/territorial variant is tailored to attracting applicants to fill jobs deemed critical to the province/territory, each has different targets (e.g., students, businesspeople, skilled workers). Under Provincial and Territorial Nominee Programs, the two processes for obtaining entry – paper-based via employer nomination and Express Entry via provincial/territorial utilization of this federally administered system to nominate candidates who meet Canadian Experience Class, Federal Skilled Worker Program, or Federal Skilled Trades Program thresholds for settlement provincially/territorially – involve a series of requirements that are highly challenging for most former Working Holiday permitholders to fulfil based on participation in this program alone.

3. Cultural Sojourners or Migrant Workers? Experiences of Cultural Exchange Precarity among Working Holiday Permitholders

Touted by the Government of Canada as "allowing more international youth to work and travel in Canada" while "helping employers find the workers they need," the Working Holiday program is the largest subset of the International Experience Canada and a major source of international migrants for employment aged 18–25 – and the emergence of new reciprocal agreements in the late 2010s and early 2020s, alongside the enlargement of quotas in pre-existing agreements, foretell program expansion (IRCC 2023n). Yet policies and practices applicable under the Working Holiday program contribute to "cultural exchange precarity" among work permitholders: they pivot on a conception of youth mobility, casting participants as sojourners pursuing employment as a secondary activity to fund cultural exchange through travel. Meanwhile, permitholders' high rates of labour force participation, considerable concentration in jobs characterized by low levels of income from employment, and high levels of engagement in multiple jobs, often in industries facing qualitative labour shortages, together with their institutionalized insecurity of presence (i.e., given the absence of direct pathways to permanent residency) and exemption from protections accorded to closed work permitholders, confound this policy construction. Still, Working Holiday permitholders experience precariousness at the nexus of employment and residency status to different degrees. Policies assuming that Working Holiday permitholders are sojourners seeking adventures abroad (i.e., migrating for non-work purposes) open space for corrosive conditions of employment overall. Yet the experiences of permitholders from a narrow group of affluent countries of origin with the highest quotas and lengthiest permits in which one of Canada's official languages is dominant, several of which belong or previously belonged to the British Commonwealth, more closely approximate this archetype than those of permitholders from less affluent countries of origin, wherein neither English nor French is dominant, and whose nationals are often racialized as non-white.

3.1 Cultural-Exchange Assumptions Shaping Work Permit Conditions and Their Effects

For prospective permitholders, cultural exchange precarity takes shape prior to entry via the Working Holiday program, a program that offers the dual promise of adventure travel and work for remuneration.

In keeping with the formal orientation of government policies promoting the Working Holiday program, which suggests that "Canada benefits when diverse, engaged, and empowered youth are able to come from abroad to gain meaningful work and life experiences here," and aware of the constraints on mobility imposed on those with closed work permits, many Working Holiday permitholders prioritize their mobility (IRCC 2023n). That is, the issuance of prized open work permits marks one side of this dualism. Holding such permits offers some security. As Samuel, a Working Holiday permitholder from Ireland employed in the high-tech sector as a software developer, notes, "I can lose my job without worrying about losing my visa and I can look for a[nother] job while I'm here." Commenting on the significance of the freedom to move within the Canadian labour market, a feature unavailable or constrained under other work permit types, Mila, a permitholder from Germany, likens the open work permit to a treasure: "It was like gold. It was worth gold. An open work permit opens ... so many doors. You don't even realize, when you have it the first time, how precious that is, because it's so hard to get open work permits here."[12] At the same time, marking the "hard" external edges (Bosniak 2006) of this dualism, Working Holiday permitholders recognize that, despite the mobility that open work permits afford them in the labour market, they are of short duration, posing significant challenges. As one respondent, Reiko, points out, "[they are] only [for] a year ... [and are] something you can't renew. And ... the less time you have, the more challenging it gets." So-hyun expresses concern that the short duration of the permit can mean that "no one wants to hire you," while Freya explains it is "a little harder to get professional jobs because you [are] considered a traveller." Freya also went on to highlight other shortcomings of the open work permit, stating that "because you have an open work permit ... [employers] [are] ... not so sure to give you a position of a higher level because you could leave any time." In these ways, open work permits of short duration can contribute to harmonizing down in employment opportunities. That permits of longer duration (i.e., two years) are provided to Working Holiday permitholders from a few affluent countries, those identified with whiteness and which also have relatively large quotas, also threatens to intensify and bifurcate this downward levelling by exacerbating divisions among Working Holiday permitholders, thwarting the potential, albeit limited, for collective action directed at improving conditions of employment and security of presence across the board.

In the absence of a direct pathway to permanent residency under the Working Holiday program for those seeking to settle in Canada,

Table 3.3 Transitions between International Mobility Program Permits among Working Holiday Permitholders, 2011–19

Number of Work Permits	
One	77%
More than one	23%

Transitions among Working Holiday permitholders who held more than 1 permit	
Working Holiday to Post-graduation Work Permit program	0.04%
Working Holiday to Spousal Work Permit program	9%
Working Holiday to Working Holiday program	25%
Working Holiday to International Co-op program	0.27%
Working Holiday to Young Professionals program	12%
Working Holiday to other temporary work permit program	45%
Working Holiday to International Study Permit program	3%

Source: Statistics Canada (2020).
Note: Percentage represents cumulative totals.

the short duration of open work permits and limited opportunities for repeat participation pose other problems as well. As So-hyun asserts, "I couldn't renew my visa and if I wanted to stay longer as a resident … that required you to have at least one year of Canadian experience and, technically, because the [Working Holiday] visa is one year, it's not a very feasible option to stay longer." In theory, Working Holiday permitholders may program jump from one International Experience Canada stream to another to either extend their time in Canada or to work towards qualifying for permanent residency. In practice, among those Working Holiday permitholders that transition to another permit, a notable proportion join the Young Professionals component of International Experience Canada, where they receive closed work permits. Among migrants who first entered Canada as a Working Holiday work permitholder between 2011 and 2019 and transitioned to another temporary work permit, approximately 25 per cent transitioned to a second Working Holiday permit, while 12 per cent transitioned to a Young Professional permit (see Table 3.3)

Furthermore, technically, those from countries where reciprocal agreements provide for multiple streams of entry under International Experience Canada and/or for more than one participation have the greatest chance of fulfilling requirements under the Canadian Experience Class, Federal Skilled Worker, or Federal Skilled Trades immigration pathways, especially if they manage to secure multiple participations or permits (i.e., a combination of Working Holiday,

Co-op and Young Professionals permits). Illustrating one creative strategy used by Working Holiday permitholders to extend their time in Canada, often in the hope of fulfilling criteria for applying for permanent residency under one of Canada's immigration streams, three interviewees shared that they engaged in flagpoling (i.e., crossing Canada's border with the United States and immediately returning to receive same-day immigration services) to expedite their transitions between the Working Holiday program and other IMPs, including the Young Professionals program (Fabrício, Freya, and Samuel). As Sophia from Germany (a country where the reciprocal agreement provides for multiple streams of entry) explains,[13] "I wanted to stay longer ... [but] I didn't have enough points at that time to apply for the PR ... So then I talked to my boss and ... they got [me into the] Young Professionals [program] ... and from the Young Professionals I could go and apply for PR."[14] Similarly, Working Holiday permitholders utilizing recognized organizations are permitted to engage in more than one "participation" and may thus also be able to attain permanent residency, although such opportunities are few and far between and the costs involved in working through registered organizations can be prohibitive. Speaking to the excessive fees charged by registered organizations, Jusa, a permitholder from the Czech Republic who obtained a second one-year Working Holiday permit through a registered organization, notes that:

> Using recognized organizations ... is super expensive. For my first visa, considering all the paperwork, I had to pay fees to the IRCC and, all in all, I paid $1,000 Canadian. For the RO [recognized organization], I paid $6,000 ... Because I have some work experience, I have some savings, I knew that I would be able to pay for it. But, for really young people, especially from the countries that are not in [International Experience Canada; i.e., without reciprocal agreements with Canada], it's unreal for them. And there are many people who are trying to get Working Holiday via ROs.

This situation flows from systemic issues; namely, the dearth of reciprocal agreements between Canada and countries in the Global South and the smaller quotas for those where agreements do exist. Facing such fees, Davi, who moved to Canada to advance his career in an area of specialization (veterinary sciences) where it is difficult to obtain credentials in his country of origin (Brazil), expresses his frustration this way: "I don't know why [young people] from some countries have the opportunity to apply directly [for Working Holiday permits] and other countries don't, but I feel like those from the countries that do are people [from] 'First World' countries. And I think that people who would need [the ability to apply directly] most would be from developing countries. I had to spend a lot of money before coming here. And so, when I came here, I was really short on money. That really made for a hard time for me in the first place."[15]

Despite such barriers and permitholders' recognition of how global inequalities shape the countries with which Canada has reciprocal agreements under the Working Holiday program, many remain undeterred in pursuit of permanent residency. Fabrício is one such permitholder. He first moved to Canada from Brazil on a study visa to enrol at a private college, and then obtained a one-year Working Holiday permit, during which time he worked full-time as a sales manager. His motivation was "to work and then immigrate. That is my final goal." Both Fabrício and Sophia, could enter and work in Canada only through the Working Holiday program. Sophia underlines the paradoxical nature of their situation: "Obviously, Canada needs immigrants and wants immigrants, but ... only ... a specific category, 'the skilled,' have direct routes for PR" (Sophia). As a consequence, even when their efforts to utilize the Working Holiday program as a route towards permanent residency are thwarted, some permitholders, whose skillsets may be at odds with the Comprehensive Ranking System insofar as they lack the qualifications to secure certain jobs deemed as "skilled," resort to other avenues. For example, permitholder Freya, who was able to extend her time working in Canada by jumping from the Working Holiday program to the Young Professionals program, considers abandoning obtaining permanent residency independently given the limited pathways. She concedes: "I think my boyfriend's just going to sponsor me. That's the easiest thing ... 'You want to stay in Canada, you have to get married!' Lots of people get married faster to stay in Canada ... Once you are common law or a spouse, you actually have the right to retrieve a permanent residence card." Despite not being "a fan of this idea to marry into Canada because I think I can do better," Freya reports that she is taking this route even though she has high levels of socially recognized skills: "I'm qualified, but it's hard to find a way ... I talked to my boss about that, and he [said] 'if you plan on staying with him, apply through common law, which makes you basically married [according to] the state. Why don't you just do that? ... A lot of people do this because it's so much easier than actually using their expertise because there's always [a chance that] ... they won't get in."

3.2 Working Holiday Permitholders' Experiences on the Job

Even though the Working Holiday program has a "non-work" purpose by design – namely, cultural exchange – many permitholders pursue employment. A program evaluation surveying permitholders in 2017 found that an overwhelming majority (93 per cent) of Working Holiday permitholders reported engaging in paid employment,[16] fully 78 per cent of whom reported working full-time.[17] According to permitholders, the relatively short duration of Working Holiday permits, limited opportunities for repeat participation, and other features of the Working Holiday program that make participation costly, such as fees charged by registered organizations, not only heighten the imperative to secure work for remuneration but to do so promptly upon arrival. As So-hyun notes: "I think having a one-year visa is okay. But in case you are laid-off or fired ... it gets extremely hard to get a [new] job. Some of my friends had that difficulty, finding a stable job, because they didn't have that stable job in the beginning." Part of the reason, as permitholder Jusa, who, at the time of the interview, had not secured employment in Canada but was actively looking for work in IT, explains, is that "employers don't trust that people ... here on open work permits ... will stay here. They don't want to invest money in them and let them disappear after a few months ... Unless you are really experienced or a smart person who's got, for example, a nuclear physics degree, you won't get easily hired here."

In light of such pressures to obtain and retain employment, an examination of prominent indicators of labour market insecurity among Working Holiday permitholders in their main job, together with their experiences in the labour force, tells an interesting story.

Considering indicators individually, income level is where Working Holiday permitholders' precariousness stands out most; while most prioritize wage-earning (e.g., less than 2 per cent who submitted T1 tax returns for 2018 report zero income from employment), more than 70 per cent reporting earnings from employment in their tax returns earn less than $30,000 annually (see Table 3.4).[18] Moreover, where country of origin is concerned, Working Holiday permitholders from Japan, Korea, and Taiwan are significantly overrepresented in the lower income-earning category, with more than 90 per cent of Working Holiday permitholders from these countries reporting on their tax returns that they earn less than $30,000 per annum. In comparison, such low earnings are reported by only 64 per cent of Working Holiday permitholders from

Table 3.4 Annual Income among Working Holiday Permitholders, 2018

	Less Than $30,000	% with Income Less Than $30,000	More than $30,000*	% of with Income More Than $30,000*
By Country of Origin				
France	7,795	64%	4,475	36%
Australia	6,835	74%	2,420	26%
United Kingdom	4,885	63%	2,865	37%
Ireland	3,585	57%	2,695	43%
Japan	3,485	96%	155	4%
Germany	2,235	88%	305	12%
Korea	2,790	91%	290	9%
Aotearoa New Zealand	1,585	67%	785	33%
Czech Republic	980	86%	160	14%
Taiwan	1,015	93%	80	7%
Other	4,495	81%	1,030	19%
By Sex				
Male	17,405	77%	5,255	23%
Female	22,270	84%	4,400	16%
Overall Total				
	39,680	72%	15,255	28%

Source: Statistics Canada (2020).
Note: *Income categories above $30,000 are combined due to low representation of Working Holiday permitholders in higher income categories.

France, by 63 per cent of those from the United Kingdom, and by 57 per cent of those from Ireland. Working Holiday permitholder Sophia attributes her relatively low earnings as a homestay assistant to her status: "it was $17 [an hour] during the Working Holiday visa … [but] given my background, my skills, and … my education, I definitely thought that was not high enough, but I also knew that you have to start a little bit lower as a work holiday person, especially if you're only on a limited visa." Another permitholder, Fabrício, has reservations: "I don't know … if the companies are aware that immigrants need the employment. In my case, my employer knew that I need[ed] this job offer to be able to get my permanent residency. I really didn't think that was fair … but that was [the job] I had." Still another, Freya, ascribes her minimum wage job – and those of her peers – to visa status and industry of employment, two features that come together in practice: "We were all getting minimum wage. There were a lot of Working Holiday visa holders, so we all got minimum wage."

Table 3.5 Indicators of Precariousness among Working Holiday Permitholders, 2018

	Non-unionized /non-professionalized	More Than One Job	Small Firm
Country of Origin			
France	71%	44%	24%
Australia	57%	44%	23%
UK	66%	43%	24%
Ireland	54%	37%	22%
Japan	42%	42%	33%
Germany	45%	36%	26%
Korea	57%	45%	44%
Aotearoa New Zealand	61%	39%	26%
Czech Republic	75%	52%	30%
Taiwan	75%	48%	31%
Other	62%	40%	28%
Overall Total			
	60%	42%	26%

Source: Statistics Canada (2020).

Regardless of the roots of income disadvantage, it is notable that, despite a significant proportion of Working Holiday permitholders who filed tax forms reporting low incomes, employer reported data show that fully 42 per cent of Working Holiday permitholders work more than one job, further illustrating a clear imperative to work among this group (see Table 3.5).[19] As Mila, who worked part-time in hospitality as a housekeeper and in food services as a restaurant hostess, explains, "Lots of Working Holiday travellers … they really make use of that open work permit, so they could have two or three jobs at the same time." Highlighting a correlation between low wages and the compulsion to work multiple jobs, Maya, a permitholder from Australia, explains that her minimum wage job "meant I was working five jobs from August to December … I was working seven days a week, almost 60 hours a week," yet "it was just not possible to keep all of them up" because "struggling to make money" "meant staying up all night, getting three hours of sleep and then going to the next job."[20] Another permitholder, So-hyun, with multiple jobs, shares that she found a customer service job in the food service sector to be very intense – "while I was working at Tim Hortons, the workload was a bit much for me … very fast paced and just too busy" – but she retained this job for 11 months while also working in a local bakery and as a freelance photographer until her "visa expired." Further suggesting an intersection between low income and source country dynamics, So-hyun also shares this observation

Table 3.6 Industry of Employment among Working Holiday Permitholders, 2018

	Accommodation and Food Services	Retail Trade	Administrative and Support Services	Arts, Entertainment, and Recreation	Scientific, Professional, and Technical Services
		By Country of Origin			
France	16%	13%	13%	3%	10%
Australia	28%	7%	7%	15%	3%
UK	21%	9%	10%	9%	6%
Ireland	21%	9%	14%	3%	7%
Japan	67%	10%	3%	1%	1%
Germany	31%	10%	11%	8%	3%
Korea	63%	10%	2%	1%	1%
NZ	21%	7%	8%	13%	6%
Czech	39%	6%	12%	4%	2%
Taiwan	53%	11%	4%	2%	1%
Others	27%	10%	10%	6%	5%
		By Sex			
Men	21%	7%	10%	6%	7%
Women	28%	11%	9%	5%	6%
		Overall Total			
	30%	10%	9%	6%	5%

Source: Statistics Canada (2020).

about her food services workplace: "In Tim Hortons … at the time, there were different … categories of workers … the low[est] paid one [included] Japanese and Korean working holidaymakers." Low income from employment, and the propensity to engage in more than one job, must also be contextualized by industry dynamics among Working Holiday permitholders. The top four industries in which these permitholders are concentrated are accommodation and food, retail, administrative and support services, and arts, recreation, and culture. The first of which, accommodation and food services, an industry in which fully 30 per cent of Working Holiday permitholders work, is known to be a gendered domain, with larger proportions of women than men, and one that relies heavily on recruitment of migrants to meet the demands of employers facing qualitative labour shortages (see, for example, Hari 2018; Fudge & Tham 2017).

Considering country of origin, Working Holiday permitholders from Japan and Korea are also significantly overrepresented in the top industry grouping – accommodation and food (i.e., more than 60 per cent of both groups of Working Holiday permitholders work in this industry, compared to approximately 30 per cent across all countries of origin), as are Taiwanese Working Holiday permitholders. At the same time, patterns of racialization via country of origin are also apparent in professional, scientific, and technical services; in this industrial context, characterized by relatively decent conditions of work and employment, Working Holiday permitholders from Japan, Korea, and Taiwan are significantly underrepresented in contrast to those from France, who are overrepresented. Similar patterns of underrepresentation among Working Holiday permitholders from Japan, Taiwan, and Korea are evident in administrative support services. Then there are the Working Holiday permitholders whose trajectories more closely approximate adventure travellers engaging in more "lifestyle"-oriented types of employment (e.g., recreational positions such as whitewater rafting guides, ski instructors). Working Holiday permitholders from Australia and Aotearoa New Zealand are overrepresented in arts, recreation, and culture (15 per cent of Working Holiday permitholders from Australia and 13 per cent of those from Aotearoa New Zealand are employed in this industry, compared with 6 per cent of all Working Holiday permitholders). That said, while the considerable representation of Working Holiday permitholders from such countries in these industries suggests they may lean towards the stereotype of the "cultural sojourner," many of the occupations in which they are engaged, including in ski instruction, in arts, culture, and recreation, are deemed to be "skilled"; thus permitholders employed in these industries, especially those with two-year visas, may continue to hold such employment in order to have the option of pursuing permanent residency. There are also signs that Working Holiday permitholders are entering domains of employment in which abuses are well-documented, where they have been historically underrepresented in Canada, but highly prevalent elsewhere. Agriculture, where sizable subprograms of the TFWP still operate, is a case in point (On Working Holiday permitholders' participation in agriculture in Canada versus Australia, see Vosko 2022; on Working Holiday permitholders' significant representation in agriculture in Aotearoa New Zealand, see, for example, OECD 2014). Another permitholder, Freya, who relied on a registered organization to gain access to the Canadian labour force through a placement in agriculture, one of a small handful of sectors in which Working Holiday permits were issued during the pandemic, notes: "The one employer [in an essential industry, working through a registered organization] that got us into Canada, he was more likely abusing that [ability] … He made us work the whole weekend through; we were not allowed to leave the farm. As for the accommodation that we got and the working conditions, that was not acceptable. He was very intimidating, so we actually left."

4. Conclusion

In the first two decades of the twenty-first century, the Working Holiday program contributed to "cultural exchange precarity" among permitholders presumed, at a policy level, to be sojourners pursuing adventure travel alongside paid work in order to fund their adventures. Yet this chapter's investigation of Working Holiday permitholders' experience overturns this ideal-typical image of the "cultural sojourner," illustrating that it is at odds with the reality of the many permitholders who engage in employment with the object of securing permanent residency, principally through obtaining so-called Canadian experience. Furthermore, policies aiming to ensure that Working Holiday permitholders' time in Canada is finite – via the provision of largely non-renewable, yet open, work permits designed to compel these back-door entrants to return to their countries of origin – neither apply to nor affect all participants equally. The employment situation of Working Holiday permitholders from less affluent countries of origin, wherein neither English nor French is dominant, whose nationals are often racialized as non-white, resembles, in key respects, that of *migrant* workers. They too experience labour market insecurities, such as low wages in jobs in industries defined by qualitative labour shortages, such as accommodation and food services. Underscoring patterns of migrantization upholding a global hierarchy of nation-states, these permitholders also confront obstacles – or blocked passages – to permanent residency: independent immigration streams mandate the fulfilment of criteria virtually impossible to achieve on one-year open work permits. However, while Working Holiday permitholders are subject to corrosive conditions overall, the lengthier duration of permits, supplemented in certain instances by provision for additional participations, can contribute to greater access to permanent resident status via immigration streams valuing the accrual of "skilled" Canadian work experience among permitholders from a few affluent countries of origin identified with whiteness in which one of Canada's official languages is dominant. Thus, in the case of the Working Holiday program – the third-largest IMP in Canada – the distinction, at a policy level, between *mobility*-oriented "cultural exchange" and *migrant* work-oriented programs is porous, and those permitholders whose marginalization through differential inclusion is most acute bear the brunt of this porosity.

Chapter Four

Probationary Precarity: Post-graduation Permitholders

Educational migration to Canada is one of the most significant areas of growth under the IMP, not surprisingly given the country's prioritization of admitting well-educated workers with high levels of socially recognized skills on temporary, temporary-permanent, and especially permanent bases. From a policy standpoint, educational migrants are assumed to be among the foremost beneficiaries of Canada's selective (im)migrant admission system across the temporary/permanent divide. Yet mounting evidence, considering the situation of international students, points to stratification among this group such that, during the course of their studies, some educational migrants experience higher levels of insecurity in their employment and residency status than others, with short-, medium-, and potentially long-term consequences (Chiose 2016; Lu & Hou 2019). There is nevertheless a lacuna where the conditions of work and residency of a large and growing group of permitholders falling under the broader educational umbrella is concerned – namely, those enrolled in the Post-graduation Work Permit program of the IMP, which, in contrast to the Working Holiday program, is designed to promote pathways to permanent residency among those who secure and maintain employment defined as high-skilled. The Post-graduation Work Permit program is the largest subprogram of the IMP – fully 32 per cent (or 241,815) of all IMP permitholders arriving in Canada fell into this category in 2023. Post-graduation permitholders also account for nearly half of those transitioning to permanent residency under the IMP – fully 46 per cent in 2023 (IRCC 2024n; IRCC 2024o). Moreover, the promise of permanent residency under this program motivates many educational migrants to choose Canada as a destination in the first place (IRCC 2018, 6).

Against this backdrop, this chapter explores the interaction between the parameters of the Post-graduation Work Permit program and their effects on permitholders' labour force experience and transitions in residency status, focusing on how program requirements affect these entrants arriving initially through the back door as students. Attending to the porosity of this entry category, the analysis reveals that Post-graduation permitholders, assumed, at a policy level, to represent desirable immigrants, particularly due to their high levels of educational attainment and age, endure "probationary precarity," a protracted process during which they must fulfil a series of cascading educational and employment requirements to acquire permanent residency. Involving movement through multiple doors of entry, probationary precarity entails three stages, beginning with educational migrants' pursuit of degrees or certificates at Canadian post-secondary institutions, followed by securing time-limited open work permits offering potential pathways (albeit narrower channels than those applied to temporary entry as Post-graduation permitholders) to permanency, followed by requirements to fulfil mainly employment-related conditions, culminating frequently in applications for permanent residency. Throughout this trial period, during which time Post-graduation permitholders' residency status is tenuous, those that wish to remain must demonstrate their value to the Canadian labour force, leading many to accept employment that is out of sync with their credentials, skills, and experience. Close examination of this staged process reveals the institutionalized pressures that Post-graduation permitholders face across the board and their deleterious effects. Yet it also discloses stratification, particularly on the basis of country of origin, among permitholders admitted initially as international students, and with regard to the top industries in which they are employed, several of which are characterized by multiple dimensions of labour market insecurity and qualitative labour shortages.

Advancing these contentions in three parts, the ensuing exploration begins in Section 1 by elaborating the concept of probationary precarity. Section 2 then describes the evolution of Canada's Post-graduation Work Permit program, with a focus on criteria applied to permitholders in pursuit of permanent residency. Utilizing administrative data on entry and transitions to permanent residency, it illustrates that permitholders fall within an expansive conception of "youth," largely between the ages of 18 and 34 (i.e., more elastic than that associated with the Working Holiday permitholders, discussed in Chapter 3), and that a sizable majority migrate from India, a country whose emigrants have long confronted immigration systems fostering their differential inclusion in settler states such as Canada (see Chapter 1). Next, Section 3 explores permitholders' labour force experiences, revealing the high degree of precariousness permitholders experience overall, correlated with the sectors in which they are most concentrated. In these sectors, often defined by qualitative labour shortages, many permitholders experience incompatibility between the jobs they hold and their educational and skills profiles, a common pattern among permitholders from countries of origin whose nationals are racialized as non-white.

1. Probationary Precarity: Hierarchically Ordered Doors of Entry Confronting Post-graduation Permitholders

Policies in high-income receiving states routinely cast educated migrants possessing post-secondary degrees as major beneficiaries of selective immigration processes; they thus represent the archetype of the *mobile* transnational worker on account of their high levels of socially recognized skills. Offshoots of educational migration programs are thus often assumed to entail streamlined front-door entry for highly educated and trained workers seeking to settle permanently in receiving countries. As such, "15–35 percent of international students [worldwide] can be expected eventually to work and settle in their host countries [and] ... *the higher the level of education is, the more graduates stay*" (She & Wotherspoon 2013, 133, emphasis added).

Such programs typically provide for open work permits and entail few rigid requirements regarding the occupations and industries in which permitholders are to be employed (see, for example, programs in the United States (Optional Practical Training (OPT)), Australia (Post-Study Work) and the United Kingdom (Graduate Visa)). Canada's variant, the Post-graduation Work Permit program, is a case in point. Fuelled, on the one hand, by Canadian universities' drive to increase revenue in the face of restricted budgets by attracting international students[1] subject to high fees and students' larger contributions to the country's economy and, on the other hand, by federal and provincial/territorial governments' desire to attract workers with high levels of socially recognized skills, it provides for limited screening upon (re)entry, open work permits, and pathways to permanent residency for participants that fulfil a series of requirements.

Yet aspects of the Post-graduation Work Permit program, especially conditions applicable to permitholders in pursuit of permanent residency, can foster precariousness in employment and insecurity of presence overall, often along racialized lines exhibiting continuities in historical practices regulating the inclusion of immigrants on the basis of the country sponsoring their travel documents (see, for example, Mongia 1999; Chartrand & Vosko 2021). Post-graduation permitholders must move through several stages and meet considerable qualifying criteria to settle permanently. As students migrating for a non-work purpose who may engage in limited work for remuneration, they enter initially through the back door. Upon completing their programs of study, and enrolling in the Post-graduation Work Permit program, notionally, these former international students can transition to a front-door program. Qualitatively, however, certain parameters of the Post-graduation Work Permit program are associated with side-door entry – including those conditions channelling permitholders into particular occupations to obtain greater security of presence (e.g., via the requirement that they hold and retain jobs deemed to be high-skilled in order to apply for permanent residency). Only subsequently, if they meet qualifying requirements to apply for permanent residency and are invited to do so, do Post-graduation permitholders gain genuine front-door access.

Applying this "doors" analytic reveals that Post-graduation permitholders confront "probationary precarity" – a staged process beginning with pursuing degrees at Canadian post-secondary institutions, often while engaging in paid work, followed by engaging in employment that may qualify permitholders to apply for permanent residency. Conceptually, probationary precarity builds on studies of the intersections between precarious employment (Vosko 2010) and precarious residency status (e.g., Goldring & Landolt 2013), attending to the relationship between insecurity of presence and precariousness in employment. It also expands upon studies of the political economy of time among migrants, casting attention to the time period "between arrival and naturalization," wherein potential immigrants are ostensibly granted the opportunity to demonstrate their capacity and desire for citizenship, despite the fact that there will always be some migrants, including undocumented migrants, "for whom no amount of time-in-residence will yield an opportunity to accrue rights" (Cohen 2015, 341). Advancing such insights, the notion of probationary precarity, as I use it here, elevates the institutionalized pressures Post-graduation permitholders face, as temporary work permitholders, to accept precarious jobs in order to achieve security of presence.

Former international students that hold legally validated temporary status in Canada, or have left the country, and have completed an appropriate academic, vocational, or professional training degree program full-time at an eligible Canadian learning institution within the preceding 180 days may obtain an open work permit. Yet Post-graduation permitholders who wish to apply for permanent residency must typically accrue the necessary employment experience, channeling some, particularly those from relatively less affluent countries whose nationals are racialized as non-white, into jobs characterized by multiple dimensions of labour market insecurity, often in industries and occupations out of sync with their skills and educational backgrounds. That is, throughout this staged trial period, Post-graduation permitholders must navigate multiple hierarchically ordered doors of entry, during which time their residency status is tenuous and their employment can be precarious, to demonstrate their value to the Canadian labour force.

2. Canada's Post-graduation Work Permit Program: A Model Program for Educational Migrants?

The origins of Canada's Post-graduation Work Permit program lie in regulations to Canada's *Immigration Act,* specifically an exemption (C-43) adopted in 2004, prior to the program's establishment, allowing international students to remain in Canada for up to a year after graduation if they have a valid job offer related to their field of study (Citizenship and Immigration Canada 2004, 37). The same year, Canada and the provincial governments of Nova Scotia and Saskatchewan signed memoranda of understanding initiating pilot programs – direct precursors to the Post-graduation Work Permit program – allowing former international students[2] who had studied for at least two years at, and graduated from, publicly funded post-secondary institutions to stay an additional year if they held jobs in their fields of study. Shortly thereafter, Alberta and British Columbia (outside of the Vancouver Census Metropolitan Area) followed suit. By May 2005, these pilot programs expanded across the country and allowed for the issuance of two-year work permits to applicants with valid job offers in areas related to their studies (i.e., permits akin to closed sectoral work permits) for those employed outside the three census metropolitan areas to "help spread the benefits of immigration to more of Canada's Regions" (Government of Canada 2005).

With the success of these provincial pilot programs, and alongside the dramatic growth of graduate student visa schemes in comparable countries long identified as settler societies, such as Australia, which saw a 15.3 per cent increase in oversees graduates remaining as workers between 2007 and 2015, and the United States, where its OPT program grew markedly over the same time period (She & Wotherspoon 2013; Grimm 2019), and as "permits issued to tertiary-level international students increased 2.8 times from 45,900 to 173,000 in Canada from 2008 to 2019" (Crossman, Lu, & Hou 2022, 2), the Canadian government introduced changes to what later became known formally as the Post-graduation Work Permit program. Between 2005 and 2008, it began to issue open work permits to

Figure 4.1 Proportion of Post-graduation Permitholders in the International Mobility Program by Year in Which the Permit(s) Became Effective, 2002–23

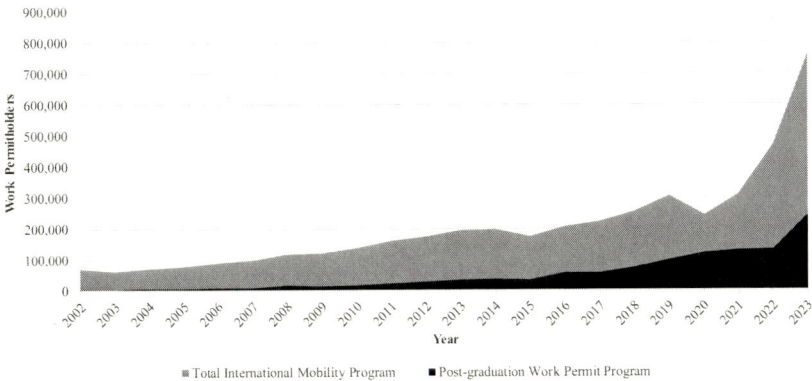

Sources: IRCC (2021a, 2023a, 2024a).
Note: Values between 0 and 5 are suppressed, all values are rounded to the nearest 5 to maintain anonymity.

former international students who had been enrolled in, and graduated from, a program of study (initially of a minimum of eight months' duration) at a designated public post-secondary institution, and were understood to have migrated for a non-work (i.e., educational) purpose. Subsequently, certain provinces (initially British Columbia and subsequently Quebec), provisionally, and controversially on account of their support for private training programs, expanded eligibility for the Post-graduation Work Permit program to a broader group of international students, including those enrolled in career training programs at select private non-degree granting institutions receiving an Education Quality Assurance Designation. By adopting these programs, the provinces aimed (1) to increase the attractiveness and improve the experience of post-secondary education for international students, (2) to increase the temporary labour supply for key industries and occupations, and, (3) to facilitate transitions from temporary to permanent status. Such pilot programs contributed to a high magnitude of growth in the Post-graduation Work Permit program.

After Canada began to issue open work permits to former international students, enrolment in the Post-graduation Work Permit program skyrocketed such that the number of permitholders exceeded 240,000 in 2023 (from less than 5,000 in 2005) (Figure 4.1). One factor driving this trend is that the Post-graduation Work Permit program allows eligible international student graduates to remain in the country as temporary work permitholders, and to engage in employment after graduating.

2.1 Entry

Contemporaneously, the Post-graduation Work Permit program allows recent international student graduates to stay and work in Canada temporarily for up to three years after graduating, pegged to their degree or program length. To qualify, graduates must hold valid temporary status or have left Canada. They must have completed an academic, vocational, or professional training program of at least eight months' total duration at an eligible learning institution[3] and have maintained full-time student status in Canada in each academic session of the program/programs of study they completed.[4] International student graduates are ineligible for the Post-graduation Work Permit program if they have already participated in the program in the past, studied English or French as a second language, taken courses of general interest or self-improvement, participated in various scholarship programs,[5] completed at least half of a study program by distance learning (online course, e-learning, correspondence), or completed a study program at a non-Canadian institution located in Canada.

With regard to education level, predictably the highest percentage of Post-graduation permitholders are college-educated, followed by those with bachelor's degrees, master's degrees, CEGEP education, and doctorates.[6] Considering age, Post-graduation permitholders are largely younger than 34, with 44 per cent younger than 25, 48 per cent falling within the 25–34 range, and 8 per cent older than 35 in 2023 (IRCC 2024r). By country of origin, India, China, the Philippines, Nigeria, and Iran were the top five countries of origin of Post-graduation permitholders in 2023 (Appendix Table A.3). Among this group, the top two countries remained constant in the 2002–3 period, although India overtook China starting in 2016. Moreover, there were approximately eight times as many Post-graduation permitholders from India (145,820) than China (17,115) in 2023. As discussed in Chapter 1, large numbers of Post-graduation permitholders arriving from India reflect the country's highest participation rate, second only to that of China, in what Suwandi (2019, 46) labels global chains of labour and value. But, while analyses of the long-term trajectories of Indian and Chinese migrant workers ultimately settling in Canada illustrate that these two groups may fare better than those from other countries of origins, Lo, Li, and Yu (2017, 328–9) show that they still confront underemployment and "brain waste." Furthermore, as Castles (2004, 223–4) has long observed, policies emerging from immigration systems enabling differential labour costs, including, in this case the Post-graduation Work Permit program, are "often really about allowing [workers arriving] in through side and back doors, so that they can be more readily exploited." Such policies may, moreover, contribute to continuities in racialized processes dating to Canada's adoption of explicitly racist immigration policies restricting permanent settlement among immigrants from China, dating to the late nineteenth century (Cho 2002), as well as the country's early adoption of requirements for passports authorizing racialized difference on the basis of nation, well-documented to affect immigrants from India profoundly (Mongia 1999) (see Chapter 1; Appendix Table A.3). Notably, there is less divergence by gender, as opposed to country of origin, in enrolment in the Post-graduation Work Permit program overall. That said, while men and women constituted 53 per cent and 47 per cent of all permitholders respectively in 2023, 57 per cent of permitholders from India, the largest country of origin, were men and only 43 per cent were women (IRCC 2024s).

2.2 Work Permit Conditions

If applicants for the Post-graduation Work Permit program fulfil the foregoing criteria, they re-enter through *quasi-front doors*. They are issued open work permits valid for between eight months and three years, attached to the length of the qualifying program of study; Post-graduation permitholders graduating from programs of between eight months and two years in length receive permits valid for the same duration as their program of study. In contrast, those graduating from programs of two years or more receive three-year work permits, the lengthiest permits under the auspices of this IMP. Post-graduation permitholders employed in "high-skilled" occupations, specifically managerial, professional, and technical/skilled trades (NOC TEERs 0, 1, 2, and 3 respectively), holding work permits valid for at least six months and residing in Canada, may also be accompanied by spouses, who are also eligible for open work permits. In April 2022, in the wake of the global pandemic, faced with many Post-graduation permitholders with expiring open work permits, the federal government issued a policy permitting extensions of up to eighteen months for all those with Post-graduation work permits scheduled to end between January and December 2022 (IRCC 2022b). Then, starting 6 April 2023, it allowed permitholders who wished to remain in Canada longer to opt into a facilitative process of work permit extension "to allow Canada to retain high-skilled talent" (IRCC 2023o).[7]

2.3 Access to Permanent Residency

Once Post-graduation permitholders are admitted, they can become eligible to apply for permanent residency through several avenues. The two most prominent options are the Canadian Experience Class, and the Provincial and Territorial Nominee Programs. As illustrated in Chapter 2, the foremost option, the Canadian Experience Class, a subset of the federal Express Entry program, was introduced in 2008 explicitly to attract more "skilled workers," including students from abroad with the goal of retaining them as permanent residents as appropriate. In its current form, with the overarching objective of "increasing Canada's labour market responsiveness and global competitiveness in attracting and retaining highly skilled workers and international graduates who [have] demonstrated their ability to integrate into the Canadian labour market" (IRCC 2015, 1), especially those who have experience studying and/or working in Canada and are fluent in an official language, the Canadian Experience Class enables participants in Canada's TFWP and post-graduates to apply for permanent residency if they meet minimum language requirements and have at least one year of full-time (i.e., 1,560 hours) skilled work experience in Canada in the three years prior to applying.[8] Under the Canadian Experience Class, recall that "skilled work" is defined as work experience in one or more jobs classified as NOC TEERs 0 to 3. To apply, Post-graduation permitholders must demonstrate that they have performed duties set out in the lead statement of the occupational description in the NOC, including all essential duties and most of the main duties listed therein. And they must have gained this employment experience while working under temporary resident status where the performance of work is authorized – that is, they must apply on the basis of their employment experience as Post-graduation permitholders, not as international students. After fulfilling these requirements, permanent residency applicants who are former Post-graduation permitholders are ranked in accordance with the Comprehensive Ranking System (described in Chapter 2), which serves as the basis for issuing invitations to apply to those with the highest scores. Recall too that Post-graduation permitholders may, in turn, apply for permanent residency under Provincial Nominee Programs, which offer both paper-based entry and entry via the Express Entry system, if they have the skills, education, and/or work experience deemed critical at a provincial/territorial level, and wish to live in the Canadian province/territory in question. During the COVID-19 pandemic these routes of entry were modified, and Canada introduced travel restrictions effectively closing the border to overseas permanent residency applicants (see Chapter 2). Yet to meet immigration targets, the federal government boosted Canadian Experience Class invitations for eligible candidates already resident in Canada, and introduced a new temporary pathway for not only "essential workers" but "international graduates" already in the country on temporary work permits (IRCC 2021b, 2021c). This Temporary Resident to Permanent Resident Pathway encompassed six streams, three for English and French speakers, with caps, and three for French speakers, without caps. Established to offer as many as 40,000 spaces between 6 May and 5 November 2021, the stream devoted to recruiting international graduates of Canadian institutions was, by far, the largest (IRCC 2021c). Eligibility requirements for those seeking permanent residency through the Temporary Resident to Permanent Resident Pathway were also less stringent than those tied to the Post-graduation Work Permit program; applicants did not have to hold a Post-graduation Work Permit and could hold any job that exists in the NOC classification system so long as they could demonstrate at least one year of Canadian work experience and they had paid taxes.[9]

In terms of securing permanent residency, Post-graduation permitholders represented 46 per cent of all IMPs transitioning to this status in 2023 – a percentage that nearly doubled in just over a decade (IRCC 2024m; IRCC 2024n). Examined from another angle, the number of permanent residents who have been Post-graduation permitholders quadrupled between 2008 and 2016 (from 4,888 to 18,801), and those who held a Post-graduation work permit immediately prior to securing this status more than quadrupled in this period as well (from 2,393 to 10,983) (IRCC 2018, 27). Among those transitioning from 2008 to 2023, the majority of entrants were consistently between 25 and 29 years of age upon arrival, a group assigned the maximum points for age under the Canadian Experience Class (IRCC 2024t). This growth of relatively younger educational migrants engaged in transitions to permanency is notable insofar as age has, in the Canadian context, been long accepted as a justification for precarious employment among young people (McBride 2004).

Among those that transition to permanent residency status, most Post-graduation permitholders move through front-door (economic class) entry categories (93 per cent in 2023). Historically, the Canadian Experience Class has been the largest entry stream annually, accounting for 45 per cent of entrants of former Post-graduation permitholders between 2008 and 2021 (IRCC 2024m; see Table 4.1). Over this same period, Provincial and Territorial Nominee Programs, which are largest in Ontario, British Columbia, and Alberta,

Table 4.1 Admission of Permanent Residents with Prior Post-graduation Permitholder Status by Immigration Program, 2008–23

	CEC (Canadian Experience Class)	CEC%	PNP (Provincial Nominee Programs)	PNP%	Other	Other %	Total (annual)
2008	0	0%	545	22.7%	1,855	77.3%	2,400
2009	905	22.5%	890	22.2%	2,215	55.2%	4,010
2010	1,265	29.9%	650	15.4%	2,310	54.7%	4,225
2011	1,800	42.6%	650	15.4%	1,775	42.0%	4,225
2012	2,535	39.5%	1,365	21.2%	2,525	39.3%	6,425
2013	1,475	21.4%	2,345	34.0%	3,080	44.6%	6,900
2014	4,110	40.9%	3,330	33.2%	2,600	25.9%	10,040
2015	2,040	20.0%	4,470	43.8%	3,705	36.3%	10,215
2016	1,675	15.2%	3,730	33.9%	5,590	50.8%	10,995
2017	8,610	45.9%	4,820	25.7%	5,335	28.4%	18,765
2018	10,165	41.4%	7,605	31.0%	6,765	27.6%	24,535
2019	11,115	40.4%	10,750	39.1%	5,650	20.5%	27,515
2020	9,145	47.2%	6,440	33.2%	3,810	19.6%	19,395
2021	52,960	60.0%	8,105	9.2%	27,360	31.0%	88,245
2022	8,650	16.4%	8,755	16.6%	35,330	67.0%	52,735
2023	17,105	25.2%	20,720	30.5%	30,035	44.3%	67,860
Total (2008–2023)	133,555		85,170		139,940		358,485

Source: IRCC (2024n).
Notes:
1. Values between 0 and 5 are suppressed; all values are rounded to the nearest 5 to maintain anonymity.
2. "Other" comprises all other entry routes, including the TRPR, skilled trades, skilled workers, family sponsorship, and refugee settlement. As noted in the text, the significance of this category in 2022–3 is explained by the expansion of the TRPR category in response to the COVID-19 pandemic.

have served as primary vehicles for obtaining permanent residency, especially in certain years (e.g., 2011–13), accounting for 23 per cent of admissions to permanent residency among former Post-graduation permitholders. As evidenced by the increase in the "Other" category in Table 4.1, in 2022 and 2023, however, the time-limited pandemic-related Temporary Resident to Permanent Resident Pathway outpaced both entry streams, which accounted for 67 and 44.3 per cent of entries of former Post-graduation permitholders in those years (IRCC 2024m).

3. Experiences of Probationary Precarity among Post-graduation Permitholders

Even though Post-graduation permitholders represent nearly half of all IMP participants that ultimately secure permanent residency, not all former students participating in the Post-graduation Work Permit program pursue this path. Many educational migrants have this goal upon graduation, particularly those migrating from countries with relatively lower GDP per capita (Lu & Hou 2019). Aside from this objective, a study of international students conducted by the Canadian Bureau for International Education found that two-thirds (65 per cent) rated post-graduation employment opportunities, in and of themselves, as vital to their reasons for electing to study in Canada in the mid-2010s (IRCC 2018, 17). Shaped by the common mismatch between Post-graduation permitholders' relatively high levels of educational attainment and credentials, acquired paradoxically as educational migrants, and their occupational and industrial locations, probationary precarity reaches its apex as they navigate the penultimate set of doors, and is experienced acutely by those migrating from top countries of origin whose nationals are often racialized as non-white. A profile of permitholders' earnings from employment, attentive to the quality of their jobs, together with current and transitioning permitholders' reflections on how the terms of their employment and residency status affect their major life choices, attests to this experience.

3.1 Precariousness on the Job

While Post-graduation permitholders arrive through the back door, as educational migrants with "non-work" objectives, many of those that reach the penultimate stage of their trial period engage in paid employment (92 per cent in 2021; see Table 4.2). Moreover, considering the top five countries of origin of Post-graduation permitholders, those with the largest shares reporting taxable earnings in 2021 were India (98 per cent) and the Philippines (98 per cent), followed by Nigeria (97 per cent), Bangladesh (97 per cent), and Iran (96 per cent). In comparison, Post-graduation permitholders with relatively lower shares of taxable earnings migrated from China (71 per cent) and Korea (84 per cent) (Table 4.2).[10] Despite such differences, large shares of permitholders engaged in wage-earning across the board, reflected in the profiles of those from top countries of origin for the Post-graduation Work Permit program, call for inquiring into the nature of permitholders' employment.

Table 4.2 Labour Force Participation among Post-graduation Permitholders by Top Ten Countries of Origin, 2021

Declared Earnings in 2021	
Top Ten Countries of Origin	
India	98%
China	71%
France	86%
Vietnam	94%
Brazil	94%
Korea	84%
Iran	96%
Nigeria	97%
Philippines	98%
Bangladesh	97%
Others	90%
Overall Total	
	92%

Source: Statistics Canada (2023).

Considering indicators of labour market (in)security among Post-graduation permitholders in their main jobs individually, overall their precariousness stands out where income level is concerned. While most permitholders engage in wage earning (e.g., only approximately 2 per cent who submitted T1 tax returns for 2021 report zero income from employment), not surprisingly, given requirements for completing the equivalent of two years of qualifying full-time employment to gain access to permanent residency, among those who report earnings, nearly 40 per cent earn extremely low and nearly 40 per cent earn relatively low incomes from employment (i.e., less than $30,000 and $30,000–$50,000 per year respectively). Furthermore, relatively high proportions of those from Vietnam (47 per cent), China (46 per cent), Korea (45 per cent), and Bangladesh (42 per cent) earn less than $30,000 (see Table 4.3). Shahriar, a permitholder from Bangladesh employed full-time as a support adviser for an e-commerce company and earning $42,000 per year, makes the following observation: "I definitely feel we are underpaid because our disposable income is not a lot at the end of the day. I have a full-time salary position … but I am not too far off from minimum wage when I calculated down to the hours." Such low earnings reflect Post-graduation permitholders' relatively low income from employment compared to permanent resident/citizen-workers with corresponding levels of education. For example, a 2018 IRCC study found that, in 2013,

Table 4.3 Annual Income among Post-graduation Permitholders, 2021

	Less Than $30,000	$30,000– $50,000	$50,000– $70,000	$70,000– $90,000	$90,000+
		By Country of Origin			
India	38%	42%	14%	4%	2%
China	46%	27%	14%	7%	7%
France	37%	31%	21%	8%	3%
Vietnam	47%	37%	11%	3%	2%
Brazil	29%	33%	20%	10%	7%
Korea	45%	34%	14%	5%	3%
Iran	38%	28%	16%	10%	9%
Nigeria	30%	33%	21%	9%	7%
Philippines	37%	44%	13%	4%	2%
Bangladesh	42%	31%	15%	7%	5%
Others	37%	33%	18%	7%	4%
		By Sex			
Men	36%	37%	17%	6%	4%
Women	41%	40%	13%	4%	2%
		Overall Total			
	38%	38%	15%	5%	3%

Source: Statistics Canada (2023).

the median employment income of Post-graduation permitholders (i.e., including all post-secondary study levels) was $23,690, whereas at the time the median gross annual earnings of Canadian graduates of colleges (i.e., citizens and permanent residents) was $41,600, university-based bachelor's programs was $53,000, and university-based master's programs was $70,000 (IRCC 2018, 19).

Despite the dearth of evidence indicating that the requirement that Post-graduation permitholders have the equivalent of one year of full-time Post-graduation work experience within a narrow band of NOCs in the three years prior to applying for permanent residency through the Canadian Experience Class yields long-term earnings advantages (Lu & Hou 2017), many endure low-wage jobs in the short term in the hope of long-term gains. As Sadia, a permitholder from Bangladesh who worked full-time on contract (through a temp. agency) as an accounting coordinator for a company in the fashion/apparel sector, puts it, "It was just what I had to do. I was on the clock … and I needed that one year of work experience. After six months of looking for a job and not finding anything, I was prepared to work at $15 an hour if need be." Faced with difficulties securing full-time employment providing sufficient wages,

Table 4.4 Indicators of Precariousness among Post-graduation Permitholders, 2021

	Non-unionized/ non-professionalized	More Than One Job	Small Firm	Precarious*
		Country of Origin		
India	80%	69%	22%	63%
China	84%	36%	37%	52%
France	64%	45%	22%	38%
Vietnam	83%	57%	36%	64%
Brazil	83%	48%	23%	49%
Korea	82%	44%	38%	56%
Iran	74%	55%	24%	51%
Nigeria	70%	62%	13%	47%
Philippines	68%	66%	21%	53%
Bangladesh	79%	60%	17%	53%
Others	73%	52%	20%	46%
		By Sex**		
Men	84%	61%	23%	60%
Women	82%	62%	24%	61%
		Overall Total		
	78%	61%	24%	58%

Source: Statistics Canada (2023).
Notes:
1. *Precarious employment is a compound variable capturing whether or not a respondent experiences two out of three indicators of precariousness.
2. **Due to the nature of the CEEDD, which is based on linkable files from administrative sources, different variables come from different datasets. The harmonized variable capturing gender comes from the T1 Personal Master tax file, submitted by employees, whereas other variables included in this table come from the Longitudinal Immigration Database or employer-provided datasets. Because some employees do not submit T1s for various reasons, the number of responses is smaller when examining gender in relation to precariousness than when examining precariousness among all respondents, regardless of whether their gender is known. For this reason, the proportions depicted for men and women differ from that of the overall total.

many permitholders resort to multiple jobholding – indeed, nearly half hold more than job. There is also evidence of stratification by country of origin along this dimension: for example, particularly large proportions of Post-graduation permitholders from India (69 per cent) and the Philippines (66 per cent) are multiple jobholders. Reshma, a permitholder from India who, despite completing two post-graduate nursing diplomas in Canada, could not acquire sufficient income from a main job and faced excessive demands in her second job, characterizes her situation this way: "Employers ... know that you need the hours and the position, [and] they do take advantage of that."

Indicative of Post-graduation permitholders' lack of control over the labour process overall, fully 87 per cent are non-unionized/non-professionalized; attending to country of origin further reveals that lower proportions of permitholders from France (64 per cent), the Philippines (68 per cent), and Nigeria (70 per cent) are non-unionized/non-professionalized than those from other top countries of origin, such as China (84 per cent), Vietnam (83 per cent), Brazil (84 per cent), Korea (82 per cent), and India (80 per cent). Coupled with their insecure residency status, these permitholders' low rates of unionization/professionalization reflect a dearth of access to rights at work overall, prompting some to avoid challenging the status quo. Leela, a permitholder from India who, after completing a diploma in gerontology and palliative care, worked in a fast food chain, characterizes the compulsion to accept excessive hours this way: "I am worried if I say no to overwork, then that can [have a] bad impact of my profile ...You are [so] insecure ... Even though sometimes I want to say 'no' to them, I have to say 'yes' ... to come in when I have day off ... to [be] cooperative." Reshma reflects on the tension between her rights at work on paper and the need to maintain employment in the interest of attaining greater security of presence this way: "I do feel like we do have rights but ... sometimes you are in a position where you cannot really use them ... For example, [at] my job, something did happen ... there was an incident [of harassment] ... I wanted to file a complaint against my employer, but I couldn't ... because it would jeopardize my employment." Another permitholder, Rahee, who came to Canada from South Korea to pursue a diploma in international transportation and customs, was also motivated to retain her employment because she feared returning to the social conditions in her country of origin, specifically growing gender-based violence. She soberly reflects, "it's getting harder for women to live in Korea ... I genuinely felt that I was in danger ... unsafe staying in Korea." Thus, while the decisions of permitholders to (at least temporarily) endure otherwise undesirable conditions of employment may reflect their limited agency at one level, they may also be motivated by longer-term aims (i.e., to pursue better life chances) and signify agency of another order.

Further attesting to the dearth of access to regulatory protection, about 24 per cent of permitholders are employed in small firms. Yet permitholders from certain countries experience this dimension of precariousness more than others. For example, relatively high proportions of those from Korea (38 per cent),[11] China (37 per cent), and Vietnam (36 per cent) work in small firms. In the case of Jia,[12] a permitholder from South Korea working for a family business as an office manager, the

Table 4.5 Industry of Employment among Post-graduation Permitholders, 2021

	Accommo-dation and Food Services	Administrative and Support Services	Retail Trade	Scientific, Professional, and Technical Services	Manu-facturing
		By Country of Origin			
India	20%	19%	15%	6%	8%
China	13%	4%	10%	19%	6%
France	5%	5%	10%	22%	8%
Vietnam	29%	5%	11%	10%	7%
Brazil	7%	7%	11%	16%	9%
Korea	24%	3%	10%	12%	7%
Iran	5%	6%	14%	19%	8%
Nigeria	3%	17%	8%	12%	6%
Philippines	22%	7%	10%	6%	5%
Bangladesh	15%	15%	13%	14%	5%
Others	8%	11%	10%	14%	6%
		By Sex			
Men	14%	16%	13%	10%	10%
Women	20%	13%	13%	9%	4%
		Overall Total			
	16%	14%	13%	10%	7%

Source: Statistics Canada (2023).

size of firm she was working for had implications for compensation as well: "Being a small business and ... family-owned ... it was very much like a 'mom and pop' store. I do feel like I would have been compensated more fairly if I wasn't a post-graduate permitholder or if I had PR or citizenship." Considering indicators cumulatively, while a large share of all Post-graduation permitholders (61 per cent) hold precarious jobs, there are considerable differences with reference to permitholders' country of origin. For example, fully 63 per cent from India hold precarious jobs in comparison to a still sizable, yet considerably lower, percentage from France (38 per cent).

Industry of employment is central to such high degrees of precariousness. The top four industries of employment among Post-graduation permitholders are accommodation and food services, administrative support, retail trade, and professional, scientific, and technical services, followed by manufacturing in fifth place (Table 4.5). Furthermore, professional, scientific, and technical services, arguably the least precarious industries in this group, moved from the first- to the third-ranked industry from 2008 to 2013 (IRCC 2018), a trend that continued in 2021 when professional, scientific, and technical services was the fourth most common industry (Statistics Canada 2023). Meanwhile, retail trade ascended from the fifth- to the third-ranked sector of employment (IRCC 2018). Correlated with a high concentration of Post-graduation permitholders in industries defined by qualitative labour shortages (i.e., in which precarious jobs undesirable to permanent residents and citizen-workers are the norm), such shifts offer insight into the relatively low employment income of Post-graduation permitholders overall – as well as their marginal wage growth between 2008 and 2018 – (Crossman, Lu, & Hou 2022) and their cumulative precariousness. Yet, more broadly, Post-graduation permitholders' concentration in these industries also reflects the challenges they confront in obtaining and maintaining employment requirements for permanent residency, particularly in acquiring jobs in professional, managerial, and technical occupational categories deemed desirable under immigration policy.

4. The Price of Front-Door Entry: Strategies to Attain Permanent Residency

As Post-graduation permitholders navigate entry through the final set of doors, challenges that they face, despite holding open work permits, become starkly apparent. Post-graduation permitholders appreciate their relative mobility compared with those with closed work permits. Yet, attesting to tensions flowing from the "probationary" nature of their status, permitholder Jia notes, while "I do have mobility ... I do feel constraints ... because I'm not a PR holder, because I'm not a citizen." Another permitholder, Leela, indicates that she cannot return to her country of origin (India) for fear of losing her managerial position because, like other people in her situation, even if there is a "family emergency, they can't quit their job." Foremost among such constraints is the requirement to sustain full-time employment in a narrow band of NOCs. As a consequence, Sadia, a permitholder that would prefer a different job, asserts that, while her open work permit seemingly provides for mobility on the labour market, this gesture is limited in practice: "It would be easy to switch jobs because of the nature of the work permit but then [there are] all the PR considerations: having to work for a year and not wanting to go into the problem of explaining that 'this is how many months I worked on this job and then this many days of gap and then this more many months of the job, they all add up to one year' ... That restricts me from switching jobs." To secure the ability to apply for permanent residency, Post-graduation permitholders also resort to occupations in industries such as accommodation and food services and retail because of difficulties securing other employment falling under required NOC codes. While they may hold qualifications for positions outside the occupations falling within such codes, permitholders seeking permanent residency must secure and retain jobs classified as NOC TEER 0, 1, 2, or 3 (i.e., professional, managerial, and technical). Leela, who took on managerial work in the fast-food industry rather than pursuing her profession (as a nurse), describes their quandary: "Its only due to this [NOC] restriction that I am working [at] McDonalds right now."

Criteria requiring Post-graduation permitholders to hold NOC level TEER 0–3 positions can also delay professional certification. In order to secure permanent residency through the Canadian Experience Class pathway, Reshma, another permitholder holding a nursing degree from a Canadian institution, yet working in a managerial position in fast food to satisfy NOC requirements, spoke of how her earnings were insufficient to undertake the nursing practicum required for registration as a nurse (e.g., 400 hours in Ontario) and of the difficulties in writing the NCLEX, a nursing exam that requires concentrated preparation time, unavailable to her given the short window of the work permit period. To fulfil such requirements for licensure, and avert occupational downgrading in the long run, Reshma needed a higher-paying job first. She was therefore seeking work as a personal support worker, a better-quality position than her job in a fast food restaurant but still one for which she was overqualified and one requiring her to purchase a vehicle:

> I am just waiting for my PR card … I can't directly work in the nursing field yet [until I pass my NCLEX and get the hours of nursing work required for licensure] but I can work as [a] PSW (personal support worker) and get paid more than this job. But [I need] to buy a car first. For that, I need my PR card so I can … get [a good] … interest rate; after that, I want to go to India [to get the 400 hours of nursing experience required to qualify for registration]. For now, everything is on hold, I am just waiting for my PR card to arrive.

Underlining the multiple doors of entry characterizing probationary precarity, Reshma also notes that, for those in her situation, the Canadian Experience Class pathway – compelling her to secure a managerial position in a fast food restaurant initially – was her only option because requirements for applying for permanent residency under the Provincial and Territorial Nominee Program in the province in which she resides (Alberta) are prohibitive: "To apply through the PNP, you need to have a job related to your studies, [meaning that] if I'm apply-ing for PNP, I have to get a job as an RPN or LPN. That is not possible without completing [the] NCLEX." Still, having invested in their edu-cation, permitholders whose end goal is permanent residency persist along such pathways. As Shahriar, who completed an undergraduate degree in Canada notes, "As an international student you are paying, annually, five times a fee that a Canadian student is paying ... coming from that perspective, I see my undergrad experience as an investment. For my parents, it's not just a degree that I want to take but everything else that Canada can offer me as well, because I have invested a signifi-cant amount of foreign money into this country ... I have seen this as a direct route for my citizenship here." Probationary precarity is nev-ertheless a highly protracted process for some Post-graduation permit-holders, particularly those who "program jump" prior to entering the Post-graduation Work Permit program. Jia, who moved from a Spousal to a student visa to the Post-graduation Work Permit program puts it this way: "When people find out about my situation, they can't fathom that I'm having such a hard time [reaching the stage of] applying for PR ... I hold a secure TEER 3-level job. My previous position also qualified. Someone who holds a bachelor's degree, an advanced diploma, like a perfect English score, who has a child who grew up in Canada for all his life, is ... still ... a foreigner ... it's hard." In light of challenges to fulfill-ing requirements for permanent residency independently, another post-graduate, Rahee, without a history of program jumping, sees pursuing permanent residency through spousal sponsorship as a back-up: "It's easier to get PR through the Canadian spouse. But I already started all the processes for applying for it, applying for PR, [as a Post-graduation permitholder] so I couldn't stop it at this moment. And just for ... insurance, I [will] just apply for another PR program through him." Despite clear and, indeed, direct pathways to permanent residency under the Post-graduation Work Permit program, some permitholders may ultimately resort to spousal sponsorship for permanent residency, the dynamics of which may reflect relational precarity, discussed next in the context of the Spousal Work Permit program explored in Chapter 5.

5. Conclusion

Post-graduation permitholders are assumed beneficiaries of Canada's highly selective immigration system. Yet the employment on offer to these former educational migrants, first entering through the back door, with credentials from Canadian post-secondary institutions, by no means guarantees access to permanent residency. Furthermore, the jobs that many permitholders ultimately secure in their bids to improve their security of presence (i.e., that may permit front-door entry) do not necessarily align with their training and experience and thus can contribute to occupational downgrading. Despite possessing high levels of education and socially recognized skills, permitholders thus typically pass through multiple, and often hierarchical, doors of entry as students and degree-holders. In this process, they experience probationary precarity overall – a protracted and staged experience functioning to filter out "economically undesirable" *migrants* and to promote front-door entry among "economically desirable" immigrants. Many permitholders, particularly those from countries of origin whose nationals have historically faced discrimination via racialized immigration policies fostering differential inclusion, such as India, confront acute labour market insecurity.

Immigration, labour, and employment policies aimed ostensibly at promoting smooth transitions to permanent residency shape Post-graduation permitholders' experiences fundamentally; criteria for participating in the Post-graduation Work Permit program and obtaining the opportunity to apply for permanent residency test these assumedly mobile workers' potential value to Canada in the long run through requirements to fill and retain jobs in a narrow band of occupational classifications, jobs that do not necessarily align with Post-graduation permitholders' credentials and career paths. Such requirements come at a price: to fit into the required national occupational codes, permitholders may engage in employment ill-suited to their skillsets and outside their areas of expertise in industries in which many jobs are characterized by high levels of precariousness, such as accommodation and food services and retail trade. Despite having completed costly degree programs at Canadian post-secondary institutions, these permitholders are also constrained until they obtain the equivalent of one year of full-time qualifying employment. During that time, many endure low income, lack of control over the labour process, and limited access to regulatory protection – in exchange for the possibility of greater security of presence in the future, as well as the potential to earn more money, sponsor family, and so on.[13] Moreover, if they experience rights violations or other forms of exploitation (e.g., pressure to undertake excessive hours of work), permitholders are often hesitant to seek recourse – especially if this means unsettling already fragile relations with the very employers upon whom they depend for securing qualifying employment.

Chapter Five

Relational Precarity: Spousal Permitholders

Spousal permitholders represent a growing number of transnational workers in high-income receiving countries in the OECD. Despite this growth, Spousal permitholders are not typically approached as workers; rather, laws and policies often characterize them as "dependants"[1] pursuing family reunification[2] and as destined ultimately for permanent immigration and settlement. Given Spousal permitholders' growth as a group of transnational workers, the Canadian case confounds the long-held assumption that they are properly conceived as accompanying family members. In Canada, such spousal entrants, many of whom are women arriving from source countries with a history of differential inclusion, grew in number from 5,420 to 165,600 between 2002 and 2023. Concomitantly, programs granting work permits to common-law or married partners of "full-time students" and "skilled workers"[3] came to represent a sizable subset of programs under the IMP – and fully one-fifth of arrivals under its auspices in 2023.[4] At the dawn of 2025, IRCC's decision to limit such accompaniment to international students enrolled in graduate-level university programs suggests that Spousal accompaniment for students is poised to decline (IRCC's 2024u). Overall, however, the availability of Spousal Work Permits is mainly poised to shift as policy changes seek both "to address labour shortages" (IRCC 2022c; IRCC 2025) and "strengthen the integrity" of temporary labour migration programs, by restricting students' access to Spousal permits to only those students enrolled in graduate-level programs (i.e., master's programs that are 16 months or longer and PhD programs) or select professional programs (e.g., medicine, law, nursing, education) while granting migrant workers deemed to be "low-skilled" yet employed in sectors characterized by labour shortages and/or linked to government priorities, such as natural and applied sciences, construction, health care, natural resources, education, sports and military sectors, and who have at least 16 months remaining on their work permit, access to open work permits for spouses (IRCC 2025).

Despite their mounting importance, the nature, operation, and effects of the Spousal Work Permit program are poorly understood. Responding to this lacuna, this chapter explores programs established for spouses of full-time post-secondary students and "skilled" workers, and addresses Spousal permitholders' experience in the labour force as temporary and temporary-permanent residents. My central contention is that, in the first quarter of the twenty-first century the Spousal Work Permit program contributed to "relational precarity" among permitholders admitted and permitted to work as spouses or common-law partners of "principal foreign nationals" (i.e., "principal" permitholders) deemed high-skilled and thus desirable as long-term immigrants, a gendered experience affecting, in particular, the many women reuniting with partners entering as skilled workers. The notion of "relational precarity" developed herein seeks to disclose patterns of dependence (Fraser & Gordon 1994) perpetuated by policies pegging spouses' criteria for admission, labour force participation, and access to permanent residency to ties, and conditions applicable, to so-named principal permitholders. This precarity flows from a framework designed around normative understandings of "the family," a notion reduced to that of "household" at a policy level (i.e., assuming cohabitation in a single geographic location, thereby obscuring transnational ties and non-nuclear modes of social organization), which differentially includes transnational workers, often in gendered ways. Reflecting continuities in the historical restriction of spousal accompaniment to (im)migrants deemed to be appropriate settlers (Dua 1992; Arat-Koç 1992; Rajkumar et al. 2012, 487), such policies promote gendered family/household forms while simultaneously supporting receiving-country employers' demands for workers in the face of qualitative labour shortages. These dynamics are, moreover, poised to become entrenched. Despite changes in late 2024 and early 2025 limiting spousal accompaniment to international students enrolled in MA and PhD programs as well as professional programs (IRCC 2024u; IRCC 2025), Canada is, in fact, extending opportunities for spousal accompaniment to some principal work permitholders deemed, at a policy level, to possess lower levels of socially recognized skills than those targeted originally (i.e., full-time post-secondary students and skilled workers), including those employed in industries and occupations characterized by qualitative labour shortages (IRCC 2025).

In exploring these contentions, the analysis to follow unfolds in four parts. Section 1 elaborates the notion of relational precarity through a review of literature on spousal migration. It prepares the ground for delineating relational aspects unique to Canada's Spousal Work Permit program, namely, those design features that allow Spousal permitholders to engage in employment due to their status as "dependent" entrants and position them to help alleviate qualitative labour shortages in the process. Within this framing, Section 2 describes and analyses how Canada's main programs for spouses, falling under the IMP, operate. It then goes on to explore the parameters of emerging policy changes piloting their phased-in expansion to all categories of so-named principal permitholders under the IMP and ultimately, albeit contingently, to the low-wage and agricultural streams of the TFWP. Rather than focusing on Spousal permitholders' educational backgrounds, credentials, and employment experience in their own right, policies on admission and conditions attached to their work permits, as well as pathways to permanent residency, where available, centre on the relationship between a so-called dependent spouse and a so-called principal work permitholder. As such, Spousal permitholders' residency status and access to the labour force are conditional upon demonstrating a conjugal relationship with the principal migrant, which they must maintain to renew work permits and, where applicable, meet qualifying requirements for permanent residency.

Historically, this attachment requirement has impeded scholarly inquiry into Spousal permitholders' labour force experience and security of presence. Because data collection has centred on principal work permitholders, and because spouses admitted temporarily are issued open work permits allowing them to enter without an LMIA, the primary basis for administrative data collection, historical data on Spousal permitholders' occupational and industrial location, conditions of work, and other aspects of their labour force participation and settlement patterns are limited. To address this knowledge gap, Section 3 profiles Spousal permitholders, drawing first on administrative data collected upon entry, which allow for the consideration of Spousal permitholders' age, gender, and country of origin. Next, utilizing open-ended interviews of spouses of students and skilled workers together with novel administrative data, the section explores Spousal permitholders' labour force experience, focusing on the effects of policies and practices fostering ideal-typical family/household forms, on the one hand, and responding to employer demands for "flexible" labour, on the other hand. An examination of Spousal permitholders' employment rates and the occupations and industries in which they are employed, as well as their terms and conditions of employment, reveals the multiple dimensions of precariousness in employment and residency status that many endure, shaped profoundly by gendered dynamics, via the relational conditions of the work permits spouses hold as entrants through the back door and in transition to permanent residency, especially those of permitholders from countries of origin, such as India, subject historically to racialized barriers to entry erected on the basis of nationality. Against this backdrop, Section 4 shows how program expansion, rationalized as a means of easing post-COVID-19 pandemic labour shortages through the provision of work permits to spouses of a wider array of principal permitholders, is poised to perpetuate such insecurities. Given that policy enhancement has yet to introduce concurrent expansions to pathways to permanent residency beyond those geared towards "skilled" workers, it also risks entrenching these insecurities.

1. Spousal Labour Migration under Canada's IMP

Even though (im)migration policies are premised increasingly on the labour force participation of Spousal permitholders, their employment experiences are largely understudied – arguably more so than other back-door entrants, such as those issued open work permits under the Working Holiday and Post-graduation Work Permit programs. One potential explanation for the notable lack of attention to Spousal permitholders' labour force experience in scholarly discussions of international migration for employment is the assumption, at a policy level, influencing prevailing research, which centres on those destined for immigration and permanent settlement, that family reunification is *the* overriding reason this group of entrants comes to Canada. Scholarship on Spousal permitholders tends to cast their labour force participation as ancillary to that of their partners, a questionable assumption on its own terms. A segment of studies sheds light on spousal migration controls – a.k.a. "marriage migration" – and explores how they support receiving countries' overarching *im*migration policy goals, especially controls facilitating transitions to permanent residency among "economically desirable" (i.e., highly skilled and educated) temporary work permitholders, on the one hand, and promoting particular types of intimate partnerships (i.e., conjugal or common-law unions), and thus family/household forms and (masculinized) norms of worker-citizenship, on the other hand. For Wray (2022, 87, see also 91), "spousal migration controls act upon three overlapping social domains: first, they reinforce immigration controls generally, ensuring that principal migrants perceived as less desirable are excluded. Second, they promote certain conceptions of marriage and intimacy. Third, they contribute to the construction of models of citizenship." Consequently, receiving countries do not – indeed they cannot – treat Spousal permitholders' presence as flowing purely from economic interests (i.e., the intention to engage in paid employment in the receiving country) because their admission and permission to work for pay involves and upholds the value of claims-making – for family reunification – by citizens or permanent residents.

For much of the late twentieth and early twenty-first centuries, consistent with norms of male breadwinning and female caregiving as well as household forms organized around the heterosexual nuclear family, as Wray (2022) shows for high-income receiving countries in Western Europe (e.g., the United Kingdom, France, and Denmark), but also in countries such as Canada, spousal (im)migration was largely invisible because it was presumed; (im)migrating spouses (typically married women) were routinely assumed to take their partners' (typically husbands') nationality (there were few formally bi- or multi-national families). Even following changes to nationality laws in Western European countries, making their terms more consistent with the US model, wherein such laws were always more restrictive in the admission of spouses (i.e., ultimately as permanent residents), the number of intimate partnership/marriage-based admissions of non-nationals was also deemed insufficient to merit intervention, especially since the descendants of such marital unions were assumed to partner in-country going forward (Bonjour & Kraler 2015, 1409, as cited in Wray 2011). State actors also viewed family reunification as a desirable means to contain migrant men's sexuality (Wray 2022, 89).

Starting around 2020, to the marginal extent that "marriage migration" came to be problematized, some scholarly literature has documented and analysed efforts by high-income receiving countries to address "sham marriages" to prevent intimate partnerships from functioning as immigration pathways "for undesirables." A subset of this scholarship, focusing on Canada, illustrates how an emphasis on stemming "marriage fraud," posing it as a threat to the country's immigration regime, effectively "naturalizes neoliberal, hetero-patriarchal, and white settler-colonial values that animate the exclusionary nature of family class migration," while reinforcing precarious residency status among Spousal permitholders (Pringle 2020; see also Gaucher 2018). Insights offered in this literature are important for this inquiry because they bring to light sex/gendered policy assumptions, which may reinforce prevailing and/or give rise to "new," and often multi-dimensional, relations of inequality. For example, in their exploration of the regulation of spousal immigration as part of Canada's multiple border strategy, Bhuyan, Korteweg, & Baqi (2018, 346) show how Canada's brief adoption of Conditional Permanent Resident Status (repealed in 2017), while aimed officially at deterring "marriage fraud," increased national anxiety motivating "the use of new digital technologies ... to expand border enforcement practices internally and outside the territorial boundaries of the nation," effectively creating "structurally embedded borders [that] continue to regulate racialized immigrants in exclusionary ways that disproportionately impact women." One consequence of Spousal permitholders' awareness of mechanisms for detecting "marriage fraud" is the intensified threat of intimate partner violence confronting many women; as documented by Jayasuriya-Illesinghe (2018), coupled with growing state capacity to engage in monitoring, factors, including requirements to demonstrate that relationships are "genuine" and, starting in 2012, "conjugal," encourage women less likely to accrue sufficient points under Canada's prevailing immigration system to be deemed economic class immigrants to remain with violent partners. Such scholarship illustrates how program parameters making spousal (im)migrants dependent upon a principal, typically a man, can exacerbate violence, underlining the perils of assuming that resources are shared in households, that is, that household relations of distribution are equitable (Acker 1988).

Less examined is the relationship between conditions applicable to persons admitted temporarily as spouses (i.e., through the back door), and the dependencies they foster, and spouses' experiences as work permitholders lacking security of presence. There is, however, growing scholarly consensus that a conceptual separation between migration for family reunification and employment is unsustainable given the large numbers of migrants of all genders engaged in employment transnationally. Consequently, socio-economic considerations also no doubt now play a central part in "family migration policies" in Europe and North America (see, for example, Kofman 2018); accordingly, it can no longer be assumed – if this were ever a fair assumption – that entrants issued temporary work permits categorized as "spouses" are necessarily women whose foremost contributions to sustaining families/households lie outside the labour force. Greater recognition of this false separation is, moreover, occurring alongside mounting pressure from employers in affluent receiving countries for continued access to transnational workers in meeting their demands for "flexible" labour.

Such acknowledgments are evidenced in the Canadian case by the expansion (provisional, in key instances) of access to work permits for spouses and dependent children of permitholders enrolled in a greater variety of programs under both the IMP and the TFWP. Announced in December 2022, the spousal pilot program comprises three phases of expansion, the first of which came into effect at the end of

January 2023. Phase 1 opened eligibility to spouses of principals under the IMP in its entirety and the high-wage stream of the TFWP; starting in late 2023 and slated to continue through to May 2025, spouses of principal permitholders enrolled in a new Agri-Food Pilot, which offers a potential pathway to permanent residency, regardless of the principal's job skill level, will be included in the mix (IRCC 2023p). Following consultations, Phase 2 aims to expand the measures to spouses of principals engaged under the low-wage stream of the TFWP. Finally, Phase 3 is to comprise discussions with respect to the operational feasibility of opening spousal access for principals engaged under agricultural streams of the TFWP (i.e., beyond the Agri-Food Pilot Program) (IRCC 2022c).

Nevertheless, while pending policy changes could amount to a move away from migrantization among principals enrolled in the TFWP, insofar as spousal reunification has historically been preserved for migrants with high levels of socially recognized skills normally with pathways to permanent residency (Rajkumar et al. 2012), the demands to which such measures respond (e.g., changes envisioned for Phases 2 and 3) continue to coexist uneasily with public recognition of the high levels of exploitation confronting workers under the TFWP, described in Chapter 1 – especially workers from Mexico and other relatively low-income countries of origin in Latin America, whose nationals are often racialized as non-white and who are issued employer- or even sector-specific work permits without meaningful opportunities to transition to permanent residency (Chartrand & Vosko 2021; Marsden, Tucker, & Vosko 2021b). Recall that in an effort to limit *migrant worker* exploitation while continuing to recruit migrants deemed "economically desirable" in the long term or, in the letter of the IRPA (2002, section 3(1)(c)), "to support the development of a strong and prosperous Canadian economy," since the mid-2010s Canada has shifted towards IMPs to attract "mobile" workers with (or in the process of acquiring) high levels of socially recognized skills, such as full-time post-secondary students and skilled workers, the two principal groups permitted to apply for work permits for their spouses to date,[5] to take on assumedly high-quality jobs. This policy shift has gradually taken hold despite mounting evidence of both precarity, akin to that experienced by their TFWP counterparts, among permitholders in key IMP subprograms, such as Working Holiday and Post-graduation permitholders, as Chapters 3 and 4 illustrated, as well as among intercompany transferees (see, for example, Tucker 2020), and persistent qualitative labour shortages. As such, becoming a Spousal permitholder has come to serve as a route of entry for those otherwise deemed inadmissible on independent (or principal) bases, a development that policy expansion beginning in 2023 seeks to sustain.

Yet Spousal permitholders confront unique vulnerabilities flowing, on the one hand, from the emphasis on satisfying employer demand and, on the other hand, persistent gendered assumptions that resources are shared in households (Acker 1988) and, as such, Spousal arrivals can depend upon their marriage or common-law partners, despite the growing policy recognition that socio-economic considerations are central to all adult permitholders. The concept *relational precarity* seeks to capture these vulnerabilities, specifically the nature and effects of policies governing the labour force participation and residency status of Spousal permitholders, positioned to navigate adjacent doors of entry, in ways that both uphold certain (i.e., nuclear) family forms and meet demands for labour to address qualitative labour shortages. The concept's dual emphasis reflects how policies construct Spousal permitholders as dependants of principals, who are permitted to engage in employment on the basis of this relationship, while simultaneously exempting them, as open work permitholders,[6] from protections accorded to closed work permitholders. This emphasis is paradoxical as these permitholders' security of presence is conditional upon retaining their marital/common-law relationships in a manner akin to how *migrants* with closed work permits are compelled to retain good relationships with their employers. After a deeper look at the design of the Spousal Work Permit program and its evolution, Section 2 attempts to operationalize this notion.

2. Canada's Spousal Work Permit Programs: Criteria for Admission, Work Permit Conditions, Recourse to Protection, and Pathways to Permanent Residency, 2002–22 and 2023+

Canada's Spousal Work Permit program takes shape via LMIA exemptions (see Chapters 1 and 2) applied to spouses of permitholders seeking to enter and reside in Canada to engage in employment on a temporary basis. Inherently relational in their nature, such exemptions are available for spouses demonstrated to be in a genuine union (i.e., either a marital relationship or common-law partnership) with a "principal foreign national" denoting "the first foreign national of the couple" (IRCC 2024d), who, until the policy expansion of January 2023, had to be either engaged in full-time post-secondary studies or deemed to be a "skilled" worker and coming to Canada to work (under either an open or closed permit or pursuing permanent residency through the

Atlantic Immigration Program or Provincial Nominee Programs).[7] Such Spousal permitholders may accept employment available to the general labour force.[8] Structurally, as such exemptions fall under the "Canadian Interest – Public Policy, Competitiveness and Economy" stream of the IMP, they are viewed as a means of attracting migrants acquiring or holding high levels of socially recognized skills (see Chapter 2). At a policy level, these exemptions were established to support the retention and integration of principal migrants deemed desirable for long-term residence in Canada.

2.1 Entry: Qualifying for an Exemption

2.1.a SPOUSES OF STUDENTS
To qualify for an LMIA exemption through to 2023, spouses of students must provide evidence that they are the partner (by marriage or common law) of a study permitholder who is a full-time student at an approved educational institution.[9] Alternatively, the principal spouse may hold a Post-graduation Work Permit, having previously fulfilled requirements applicable to study permitholders (see Chapter 4). Following a processing period of a few months, entailing the payment of fees and so on, spousal applicants fulfilling the foregoing qualifying criteria are granted work permits. Consistent with their foundation in a conjugal relationship, permit validity dates coincide with those of the principal's work permit. However, if the principal foreign student takes a leave from their studies for more than 150 days, they are required to change their status (to either visitor or worker status) or leave Canada. In such cases, if the spouse or common-law partner of the student is issued a work permit before the change of status of the full-time student, the Spousal permit remains valid until it expires or becomes invalid. Similarly, children of full-time students who change status remain authorized to study at the preschool, primary, or secondary level without a study permit if the spouse of the former full-time student's work permit remains valid.

2.1.b SPOUSES OF SKILLED WORKERS
In the case of spouses of skilled workers – both those of principals working in Canada on a temporary basis (under either an open or closed permit) and of principal applicants for permanent residency under an eligible economic class permanent residence program[10] – criteria for admission are also pegged to the principal spouse. For the former, the principal must be authorized to work in Canada for at least six months after the application for a Spousal work permit is received and

be employed in a high-skilled occupation (i.e., normally in a managerial, professional, technical/skilled trade occupation, known under the NOC system as TEER 0, 1, 2, or 3 respectively).[11] For the latter, occupational criteria are less rigid for securing Spousal permits: the principal can work in any occupational category (IRCC 2024w). In all cases, the principal must also reside in Canada while employed as a skilled worker, although there are no standard minimum weekly, monthly, or annual hours of work requirements. Immigration officers have discretion in deciding whether the principal's employment or funds are sufficient to financially support themselves and their family members while in Canada, a fundamental policy requirement.

Overall, spouses' admission to Canada pivots on the stability of principals, a group limited, until recently, to full-time post-secondary students enrolled in recognized programs at eligible institutions or admitted as skilled workers typically holding TEER 0, 1, 2, or 3 jobs, as immigration policies have long accorded greatest security of presence to "economically desirable" future immigrants. Relational admission criteria thereby uphold ideal-typical family/household forms (i.e., nuclear family households led by a principal holding or poised to hold secure employment).

2.2 Work Permit Conditions and Recourse to Protection

The open work permits Canada issues to spouses of students and skilled workers correspond to the length of the work permit of the principal applicant. As open work permitholders, spouses are not required to have job offers from prospective employers in order to migrate (i.e., their work permits are not employer-tied). Nor are they mandated to work in specified occupations, industries, or regions upon arrival. Such features of the Spousal Work Permit program are desirable insofar as they afford permitholders' mobility in the labour market (i.e., a degree of choice in the jobs they accept and the ability to quit and/or change jobs). So, too, are provisions allowing Spousal permitholders to retain their permits until their expiry even if the principal is no longer a student or becomes unemployed and/or loses status in some other way. However, unlike those for other international migrants for employment, institutional arrangements facilitating spouses' labour force participation in Canada bind them to principals via familial relationships, which are often characterized by inequalities in power, further amplified by pressure to attain greater security of presence for all household members (i.e., permanent residency) (Jayasuriya-Illesinghe 2018). Despite the recognition, at a policy level, that admitting Spousal permitholders is vital to supporting principals with or in the process of acquiring high levels of socially recognized skills and credentials critical to positioning them to make long-term economic contributions to Canada, as they hold open permits, Spousal permitholders, like Working Holiday and Post-graduation permitholders, lack coverage under the regulatory regime introduced in 2015, via regulations to Canada's IRPA in 2002, in recognition of high levels of exploitation among certain categories of migrant workers, in conjunction with the overhaul of the TFWP (see Chapters 1 and 2). Albeit flawed (Marsden, Tucker, & Vosko 2021b) in key respects, as the analysis in the foregoing chapters emphasizes, the founding rationale for this regime, and key aspects of its substance, are important. Under the regime, the federal government requires employers to comply with minimum employment standards and the terms of migrant workers' contracts as a condition of their hiring – an unprecedented measure. To implement this new requirement, regulations to the IRPA broaden the enforcement and inspection powers of ESDC and IRCC to help these agencies ensure respectively that all workers migrating under TFWP and all those holding closed work permits under the IMP (fully one-third of IMP participants) can realize their rights (Marsden, Tucker, & Vosko 2021b). Spousal permitholders are, however, without recourse to such protection for two reasons implicit in the design of the Spousal Work Permit program. First is the policy assumption that Spousal permitholders' relationships with students in pursuit of post-secondary degrees and skilled workers, most of whom occupy professional, managerial, and technical NOCs, make them relatively secure economically vis-à-vis their TFWP counterparts and closed work permitholders under the IMP, a rationale premised on the questionable notion that resources are shared equitably among cohabiting spouses. Second is the assumption that, as they hold open work permits, Spousal permitholders have access to decent jobs despite growing evidence that workers holding these permits, such as the bulk of permitholders under the IEC umbrella, experience precariousness (see, for example, Nakache & Corderre 2021).

That the length of their work permits is also pegged to the duration of those held by principals' study or work permits further amplifies Spousal permitholders' precarity even though they hold open work permits. This policy design feature aims to ensure that neither those principals deemed undesirable (e.g., those that cannot complete their studies or sustain employment in skilled jobs) nor their spouses are able to remain in Canada indefinitely (IRCC 2022d). In instances in which the principal pauses their studies, is unemployed temporarily, and/or briefly loses status, Spousal permitholders can see their work permit through. There are features built into the Spousal Work Permit program that allow spouses to help principal applicants bridge labour market insecurities, as well as insecurity of presence, premised on the assumption that the spousal relationship at the crux of the family/household is solid. However, apart from under exceptional circumstances in which they are able to secure high-skilled employment enabling them to become principals themselves (i.e., to apply independently), circumstances that should not be discounted given the agency of spouses migrating for employment, Spousal permitholders lose security of presence and access to the labour force with the expiry of their work permits, that is, if principals cannot retain status, secure Bridging Open Work Permits, or obtain permanent residency.

2.3 Access to Permanent Residency

Assuming that Spousal permitholders remain attached to eligible principals, they may also gain access to permanent residency on a relational basis. From 2010 to 2021, entrants previously holding Spousal permits obtained access to permanent residency as dependants via principal applicants transitioning under three main immigration entry categories: the Canadian Experience Class, Provincial and Territorial Nominee Programs, and the Federal Skilled Worker Program.[12]

Principal applicants under both the Federal Skilled Worker Program and the Canadian Experience Class who fulfil the requirements, described in Chapter 2, are then ranked via the federally administered Comprehensive Ranking System. Recall that under the Comprehensive Ranking System, a maximum of 1,200 points are allocated across several categories, including not only core human capital (e.g., age, education level, official language proficiency) and skill transferability (e.g., foreign work experience) factors but also spousal factors. Most important regarding access to permanent residency among Spousal permitholders, the Comprehensive Ranking System applies a 40-point penalty to all principal applicants accompanied by a spouse. Spousal permitholders may mitigate this penalty by enabling the principal to secure 10, 20, and 10 points respectively for their education level, official language proficiency, and Canadian work experience. Yet spousal points may be challenging to accrue. For instance, in order to earn any points for Canadian work experience, all Spousal permitholders attached to a principal must have skilled work experience (TEER 0, 1, 2, or 3). To earn the full 10 points, Spousal permitholders must also have at least five years of skilled work experience. And, to receive full points (10) for education, they must have either a graduate degree or an entry-to-practice professional degree for a TEER 1 occupation for which licensing by a provincial/territorial regulatory body is required (IRCC 2023q).[13] Regardless, such penalties encourage Spousal permitholders seeking to transition to permanent residency under the Federal Skilled Worker Program or the Canadian Experience Class to secure employment immediately upon arrival and, as appropriate, take up opportunities to improve official language competency and/or educational credentials.

Provincial Nominee Programs, however, do not impose such penalties on Spousal permitholders. As such, they are desirable to many principals with spouses seeking permanent residency. At the same time, principal applicants through Provincial Nominee Programs must normally have high levels of socially recognized skills, education, and work experience. Moreover, as Chapter 2 illustrates, the terms of Provincial and Territorial Nominee Programs vary, as each province/territory has different emphases and targets, limiting its program's suitability to particular principal applicants.

Spousal penalties thus put principal applicants for permanent residency under the Federal Skilled Worker Program and the Canadian Experience Class at a disadvantage vis-à-vis their counterparts applying via Provincial Nominee Programs, fostering relational precarity in the process. Spouses of Federal Skilled Worker Program and Canadian Experience Class applicants are particularly driven to excel in language tests and compensate for points penalties by obtaining Canadian work experience (at the potential cost of accepting jobs characterized by multiple dimensions of labour market insecurity rather than taking time to obtain more secure employment or to advance their education). But, when a principal applicant is in sufficient demand, on account of their skills, experience, and/or occupational location, to receive a job offer, or is defined as having a suitably high level of human capital to be admitted under a provincial program, having an accompanying spouse is points neutral. In such cases, where the principal applicant is deemed economically desirable, they are not penalized for having a spouse; paradoxically, the presence of a spouse is presumed to facilitate integration.

Shaped by the foregoing dynamics, admissions of permanent residents previously holding Spousal permits represented 17 per cent of all prior IMP permitholders transitioning to permanent residency in 2023 (IRCC 2023r; IRCC 2023s; IRCC 2024a), an 11 percentage-point decline from 2010. Overall, the number of permanent residents who have been Spousal permitholders increased between 2002 and 2023 (from 525 to 25,365), despite accounting for a smaller proportion of all former IMPs transitioning to permanent residency (IRCC 2024x). Across the 2002–23 period, Spousal permitholders transitioning to this status were most likely to be between 30 and 34 years of age, a group accounting for 29 per cent of all Spousal permitholders who transitioned to permanent residency, interestingly since independent applicants in this group fall within the category awarded the highest number of points for age (IRCC 2023s; IRCC 2024z).

3. Experiences of Relational Precarity among Spousal Permitholders

Policies and practices applicable to Spousal permitholders shape their experiences upon entry by fostering nuclear family households, on the one hand, and responding to employer demands for "flexible" labour, on the other hand. Indeed, they position many such permitholders for relational precarity, a gendered experience affecting, in particular, the large percentage of women reuniting with partners entering as skilled workers or students, a sizable subset of whom arrive from countries of origin subject historically to discriminatory immigration policies.

3.1 A Profile of Spousal Permitholders at Point of Entry and in Pursuit of Permanent Residency, 2002–23

Even prior to its expansion, the Spousal Work Permit program was Canada's third-largest IMP after the Post-graduation program and International Experience Canada as a whole. Though larger than its Working Holiday component – in 2022, Spousal permitholders represented fully 24 per cent of the IMP. In 2023, the Spousal Work Permit program outstripped International Experience Canada, with 165,600 permitholders entering Canada under its auspices (see Table 2.2). Approximately 56 per cent of entrants (93,285) were spouses of skilled workers and approximately 44 per cent of whom (72,315) were spouses of students. Moreover, the program experienced considerable growth from 2002 to 2023 – in these years, permitholders increased from just 5,240 to 165,600 (Figure 5.1).

Women were dramatically overrepresented as spouses of skilled workers in these decades. In 2023, their numbers were nearly one and a half times those of men, raising concerns about the gendered effects of policies facilitating Spousal permitholders' access to employment and routes for obtaining security of presence conditional upon the presence of specific types of relationships (i.e., conjugal relations between married or common-law partners) and household forms (i.e., nuclear

Figure 5.1 Spousal Permitholders by Year in Which the Permit(s) Became Effective, 2002–23

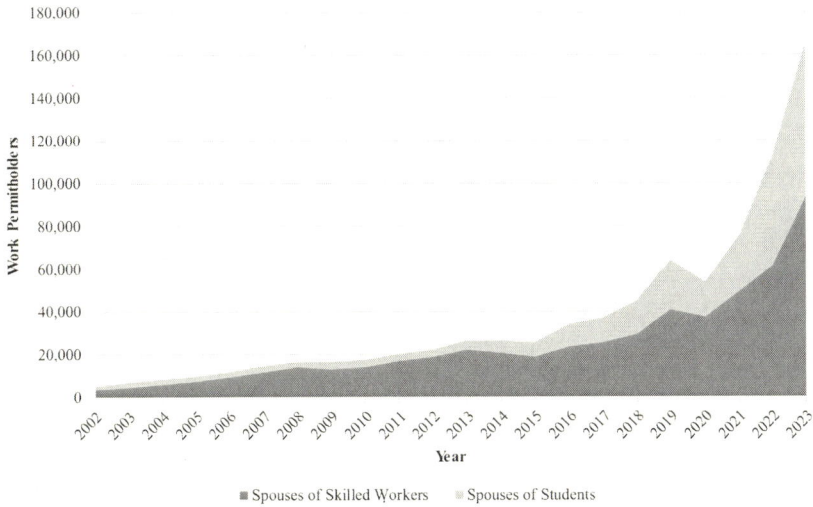

Sources: IRCC (2021a, 2023a, 2024a).
Note: Values between 0 and 5 are suppressed; all values are rounded to the nearest 5 to maintain anonymity.

families). Yet, starting in 2016, the number of male spouses of students exceeded female spouses. Indeed, men accounted for nearly 70 per cent of such permitholders in 2023 (IRCC 2023t; IRCC 2024z); however, as permits for spouses of students are set to decline with the recent cap on all international student entries as well as the limitation of Spousal permits to students enrolled in graduate-level programs, this ratio between men and women across both categories of Spousal permitholders is poised to shift towards women in the future. As far as age is concerned, the three top age groups of Spousal permitholders as a whole in 2023 were 30–34, 25–29, and 35–39 respectively, although more spouses of skilled workers, especially women, are in the 35–39 group.

By source country, the top five countries of origin of spouses of students were India, the Philippines, Nigeria, Iran, and Brazil in 2023, although permitholders from India represented over a third of all such spousal admissions, whereas the next four countries of origin each represented between 4 and 14 per cent. That year, spouses of skilled workers migrating from India represented the largest group by country of origin (over 43 per cent); while spouses migrating from the Philippines, France, Mexico, and China also ranked in the top five origin countries, their proportions ranged from just 3.6 to 7 per cent (IRCC 2024a). As I suggest in Chapter 4, the high proportion of spousal migrants from India is arguably tied to the country's standing in global chains of labour and value, through which global firms pursue lower labour costs, shaped partly by (im)migration systems operating contemporaneously in more affluent countries (Suwandi 2019, 46) and their precursors. At the same time, the gendered character of such systems merits emphasis in the case of Spousal permitholders, pointing to the significance of the relational conditions characterizing the Spousal Work Permit Programs.

3.2 Experiences of Spousal Permitholders

Spousal labour migration programs represent a major component of Canada's IMP and a considerable source of future permanent residents in the country – one poised to grow given plans to offer migrants enrolled in all IMPs and a wider range of TFWP subprograms the opportunity to apply for open work permits for their spouses going forward. Yet Spousal permitholders' experiences of relational precarity, from the time they apply for temporary work permits through to when they seek permanent residency, as appropriate, belie the optimism expressed by government officials announcing that program expansion – characterized by Associate Minister of Finance Randy Boissonnault as an "innovative family-based solution" (IRCC 2022c) – will "help employers *overcome labour shortages,* while also *supporting the well-being of workers* and uniting their families" (Sean Fraser, Minister of Immigration, Refugees and Citizenship, IRCC 2022c, emphasis added).

3.2.a RELATIONAL CONDITIONALITIES AND THEIR EFFECTS ON SPOUSAL PERMITHOLDERS

For Spousal permitholders, relational precarity takes root prior to entry via policies that peg criteria for admission to evidence of a marital or common-law relationship. Accordingly, Spousal permitholders characterize the documentation required for proof of their conjugal relationships as onerous. Some applicants, such as Spousal permitholder Valdir from Brazil, indicate that while they were only required to provide notarized marriage certificates – in the knowledge, supported by scholarly findings (Satzewich 2014), that immigration officials have considerable discretion – they felt compelled to include wedding albums, photos of previous shared residences, and letters from friends and family members attesting to the legitimacy of their unions in the document package that the principal applicant must submit for Spousal permits. As Mason, a Spousal permitholder from the United States, notes:

> it was about … 24 pounds of paper that we sent … for processing back then. Within that, a dossier or document included … my basic amendment forms and applications and family backgrounds and 35 pages of proof [attesting] to a genuine relationship. Some of them are texts. Some of them are pictures. Some of them are stories, like how we met and how she and I became engaged and how we got married.

The requirement to demonstrate a veritable partnership also leads some spouses to get married to ensure that their unions are deemed valid. As Chun-hua, a Spousal permitholder arriving from Hong Kong, indicates, because she and her partner could not afford an independent dwelling, they needed to marry before applying for a Spousal permit: "We were together for 5 to 6 years. But we didn't officially live in the same independent apartment together … to prove that we [have] common-law status. So, we just got married." Even though the documentation requirements on demonstrating genuineness of relationship from IRCC were vague, Chun-hua notes that she felt pressure to provide extensive documentation: "We married before, maybe one week before we applied … so for [my own] security reasons, I had to prepare a 30-page document for the IRCC as proof of our relationship, which included Instagram posts, Facebook posts, and family and friends photos inside, to prove that we acknowledge each other between our family groups and friends groups."

Even after Canadian immigration officials validate their permits, however, Spousal permitholders underscore the continued importance of conjugal ties. They are mindful of the need to maintain their partnerships for the duration of their work permits, particularly if they anticipate seeking extensions. Spousal permitholders are also preoccupied with avoiding the dissolution of their relationship prior to applying for and securing permanent residency, in the knowledge that their dependence on a principal is integral to achieving security of presence in Canada. Accordingly, Chun-hua, who, when interviewed, worked full-time in data management and logistics as a supply chain specialist, asserts that, "as a spouse, I just [need to] make sure that I'm not divorced from him while applying for the PR or before the PR." This situation materialized for Jia, a Spousal permitholder from Korea, who reported having to find a new means of entry after her relationship dissolved in order to maintain security of presence in Canada. Noting that her work permit was entirely based on that of her ex-partner, she comments: "[the permit] says 'accompanying spouse on work permit valid to same dates'... So it's totally tied."

Indicative of the adjunct nature of the doors through which they must pass, Spousal permitholders also routinely emphasize how the tied nature of their permit (i.e., to a principal applicant) intensifies, rather than ebbs, as they pursue permanent residency. Davina, a permitholder from Colombia, notes, "We have to apply for everything together in the future ... to make sure we can both work and [that] we can stay here. Because ... our permits are joined." For some Spousal permitholders, being tethered to a partner requires remaining agile, that is, always attempting to secure and retain employment in occupations deemed admissible for independent entry while accepting that they may ultimately need to resort to spousal sponsorship. For instance, Davina, who was unemployed due to challenges finding work in Newfoundland, spoke to this uncertainty, noting that in her case, who will be the principal applicant for permanent residency depends on what type of work she's able to secure with a Spousal work permit. If it is high-skilled and/or in an occupation or a sector that qualifies under the Provincial and Territorial Nominee Program, then she could be the principal applicant. However, if Davina, who worked as a design engineer and owned her own business in Colombia, were unable to secure the right type of job, she would then anticipate being tied to her spouse (currently a student) in the long term, as he would first obtain a second Spousal work permit upon graduating and becoming a Post-graduation permitholder. Upon the expiry of this permit, he would likely become the principal applicant: "It depends on who is going to be the primary applicant. It can be me if I get the right job offer. Then, he's going to be with me, like [follow] my process, but I'm going to be the principal applicant. The other option is [for him] to apply for the PGWP, and [then] he's going to be the principal applicant." Either way, the complexities involved in obtaining permanent residency, particularly the skilled work experience requirements for principal applicants under the largest entry streams, heighten pressure to remain in "dependent" relationships with a partner to attain a greater security of presence.

Such lived experiences are corroborated by administrative data analysis, which shows that the bulk of Spousal permitholders transition as "secondary applicants." Although a significant number of Spousal permitholders transition to permanent residency, few do so as primary applicants. Reflecting how the Spousal Work Permit program fosters nuclear family households, at the expense of heightening Spousal

Figure 5.2 Proportion of Former Spousal Permitholders Transitioning to
Permanent Residency by Family Status, 2002–23

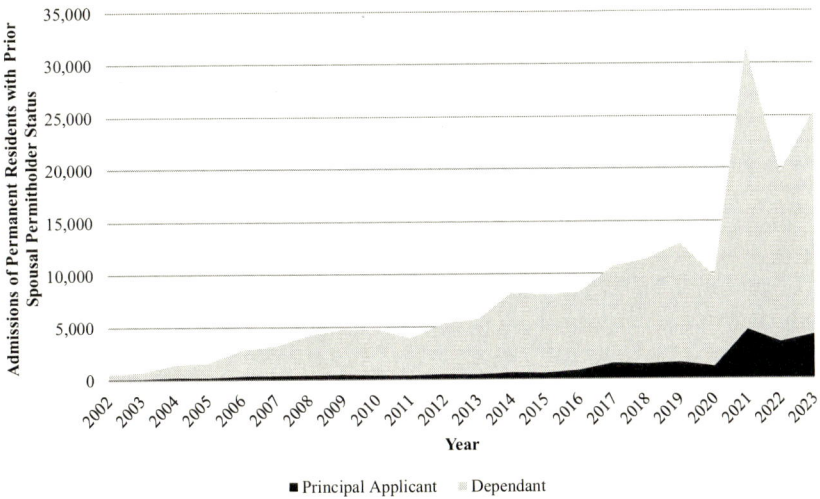

■ Principal Applicant   ▨ Dependant

Source: IRCC (2024w).
Note: Values between 0 and 5 are suppressed; all values are rounded to the nearest 5
to maintain anonymity.

permitholders' insecurity of presence, only 13 per cent of all former
Spousal permitholders who obtained permanent residency between
2002 and 2023 did so as primary applicants (IRCC 2023t, see also Figure
5.2). Such dynamics are also gendered. More former Spousal permitholders transitioning to permanent residency as principal applicants in 2023
were men (61 per cent) than women (39 per cent) (IRCC 2024x). Among
former spouses of skilled worker permitholders, 58 per cent of those
transitioning as primary applicants were men while 42 per cent were
women. This pattern was more pronounced among former spouses of
student permitholders, wherein fully 66 per cent of those transitioning
as primary applicants were men. Among those transitioning as dependants, 61 per cent of former Spousal permitholders in 2023 were women
(IRCC 2024x). However, this pattern does not hold across both categories of spouses – while nearly 61 per cent of former spouses of skilled
worker permitholders transitioning as dependants in 2023 were women,
there was gender parity among former spouses of student permitholders transitioning as dependants in that year (IRCC 2024x). These findings underscore the magnitude of the compulsion – confronting women

in particular, especially those who held permits as spouses of skilled workers, who represent, and are poised to continue to represent, the majority of Spousal permitholders overall, given their much higher rate of transition as so-called dependant rather than principal applicants compared to their counterparts who are men – to maintain marital or common-law relationships in order to achieve security of presence.

Still, the need for relational maintenance goes deeper, affecting intra-family/household relations. Spousal permitholders underline that, especially upon arrival, their main role is to support their partners by sustaining their families/households in Canada materially and socially and, in some cases, to send remittances abroad as well. Sonali, a permit-holder from Nepal and the spouse of a student, reports, "I chose the [Spousal] open work permit so I can work here [i.e., in Canada] and I can support him [my husband] while he is [a] student." Evelyn, a Spousal permitholder from Uganda, indicates that being "able to work here … somehow brought us together and made us more united because we're there for each other … financially," and reports, "I have to grind hard to provide for him because he's studying and sometimes doesn't earn as much as I do." Valdir underlines that the "main benefit" of the Spousal permit is "the possibility of coming [to Canada] and not just being a visitor … but someone who can actively work." This possibility also enables some Spousal permitholders such as Evelyn "to work in a better job… [than] the pay that I got …while I was back in Uganda … I'm in a better place financially right now, and this enables me to send some few coins back to my family and my sibling."

Spousal permitholders nevertheless cite trade-offs for holding work permits responding narrowly to the imperative to enable couples to reside together in Canada, including the compulsion to abandon educational programs, given the intense pressure to engage in employment. Mason worked in the public sector (immigration) and was a business owner in architecture and furniture design while holding a Spousal permit. He notes: "I got engaged. So, I just came to Canada. I never got to [take] education[al] leave … I never finished university. After I came to Canada, I was thinking about going back to finish it. However, there were a lot of limitations … so I decided to put that on hold and started working." Among Spousal permitholders, abandonment of individual educational goals can also stem from pressures to choose Spousal permits over other less secure alternatives (e.g., study or visitor permits). Davina had a similar experience: "We came together, but he [my spouse] came with a study permit, and I came under a visitor visa … so I applied for a study permit also, but my study permit was refused [inland]. We started studying ESL, and I applied again for a new study permit. But the new study permit was refused again. When we received the last refusal, we were talking with an adviser from the university … [who] advised us to try again, but on a spouse open permit because we had all the requirements at that time." While Davina went on to characterize her Spousal permit as "the easier and faster way to stay, joining our processes and doing it this way" and also that "it was better for both of us, for economics … and for stability," others cast the need to secure paid work is two-edged. On the one hand, Spousal permitholders appreciate that they can work for as many hours and hold as many jobs as they like. Sonali states, "Spouses [that] come like I came … because of the Open Work Permit … can do two jobs, three jobs, or whatever [they] want. That's really helped [us] out for start-ing … There are no boundaries [for Spousal permitholders] to work." On the other hand, capturing a commonly reported problem, flowing from the need to secure employment to sustain their households, Wesley, a Spou-sal permitholder from the United States who could only find work as a labourer, emphasizes the mismatch between his qualifications and his job, and views his temporary residency status as inherently limiting despite holding an open work permit: "Although they say that it's an open work permit … not every employer really values it … there's certain jobs that you apply to and they won't really consider you … I had a friend who did this process before me … he applied for other jobs and he was denied. They only accepted him for construction work." Evelyn, a certified chef, who considers herself lucky to have work in culinary services, also underlines the limits of the open work permit, noting that this permit does little to stem migrantization under other guises: "As much as I had this spous[al open] work permit, it was still a problem … They [the employers] would … be asking whether you're really a Canadian citizen and things like that. It's hard to be accepted because they're … thinking 'you're a foreigner,' 'you're an immigrant'… Somehow they don't trust that you're going to work or deliver the services appropriately."

A paradox is at work here: while Spousal permitholders are cast as "dependants" or, at best, "accompanying migrants," their contributions to households in the form of wages are often vital. In assuming depen-dency, the ideal-type marital or common-law relationship informing criteria for obtaining and utilizing Spousal permits, as well as pursu-ing permanent residency, is thus at odds with Spousal permitholders' activities. In some cases, the so-named principal permitholder may not be a classic breadwinner due to educational requirements and/or labour market conditions (e.g., until 2006, international students were only permitted to work on campus and after that their weekly hours were restricted). Some Spousal permitholders, like Mason, also view the opportunity to contribute financially to their households as a means of militating against dependencies constructed by policies: "It's a huge stress relief … [that] you can contribute to the family. Because, when a spouse is sponsoring the other partner for permanent residency, there is an undertaking financially."

A series of consequences flow from this paradox. One raised by several women is the decision to delay having children. Some such Spousal permitholders, including Chun-hua, say that they "are not planning to have any children [despite holding open work permits] because of the uncertainty. We are not sure if we can settle in Canada, or if Canada is our final place to stay." Chun-hua also emphasizes the difficulties of navigating temporary work as permitholders with children, noting that it means "more concerns, like the education for … or the future of our children. Before we settle, we will not have any children." Others, such as Marcus, a Spousal permitholder from South Africa, in turn, reports planning, upon the expiry of their permits, "[to] go back to our country [of origin] … so that we can have kids." Calling into question the characterization, at a policy level, of the expanding Spousal Work Permit program as an "innovative family-based solution," such narratives highlight how its relational features (i.e., tying spouses' criteria for entry and admission to permanent residency to a principal permitholder), and the patterns of dependence they foster, rely upon and heighten gendered power relations embedded within the normative (nuclear) family.

3.2.b RESPONDING TO QUALITATIVE LABOUR SHORTAGES?: PRECARIOUSNESS IN EMPLOYMENT AMONG SPOUSAL PERMITHOLDERS

Such relational conditions also aid Canadian-based employers in filling vacancies in jobs and industries undesirable to nationals. The imperative to contribute promptly upon arrival to household income through employment, mentioned by many Spousal permitholders, positions these permitholders as an ideal labour supply for redressing qualitative labour shortages. Analysis of administrative data reveals the multiple dimensions of labour market insecurity Spousal permitholders experience. In 2023, only about 19 per cent of Spousal permitholders did not report independent income (i.e., they reported zero income or did not file a T1). Furthermore, among those who did, fully 88 per cent reported earnings from employment. Until 2020, spouses of students were particularly motivated to contribute to household income owing to limitations on full-time international students' participation in the labour force. As Spousal permitholder Sonali notes: "[In] my experience, it's really helpful for [spouses of] students [to earn money] because many students … can work only 20 hours [a week]." Regardless, numerous spouses underscored the difficulties of finding high-quality employment due to lack of support, intense competition, and their limited mobility within Canada for family reasons, reinforced by immigration policies. While applauding the provision of open work permits, Valdir struggled to find work in his field in Canada, and therefore kept the job he had in Brazil, working remotely as a researcher for a Brazilian-based NGO. He describes the dearth of supports available upon arrival and their effects on securing high quality employment:

> You don't have any support as you're coming as a worker. You just have to get your stuff together and do what you have to do to get a job. Nobody tells you where to go, what to do. There's no orientation. In that sense, I keep thinking that maybe, for some people, that could be very like hard, [that is,] to adapt to a new culture. Even for me ... I had a lot of letters and CVs that were in Portuguese. I just translated them and tried to send them to Canadian employers and that wasn't enough ... Clearly, I wasn't doing something right. If I had some sort of orientation that could have helped me get a job, that could [have] changed things. I would have much higher pay.

Sonali recounts that even though she "applied for lots and lots of jobs," it took "two to three months ... [to] get any response ... and [for] three to four months ... [I] didn't get any job. It was really difficult for us, because he was a student [when] I came here ... How we survived, I do not know." This situation is by no means anomalous. As Chun-hua comments, "I have sent around 40 applications to different companies and positions, and I only got two interviews in return."

Considering prominent indicators of precariousness individually among Spousal permitholders in their main job in 2021, the labour market insecurities described by the previous three interviewees are relatively widespread. Rates of non-unionization/non-professionaliza-tion among Spousal permitholders are high – fully 86 per cent of those with valid work permits are non-unionized/non-professionalized. Men Spousal permitholders have a slightly lower rate of labour market insecurity along this indicator compared to women (i.e., 88 per cent of men are non-unionized/non-professionalized compared with 91 per cent of women) (Table 5.1). Furthermore, shares of non-unionized/non-professionalized Spousal permitholders from countries of origin whose emigrants have long been subject to differential inclusion via Canadian immigration policy are high vis-à-vis those from higher-income countries of origin. Specifically, rates of non-unionization/non-profession-alization among Spousal permitholders from France and the United States are 77 per cent and 83 per cent respectively, whereas those among

Table 5.1 Indicators of Precariousness among Spousal Permitholders, 2021

	Non-unionized/non-professionalized	More Than One Job	Small Firm	Precarious**
	By Country of Origin			
India	88%	46%	25%	53%
Brazil	86%	39%	22%	45%
France	77%	33%	24%	38%
Philippines	82%	51%	18%	48%
China	93%	26%	53%	62%
Iran	87%	38%	31%	51%
Korea	93%	35%	55%	67%
Mexico	90%	35%	34%	51%
Colombia	84%	48%	23%	49%
US	83%	21%	25%	32%
Others	86%	36%	27%	45%
	By Sex*			
Men	88%	44%	27%	53%
Women	91%	36%	27%	47%
	Overall Total			
	86%	40%	27%	49%

Source: Statistics Canada (2023).
Notes:
1. **Precarious employment is a compound variable capturing whether or not a respondent experiences 2 out of 3 indicators of precariousness.
2. *Due to the nature of the CEEDD, which is based on linkable files from administrative sources, different variables come from different datasets. The harmonized variable capturing sex comes from the T1 Personal Master tax file, submitted by employees to the Canada Revenue Agency (CRA), whereas other variables included in this table come from the Longitudinal Immigration Database or employer-provided datasets. Because some employees do not submit T1s for various reasons, the number of responses is smaller when examining gender in relation to precariousness than when examining precariousness among all respondents, regardless of whether their gender is known. For this reason, the proportions depicted for men and women differ from that of the overall total.

Spousal permitholders from India, China, and South Korea are even higher, at 88, 93, and 93 per cent respectively.

Similar patterns prevail with regard to firm size. Overall, most Spousal permitholders are employed in larger firms. Proportions of men and women Spousal permitholders in small firms are also balanced. At the same time, proportions of Spousal permitholders from China and South Korea employed in small firms are relatively high (53 per cent and 55 per cent respectively), compared with those of their counterparts from other countries in the Americas, such as the United States (25 per cent employed in small firms). Likewise, proportions of permitholders with more than one job are higher for spouses from India (46 per cent), the

Table 5.2 Industry of Employment among Spousal Permitholders, 2021

	Administrative and Support Services	Retail Trade	Accommodations and Food Services	Manufacturing	Scientific, Professional, and Technical Services
			By Country of Origin		
India	18%	10%	9%	11%	10%
Brazil	12%	13%	8%	12%	12%
France	6%	13%	5%	10%	15%
Philippines	11%	11%	26%	16%	4%
China	3%	14%	22%	8%	11%
Iran	8%	22%	10%	11%	9%
Korea	3%	15%	35%	7%	4%
Mexico	16%	10%	15%	11%	7%
Colombia	23%	9%	9%	17%	7%
US	6%	9%	6%	4%	16%
Others	12%	12%	12%	9%	10%
			By Sex		
Men	13%	10%	10%	14%	9%
Women	12%	14%	14%	8%	11%
			Overall Total		
	13%	12%	12%	11%	10%

Source: Statistics Canada (2023).

Philippines (51 per cent), and Colombia (48 per cent) than those from France (33 per cent) and the United States (21 per cent).

Using a combined variable, Spousal permitholders experiencing either both a lack of control and working in a small firm, or one such feature plus holding more than one job, fully 49 per cent (similar percentages of women and men)[14] would be considered precariously employed. Moreover, shares of precariously employed Spousal permitholders from South Korea (67 per cent), China (62 per cent), and India (53 per cent) exceed this overarching figure (see Table 5.1). As such, precariousness among Spousal permitholders is racialized insofar as those from countries of origin whose emigrants are racialized as non-white experience multiple dimensions of labour market insecurity most acutely.

Industry of employment also offers a window into the labour market insecurities confronting Spousal permitholders. Many are employed in domains characterized by qualitative labour shortages in which precarious jobs are the norm. The three top industries of employment for Spousal permitholders are administrative and support services, retail trade, accommodation and food services, manufacturing, and scientific and professional (Table 5.2). In retail, these trends are also gendered,

Table 5.3 Precariousness among Spousal Permitholders by Industry, 2021

Industry	Precarious (%)
Agriculture, mining utilities	49%
Construction	66%
Manufacturing	36%
Wholesale trade	44%
Retail trade	49%
Transportation	50%
Information and cultural industries	37%
Finance and insurance	29%
Real estate; rental and leasing	55%
Professional, scientific, and technical services	42%
Management	55%
Administrative support	50%
Educational services	20%
Health	41%
Arts, entertainment, and recreation	51%
Accommodation and food services	63%
Other services	66%
Public administration	12%

Source: Statistics Canada (2023).

that is, 14 per cent of employed women Spousal permitholders hold main jobs in this industry compared to 10 per cent of men.[15] Spousal permitholders from relatively low-income countries, such as Iran, are also overrepresented in retail.[16] Spousal permitholder Sonali, working two retail jobs to compensate for her low-income from employment, one in a florist shop and one at a large low-cost transnational retailer, hopes her experience of occupational downgrading will be short-lived: "I was working as a teacher in Nepal. When I came here, I didn't have any [Canadian] experience. I didn't have studies here ... I thought, for a start, it's okay for me. But, definitely not for [the] future." In contrast, 14 per cent of employed men Spousal permitholders work in manufacturing, compared with 8 per cent of women. Spousal permitholders from Colombia are also overrepresented in this industry (17 per cent work in manufacturing), whereas those from South Korea (8 per cent), China (7 per cent), and the United States (4 per cent) are underrepresented. Notably, however, while administrative and support services are a somewhat less precarious industry overall, 50 per cent of Spousal permitholders in this industry hold precarious jobs (i.e., a similar percentage of those who experience precariousness in retail) (see Table 5.3).

Table 5.4 Annual Income among Spousal Permitholders, 2021

	Less than $30,000	$30,000– $50,000	$50,000– $70,000	$70,000– $90,000	$90,000+
		By Country of Origin			
India	56%	26%	11%	4%	4%
Brazil	50%	25%	13%	6%	6%
France	44%	26%	15%	8%	7%
Philippines	61%	27%	9%	2%	1%
China	72%	17%	6%	3%	3%
Iran	68%	19%	8%	3%	2%
Korea	71%	20%	6%	2%	1%
Mexico	67%	20%	8%	3%	2%
Colombia	65%	24%	7%	2%	2%
US	54%	15%	10%	7%	13%
Others	63%	20%	9%	4%	4%
		By Sex			
Men	48%	27%	14%	6%	5%
Women	68%	19%	7%	3%	3%
		Overall Total			
	59%	23%	10%	4%	4%

Source: Statistics Canada (2023).

As in retail, the gender distribution of Spousal permitholders in accommodation and food services, the third-largest industry of employment for Spousal permitholders, is skewed towards women in this group; 14 per cent of all employed women Spousal permitholders work in this industry compared to 10 per cent of their male counterparts who are men. Moreover, those from Korea, the Philippines, and China are overrepresented in accommodation and food services (i.e., 35 per cent of Spousal permitholders from Korea, 26 per cent from the Philippines, and 22 per cent from China), compared with high-income source countries, such as France and the United States (i.e., 5 per cent of Spousal permitholders from France and 6 per cent from the United States are employed in this industry). Spousal permitholder Marcus, working as a waiter, comments on the low levels of compensation in this industry while underscoring the need to retain employment for the duration of a Spousal permit and in pursuing permanent residency: "The job is a bit stressful having to … deal with customers. So, I wouldn't say it's … 'good pay,' but then you can't really complain." Marcus's attitude may emanate from his experience at his first job as a Spousal permitholder, which paid $10 per hour as a packager in a warehouse. In retrospect, he notes that "in that moment … I was happy just to find something, to get my hands on something instead of just being idle at home … [but] the pay was way too small."[17]

Although the foregoing example is illustrative of the low hourly wages some Spousal permitholders are compelled to accept, income categories in which they are found are even more revealing of gendered patterns. As Table 5.4 shows, whereas the share of women Spousal permitholders earning less than $30,000 is high (68 per cent) compared to the share of men Spousal permitholders in that same category (48 per cent), shares of women earning more than $50,000 are exceedingly low (13 per cent compared to 25 per cent of men). Correspondingly, the share of men earning $70,000+ is almost double (11 per cent) compared to women in that same category (6 per cent). These findings underscore the income insecurity confronting many women Spousal permitholders, heightening their economic dependency and thus *relational* precarity. An exploration of country-of-origin dynamics also reveals relatively high shares of Spousal permitholders from China (72 per cent) and Korea (71 per cent) in the less than $30,000 category compared to those still high percentages among those from France (44 per cent), and the United States (54 per cent) with such low earnings. Moreover, shares of Spousal permitholders from the United States (13 per cent) and France (7 per cent) in the $90,000+ category are appreciably higher than those of Spousal permitholders from the remaining top ten countries of origin, leaving little doubt that those from the latter group of lower-income countries are relatively more insecure in income terms. Accordingly, Abel, a Spousal permitholder migrating from South Africa working as an electrician apprentice earning $15/hour in Toronto aspires to move up the wage hierarchy: "The appliances and electronics [sector] in Canada is different than [in] Africa. So, I think, [given] my learning my way around everything, my wage is okay. But, as time goes on, I hope it will increase." Wesley is more forthright about the lack of recognition of his expertise in his $13/hour job as a labourer in construction, noting, "I think I deserve more than that with my skillset."

Despite Spousal permitholders' experiences of relational precarity, members of this growing sector adopt a host of creative measures in confronting their conditions. Participants routinely utilize their social networks, friends, and social media groups to navigate complex situations and application processes. Sonali eloquently describes her observations about information-sharing in online communities of permitholders this way:

> People have communities, Nepalese communities, Indian communities ... People post their questions [and others] answer ... based on their experiences. People put a lot of information out there ... then you ... look into what kind ..., where you can match your situation to that particular person and then get more information and proceed from there.

Another permitholder, Chun-hua, received tips from another applicant: "I asked my Canadian friend. She also sponsored her spouse to Canada. And, while she's doing the PR application for the spouse, she also had to provide 30 pictures to prove that the relationship is valid and it's not a fraud ... I learned from her experience to provide more photos and evidence for IRCC to prevent any back-and-forth email or questions, which can push back our application process time." Still others speak of the importance of social networks in finding jobs quickly[18] and especially in securing employment in their fields. For instance, Evelyn underscores the importance of "a friend [that] directly connected me to another friend who was already working in the restaurant. The friend told me that there was an open position, and they're looking for someone, a chef, and I could apply to that."

Spousal permitholders also utilize other networks and services to secure advice about (im)migration processes and policies. For example, Jia highlights how she learned about accessing child benefits for her son through community connections at newcomer services: "I did go to the YMCA career centre ... those places for newcomers ... I didn't know I could apply for child benefits until somebody told me." Permitholders, such as Jia, tend to rely most heavily on community networks, connections, and supports in transitionary periods. That is, when their permits expire or their relationships dissolve and they are seeking to maintain residency in Canada, either with their spouse or by themselves. For Jia, the journey entailed "jumping" from one IMP to another to maintain employment and residency, for both herself and her dependent son, in Canada, first with her husband and then without him (following her divorce). She came initially as a spouse of a student, after holding a visitor visa, before transitioning to the spouse of a Post-graduation permitholder, a permit that was extended once, during which time her relationship dissolved. Jia then gained a student visa before becoming a Post-graduation permitholder herself, with the goal of applying for permanent residency, ideally while she could still benefit from the maximum points for her (young) age.

4. Conclusion

The Spousal Work Permit program contributes to "relational precarity" among permitholders admitted, and permitted to engage in employment, as common-law or married partners of students and skilled-work permitholders deemed potentially desirable as long-term immigrants. In revealing and investigating the dynamics behind this experience, this chapter has disclosed patterns of dependence perpetuated by policies pegging Spousal permitholders' criteria for admission, labour force participation, and access to permanent residency to ties, and conditions applicable, to principal permitholders. In the process, it has illustrated how program parameters promote deeply gendered household forms – i.e., nuclear family households led by a principal permitholder presumed (or poised) to hold secure employment – via sorting mechanisms contributing to gradations of subordination. Simultaneously, these parameters also serve to fulfil employer demands for a "flexible" labour supply to address qualitative labour shortages in industries such as retail and accommodation and food services, often with not only profound consequences for permitholders' terms and conditions of employment but the decisions they make in other areas of their lives (e.g., delayed fertility, occupational downgrading). As permitholders' narratives, together with administrative data (e.g., data illustrating that women Spousal permitholders who transition to permanent residency are disproportionately represented in the "dependant" category) attest, program conditions effectively compel Spousal permitholders to remain in partnerships as both their finite work permits and transitions to permanent residency rest on relationship maintenance, which can involve long periods of navigating complex family/household dynamics alongside accepting whatever jobs are on offer and thus deskilling/ occupational downgrading and/or delayed education or credential acquisition.

The foregoing profile of Spousal permitholders' labour force experiences, particularly related to job quality, further illustrates the limits of the "family-based solutions" that the Spousal Work Permit program offers. Spousal permitholders' considerable exposure to labour market insecurities is evident when considering indicators of precariousness such as the absence of unionization/professionalization, small firm size, and multiple job-holding as well the income groupings in which many are found. Moreover, permitholders, a group comprised primarily of women, and those arriving from countries of origin subject historically to racially discriminatory immigration policies, such as India, bear the brunt of this gendered precariousness. Analysis of Spousal permitholders' experience of dimensions of labour market insecurity cumulatively, together with holding jobs in industries defined by qualitative labour shortages, in which precarious employment is common, reveals the magnitude of relational precarity confronting those who are women and especially those women from countries of origin such as India, China, Korea, and the Philippines. Indeed, these Spousal permitholders are overrepresented in precarious jobs compared to their counterparts from wealthier countries of origin whose residents are more closely identified with whiteness. Meanwhile, considering income level alone, women earn lower incomes from employment, reinforcing socially assigned gendered dependencies and, quite concretely, women Spousal permitholders' dependency on their partners.

As Canada' extends greater opportunities for Spousal permitholders' accompaniment with "principal" work permitholders beyond those identified as "skilled workers," including those principal permitholders deemed, at a policy level, to possess lower levels of socially recognized skills than those eligible for spousal accompaniment in the 2002–22 period (i.e., solely full-time post-secondary students and skilled workers), some of whom are enrolled in subprograms inhibiting access to permanent residency, such dynamics are poised to intensify. Such expanded eligibility – no doubt fragile, as illustrated by shifting eligibility requirements implemented in 2025 – is rationalized on the bases of providing "innovative family-based solutions" and easing labour shortages, justifications first emerging in the post-pandemic period. However, in stopping short of concurrently expanding pathways to permanent residency beyond those geared towards "skilled" workers – a consequence potentially compounded by the 2024–5 policy change limiting the provision of Spousal permits to students enrolled in graduate and professional degree programs – this policy expansion is likely to result in a greater proportion of women participating in the Spousal Work Permit program as a whole.

Chapter Six

Conclusion: Contesting Differential Inclusion and Precarity under Canada's International Mobility Program

Through a study of Canada's fast-growing IMP, set against the backdrop of the reduction and recalibration of programs under the TFWP, this book has challenged the migration/mobility policy construct integral to these developments. Upholding this construct, fostered by conditions established in international agreements promoting reciprocity and competitiveness, the newly inaugurated IMP targets well-educated *mobile* workers with high levels of socially recognized skills and qualifications who are positioned as taking advantage of employment opportunities overseas. Yet the case studies of its three largest subprograms, undertaken in Chapters 3–5, reveal that this umbrella program does not entail a meaningful departure from conditions long associated with *migrant* work programs in Canada. Rather, as a product of an (im)migration policy framework fostering differential inclusion, the programs under study provide for legalized yet tenuous residency status, often coupled with precariousness in employment. By rationalizing access to temporary work permits on "non-work" bases in the face of qualitative labour shortages, the youth mobility-oriented Working Holiday program; the Post-graduation Work Permit program, targeting former educational migrants; and the Spousal Work Permit program, supporting family reunification, contribute to cultural exchange, probationary, and relational precarity. Under the auspices of these IMPs, all three groups of permitholders initially enter Canada and join its labour force through the back door. Subsequently, should they wish to extend their time in Canada and/or pursue permanent residency, these permitholders encounter blocked, multiple hierarchically ordered, and adjoining doors of entry respectively. Furthermore, in each case, those from countries of origin subject historically to racialized barriers to entry, erected via nationality, and women experience these restrictions acutely, indicative of how migrantization can act as a divisive force even though permitholders' precarity takes expression in different ways depending upon the features of the IMP in which they are enrolled. There is, therefore, evidence of differentiation not only between permitholders enrolled in different IMPs, but also among those enrolled in the three large subprograms examined in this book – reflecting inter- and intra-program polarization, challenging the assumption, promoted in laws, policies, and regulations, that IMPs provide for high-quality employment across the board, and threatening to thwart collective efforts to secure necessary reforms.

Attesting to such dynamics, in exploring how Canada's Working Holiday program operates among the "young" people it targets, Chapter 3's exposé of cultural exchange precarity reveals that while some Working Holiday permitholders reflect the ideal-typical "cultural sojourner," a large subset offer a "flexible" labour supply for employers in industries defined by qualitative labour shortages that are key sites of precarious jobs, such as accommodation and food services, as well as retail trade and arts, recreation, and culture. Patterns of stratification reflecting processes of migrantization, whereby the working conditions and residency status of permitholders from certain countries of origin, more than others, more closely resemble those facing permitholders in TFWP subprograms demonstrated to be exploitative (e.g., in food services prior to the 2014 moratorium), are also evident among Working Holiday permitholders. Policy and administrative data analysis, together with open-ended interviews exploring the character of permitholders' labour force experience, underscores the porosity of distinction between *mobility*-oriented "cultural exchange" and *migrant* work-oriented programs. They reveal "cultural exchange precarity" among Working Holiday permitholders overall – exposing corrosive conditions among many permitholders occupying jobs in the essential and/or frontline service industries in particular. At the same time, given their access to longer work permits, entrants from affluent countries of origin with the largest quotas for participation in the Working Holiday program, such as those from several countries identified with whiteness, a majority of which have ties to the British Commonwealth (e.g., Australia, Ireland, New Zealand, and the United Kingdom), more closely approximate the figure of the "cultural sojourners." Consistent with previous analyses of the ways in which privilege functions among Irish Working Holiday permitholders (Helleiner 2017), these entrants' access to permits of 23–24 months in duration effectively gives permitholders greater (albeit still constrained) access to permanent residency via immigration streams valuing the accrual of "skilled" Canadian work experience. Entrants from France are similarly privileged.

In contrast, permitholders with shorter work permits of, for example, 12 months duration, from less affluent countries with access to smaller quotas, whose nationals are often racialized as non-white (e.g., Japan, Korea, and Taiwan), deviate from the "cultural sojourner" archetype. Still, while the Working Holiday program is conceived and organized on the basis that all permitholders spend a limited period of time in Canada, as work permits are non-renewable and repeat participation is difficult to attain (i.e., program design blocks front-door entry among such back-door entrants), those attempting to utilize the program as a pitstop enroute to permanent residency engage creative strategies such as "program jumping," in the absence of pathways akin to those available to their counterparts enrolled in the Post-graduation Work Permit and Spousal Work Permit programs.

Applying the doors of entry analytic to the case of Post-graduation permitholders and exploring factors conditioning their residency status and labour force participation in Canada, Chapter 4 illustrates distinctly that the "probationary precarity" they confront institutionalizes pressures to take on precarious employment as a means of achieving security of presence. Like Working Holiday permitholders, these former international students receive open work permits. Yet, unlike the blocked doors of permanent entry institutionalized via the Working Holiday program, there is a formal pathway to permanent residency under this IMP. At the same time, accessing this pathway is challenging; Post-graduation work permitholders must accrue at least one year of employment experience in a narrow band of occupations, compelling many to fill jobs in sectors that, like those in which a large subset of Working Holiday permitholders are employed, are characterized by qualitative labour shortages. To demonstrate their value to the Canadian labour force, Post-graduation permitholders pursuing permanent residency endure a multi-staged trial period, during which time their residency status is tenuous, often culminating in their holding jobs that do not align with their education and training. Consequently, in navigating passageways between hierarchically ordered doors of entry, a considerable proportion confront multiple dimensions of labour market insecurity. However, here too, even though the design of the program does not tie permit duration to country of origin (as with the Working Holiday program), precariousness in employment is particularly severe among permitholders from countries whose nationals have been subject historically to discriminatory treatment via immigration policy.

Distinctively the examination of the Spousal Work Permit program undertaken in Chapter 5 discloses patterns of gendered dependence fostered by policies pegging permitholders' criteria for admission, labour force participation, and ultimately access to permanent residency to ties and conditions applicable to a "principal," specifically, a work permitholder deemed to be a skilled worker or, at the time of writing, a full-time post-secondary international student, a category narrowed to full-time international graduate student in 2024. Underscoring the stubbornly persistent primacy that laws, regulations, and policies accord to the nuclear family form, perpetuating continuities in sex/gendered divisions of labour in households alongside gendered precariousness in the labour force, this case study reveals how Canadian (im)migration policy sorts entrants in ways that foster gradations of inclusion on the bases of gender together with country of origin, and its consequences for Spousal permitholders' experience overall (i.e., relational precarity). Attesting to how exclusion and inclusion are continuous rather than dichotomous processes that perpetuate intersecting inequalities, the chapter also illustrates the degree of migrantization confronting women Spousal permitholders from countries of origin whose nationals are racialized as non-white. Continuities fostered by the design of the subprogram in which Spousal work permitholders enrol include not only the tendency, at a policy level, to conflate households and families but the promotion of a family form supportive of Canadian-based employers' persistent demand for workers to fill precarious jobs in occupations and industries considered undesirable by citizens with racialized gendered effects. Indeed, program parameters respond to employer demand by providing for open work permits in the interest of offering a "family-based solution" that paradoxically recognizes socio-economic considerations as key for all adult permitholders, regardless of marital/family status (i.e., not only those designated "principal foreign nationals"). At the level of program design, this contradictory emphasis heightens the unique vulnerabilities of (especially women) Spousal permitholders, particularly those from countries of origin, such as India, as they negotiate doors assigned to their common law/marital partners.

1. Principles for Meaningful Inclusion

Despite the foregoing findings, cultural exchange, probationary and relational precarity among Working Holiday, Post-graduation, and Spousal permitholders are by no means inevitable outcomes of Canada's three largest IMPs. Nor do permitholders view them as such, as evidenced by the agency they exhibit. In Canada, as elsewhere, organizing efforts on the part of permitholders and their allies are also beginning to emerge, principally through the advocacy work of organizations such as Migrant

Students United (Mathew 2022); post-secondary student collectives/
associations, such as the Canadian Federation of Students (Canadian
Federation of Students n.d.; Graduate Student Society at Simon Fraser
University 2020); and immigrant service agencies, largely at the provincial level (e.g., the Ontario Council of Agencies Serving Immigrants)
(OCASI 2011), as well as via self-help/mutual aid groups organized and
run by permitholders themselves, aided by social media (e.g., the IEC
Working Holiday Forum – Moving2Canada Facebook group). Whereas
Post-graduation permitholders tend to be most organized through
existing institutions, not surprisingly given both their typically longer
presence/histories in Canada and their ties to international students,
organizing among Working Holiday and Spousal permitholders tends
to take shape via the sharing of advice and resources as well as mutual
aid/support networks, typically via social media.[1] Together with the
creative strategies permitholders engage in to challenge the tenuous
residency status and the precarious jobs many endure, as documented
in Chapters 3–5, these initiatives highlight avenues for improving the
situation of the back-door entrants of focus in these pages in the here
and now. Granted, such avenues are not a panacea. Nor are they akin to
the more long-standing organizing efforts among, and/or on behalf of,
migrant workers under the TFWP, although finding common ground
with those enrolled in its major subprograms holds potential given not
only the shared vulnerabilities of workers across the migration/mobil-
ity policy construction but the efficacy and innovative character of
organizing strategies on the part of, for example, migrant agricultural
and care workers (see, for example, Tungohan 2023; Choudry & Smith
2016; Choudry, Hanley, & Shragge 2012). Rather, these avenues represent "waystations" geared towards incremental changes, directed ultimately at transformative ends. Recognizing and seeking to underline
that the migration/mobility distinction is a falsehood that accentuates
differential inclusion and migrantization, they are unified in challenging this policy construct and the very categories of the "migrant" versus
"mobile" worker engaged in national (im)migration policy design.

   As such, the policy options canvassed below reject two central tenets
of methodological nationalism integral to the design and implementation of laws, regulations, and policies governing IMPs. They challenge
the naturalization of "national" migration discourses and agendas and
logics, and their propensity to conceive of workers in a nation-state as a
singular, bounded social group, with the effect of marginalizing certain
non-nationals as "migrants," regardless of the program under which
they enter, and strive to achieve meaningful inclusion of all transnational workers; and, they oppose the territorial limitation in entitlements

and access to protections, supports, and services (e.g., labour and social protections, such as those provided under IRPA (2002) and via its regulations as well as settlement services), forwarding equity in coverage and, as appropriate, enforcement.

2. The Horizon of Possibility: Redesigning the International Mobility Program and Its Subprograms

The precarity experienced by permitholders under each of Canada's three largest IMP subprograms, and the extent to which the variants of cultural exchange, probationary, and relational precarity are shaped by social relations of gender and racialization via country of origin, call for rejecting (im)migration laws, regulations, and policies fostering differential inclusion and migrantization. More specifically, the experiences of permitholders in such subprograms reveal that while open work permits are preferable to closed or sector-specific work permits, they are insufficient in extending genuinely free mobility in the receiving country labour force. This insufficiency is amplified when the provision of the latter is paired with rigid policy strictures, naturalizing "national" agendas and logics insofar as they continue to foster singular conceptions of workers in a nation-state, for retaining permission to work (e.g., maintaining conjugal relationships, as is the case of Spousal permitholders), or for fulfilling criteria required for acquiring permanent residency, where pathways exist, centred, for example, on obtaining the necessary "Canadian (employment) experience" (e.g., tied to holding jobs in designated TEER categories for the requisite number of hours in a one-year period as in the case of Post-graduation permitholders). Evincing the consequences of territorialization, the experience of all three types of permitholders likewise underscore the bankruptcy of a regime for the enforcement of wide-ranging workplace protections extended only to a dwindling number of closed work permitholders, a majority of whom are enrolled in subprograms of the TFWP. As such, in opposition to territorial limitation, enforcement-related design flaws of the 2015 Immigration and Refugee Protection Regulations must be remedied (Marsden, Tucker, & Vosko 2021b) such that inspectors, via coordination between federal and provincial labour inspectorates charged with ensuring transnational workers' rights at work are protected, are mandated to engage in proactive investigations. Canada's workplace rights enforcement regime under the IRPA (2002) must also extend to cover all work permitholders, including those holding open work permits under the IMP. At the same time, to ensure that tenuous residence status neither functions to suppress permitholders' access to rights for fear of losing the good grace of employers confronting qualitative labour shortages (e.g., in the case of Working Holiday and Post-graduation permitholders) nor to compel them to remain in unsuitable, and even violent (see especially Illesinghe 2018), conjugal relationships (e.g., in the case of Spousal permitholders), creating direct and unequivocally independent pathways to permanent residency is imperative for all three categories of permitholders seeking greater security of presence so that they are not in a position where they, like Spousal permitholder Kaleb, who, on account of relational precarity "didn't know there was a possibility of permanent residency altogether." Such measures are vital in eliminating blocked doors for Working Holiday permitholders and reducing the hierarchical and adjoining doors confronting Post-graduation and Spousal permitholders respectively, and thereby minimizing conditionalities related to the nature and content of permitholders' jobs and interpersonal relationships. Fabrício, a Brazilian national who obtained a Working Holiday permit by paying a registered organization, and recognized his good fortune in eventually securing permanent residency via a unique Provincial Nominee Program operating in British Columbia, "want[s] the government ... [to] create a ... direct pathway between the Working Holiday visa and PR." Post-graduation permitholder Nita puts her interest in permanent residency more bluntly: "I am just interested in ... being free."

Instituting an across-the-board precarity premium on IMP permitholders' wages is another way to address one of the most prominent dimensions of labour market insecurity such permitholders confront (i.e., low wages), as well as to acknowledge the magnitude of their personal remittances (e.g., Canada sent 29 million USD in remittances globally in 2021). It would help ensure that entrants across the umbrella program's major categories, streams, and subprograms are not unfairly positioned to fulfil precarious jobs undesirable to workers holding citizenship or permanent residency (i.e., in the face of qualitative labour shortages). As Spousal permitholder Kaleb emphasizes, for IMP participants, "job stability is a big point ... people that come with these kind of permits, they have relationships that need them to be, you know, on top of things." More broadly, to redress global inequalities exacerbated by international migration for employment on temporary and temporary-permanent bases, particularly among permitholders from relatively low-income countries, Canada, as a high-income receiving country, must do more to compensate countries of origin (i.e., via mechanisms for global redistribution). Putting the situation of women from low-income countries of origin front of mind, particularly those engaged in paid caregiving work in high-income countries, some scholars advocate

taxing receiving countries to fund public physical and social infrastructure in sending countries (Beneria 2008, 17; see also Pearson 2004).

Above and beyond these overarching proposals, necessary short-
term reforms to the Working Holiday program to advance greater
equity include eliminating or, at a minimum, equalizing the number
(i.e., quotas) and duration of work permits among permitholders from
different countries of origin. Reciprocal agreements between nations
may be valuable tools in delineating, and facilitating access to, rights
among permitholders. Yet, there is a danger that, in the absence of a
principled basis for negotiating their terms, agreements extending
vastly different permitholder quotas to different countries, or, for that
matter, those forgoing quotas altogether, will accentuate rather than
militate against global hierarchies of nation-states fostering migrantization. This situation led Fabrício, cited above, to resort to a registered
organization, to whom he paid a considerable fee, because he could not
enter Canada through the Working Holiday program in the absence
of a reciprocal agreement with Brazil. He thus proposed that the
Canadian "government ... expand the [eligible] countries [under the
Working Holiday program]." Fabrício and others entering under either
the Working Holiday or allied Young Professionals program under
International Experience Canada often do so at excessive financial cost
to themselves. (This finding applies as well to prospective permitholders and permitholders seeking to transition to permanent residency.)
Registered organizations effectively act as labour market intermediar-
ies, and are subject only to limited scrutiny. Their role in the Working
Holiday program should thus be re-evaluated and possibly eliminated,
given especially permitholders' appreciably high concentration in jobs
in industries characterized by qualitative labour shortages, in which
precarious employment is the norm.

The situation of Post-graduation permitholders, particularly as
to the challenges they face at the penultimate stage of their probation, together with the well-documented exploitation of international
student workers, a group for whom the naturalization of "national"
migration agendas and logics institutionalized in the fee structures of
post-secondary institutions engenders financial risk and precarity from
the get-go (Hune-Brown 2021; Kim, Buckner, & Montsion 2024) – levels of mistreatment sufficient to move the federal government to make
programmatic changes limiting their numbers rather than pursuing
strategies for greater equalization[2] in January 2025 – also demands the
introduction of more straightforward and direct pathways to permanent residency for Post-graduation permitholders, most immediately,
and ultimately for international students. Not only have these students

"paid their dues," as they are typically subject to fees out of sync with those of their domestic counterparts, putting them on further probation is poised to perpetuate differentiation between Canadian-born/established immigrant workers and newcomers and to contribute to downward harmonization/skills downgrading among the latter (Spring & Vosko 2023). To limit occupational downgrading among permitholders in the short run, should incremental, rather than more radical, changes be most feasible, immediate reforms to the Post-graduation Work Permit program should entail the elimination of unprincipled occupational requirements, emblematic of territorialization, for access to pathways to permanent residency.[3]

As it extends insecurity of presence and can also lead permitholders to become trapped in precarious jobs in both the short and long term, given the danger of occupational downgrading, the requirement for 12 months of full-time employment or its equivalent in the prescribed NOC categories must be eliminated. Jia, a Post-graduation permitholder we met in Chapter 4, expressed justified frustration with the system: her work permit was due to expire while she was on the cusp of fulfilling all qualifying requirements but she was just short of those related to holding a job in a narrow band of occupations. To recall, at the time of her interview, Jia, who initially came to Canada on a Spousal permit and then obtained a student permit after a difficult divorce, found herself slightly below the official cut-off score for access to permanent residency because elements of her Canadian work experience did not fall under the correct occupational group due to the TEER/NOC code reclassification. For permitholders in such situations, as student associations such as the Simon Fraser University Graduate Student Society suggest, restrictive Canadian employment experience requirements are unjust; coupled with changing rules around occupational requirements, they promote a high level of insecurity of presence that policies should not condone.

Compared to Working Holiday and Post-graduation permitholders, Spousal permitholders are uniquely dependent upon their married or common-law partners, who may be students or skilled workers, in addition to their employers. Noting parallels between the Spousal work permit and a closed/employer-tied permit common under the TFWP, two limitations tethering these permitholders to their common-law or married partners in ways unimaginable among national (i.e., citizen and permanent resident) workers, Davina emphasizes that she can only maintain security of presence as long as her spouse can, and so long as they stay together: "I'm under his process. I'm here as long as he's here." Frustrated by the very limited and often precarious jobs available to permitholders tethered to their spouses, regardless of their skillsets, Wesley, the spouse of a student completing their educational program, notes further that "the negative part is I have six months to work ... [and] after the six months, I have to leave." Albeit in a different register, the experiences of permitholders like Davina and Wesley reinforce calls for adopting policy reforms oriented to equity; they underline the need to, at a minimum, offer the spouses of *all* work permitholders, regardless of the program in which they are enrolled, entry to Canada and access to its labour force without qualification, a proposal of, among other immigrant-serving agencies, the Canadian Council for Refugees (Canadian Council for Refugees n.d.). Jia, the Post-graduation permitholder who initially entered Canada as a spouse, also comments that such across-the-board initiatives are necessary if policies are to reduce the many "barriers, especially for people from different backgrounds and in different circumstances." This necessary shift towards universal access to work permits for spouses of temporary work permitholders of all sorts, as well as for full-time students, is, however, at odds with the 2024/25 policy change (IRCC 2024o). This change limits entry for spouses of full-time students to those accompanying principals enrolled in graduate programs; meanwhile it expands opportunities for Spousal permit holding to a wider array of principal work permitholders, rather than educational permitholders, attesting to the growing focus on attracting "economically desirable" workers – a change that also sidesteps the issue of relational precarity.

Reducing relational precarity among Spousal permitholders likewise demands independent pathways to permanent residency. It underscores the need to adapt conditions applicable to Spousal permitholders to recognize, and take into account, gendered power relations in conjugal relationships and familial/household contexts, power relations well-documented to contribute to violence against women (see especially Jayasuriya-Illesinghe 2018; see also Bhuyan, Korteweg, & Baqi 2018), in ways that transcend rather than reproduce inequalities (i.e., to augment Spousal permitholders' autonomy as transnational workers in their own right). By creating and sustaining communities of mutual care, Spousal permitholders, whose experiences and creative strategies Chapter 5 chronicles, deftly navigate constraints imposed via (im)migration policies. Yet, in solely admitting spouses via adjunct doors of entry, the very structure of the Spousal Work Permit program works against permitholders' agency with gendered and racialized consequences. While sorting mechanisms inherent in (im)migration policies may continue to prioritize prospective permitholders with conjugal relationships with legally present work permitholders (or landed immigrants) initially in admission processes applied to the latter, given how they reinforce gendered, and indeed racialized gendered, dependencies, processes for obtaining greater security of presence once a Spousal permitholder must be delinked from the "principal" permitholder. Moreover, on account of this concept's deeply gendered and racialized nature and its reinforcement of dangerous "dependencies," (im)migration policies should be stripped of this very notion (on the roots and implications of dependency as a racialized gendered concept, see Fraser & Gordon 1994). One promising policy solution to this problem would involve providing spousal entrants with work permits of a standard (and generous) length *separate and apart* from that of their common-law or married partners such that if the relationship dissolves, the now labelled "principal" applicant's work/study permit ends, or the lead applicant decides to leave the country or terminate their studies, their status would have no bearing on that of their partner. Delinking Spousal permits in this way upon arrival is in line with previous collective organizing/advocacy work vis-à-vis spousal migrants. As Chapter 5 illustrated, immigrant-serving organizations, such as the Canadian Council for Refugees and the Ontario Council of Agencies Serving Immigrants, together with women's organizations, collectively organized in opposition to the 2011 federal government proposal to make sponsored spouses' successful permanent residency "conditional" upon staying in a relationship with their sponsor (e.g., the principal) for a minimum of two years post–permanent residency (OCASI 2011). They collectivized their concerns on the basis that such a policy could compel sponsored spouses to stay in relationships even if they are facing violence, abuse, and/or harassment – and, in a major victory, the policy was repealed in 2017. Since that time, nothing has been done to untether spousal from "principal" permanent residency applicants. Yet given the relational precarity experienced by Spousal permitholders applying for permanent residency, this is no doubt a logical next step in redressing migrantization under this IMP.

Collectively, the cultural exchange, probationary, and relational precarity documented among the Working Holiday, Post-graduation and Spousal permitholders of central focus in this book amount to temporary migrant work by any other name. The experiences of permitholders enrolled in the *mobility* programs examined in these pages demonstrate boldly that addressing demands to fulfil qualitative labour shortages via the engagement of transnational workers remains a central motivation for Canada's IMP. Despite the aim of limiting the high degree of exploitation associated with *migrant* work programs under the TFWP via the inauguration of the IMP, the ways in which migrantization takes shape within this formally de-migrantized program – i.e., both across and within its three largest subprograms – are deeply engrained in laws, policies, and practices. Consequently, permitholders' ability to shed their migrancy (i.e., to obtain secure employment and residency status) is often conditioned by country of origin and/or gender, fostering polarization that can constrain the effectiveness of efforts to support and advocate for one another. This situation calls for building the political will necessary for challenging differential inclusion and precarity, and the migrantization that comes in their trail, in policy and practice. The foregoing proposals nevertheless aim to point the way to incremental changes directed at gaining momentum sufficient to initiate meaningful inclusion.

Appendix 1

List of Interviewees

International Experience Canada

Pseudonym	Location of Interviewee	Country of Origin	Education (at time of interview)	Industry and Position during Permit	Contract Type	Income	Trajectory
Sophia	Vancouver	Germany	Master's degree	Tourism (homestay assistant manager at a recognized organization)	Ongoing	$17–$19/hr	1-year Working Holiday permit – 1- year Young Professional permit – Obtained permanent residence via Canadian Experience Class
Davi	Laval	Brazil	PhD	Veterinary Services (Intern)	Fixed term, hourly	$37,000/yr	1-year Young Professional permit – Planned to apply for permanent residence via Canadian Experience Class at time of interview
Fabrício	Vancouver	Brazil	College diploma in Innovation and Entrepreneurship	Sales (sales manager)	Full-time, ongoing	$42,000/yr	Student visa in a private college – 1-year Working Holiday permit – Obtained permanent residence via British Columbia PNP
Lilly	Toronto	Germany	Master's degree in Engineering	Manufacturing (project coordinator)	Full-time, ongoing	$60,000–$62,000/yr	University exchange co-op – 1-year Young Professional permit – Bridging Open Work Permit – Obtained permanent residence

Freya	Montreal	Germany	Bachelor's degree in business administration	Tourism/hospitality (housekeeper, server); software development (tester)	Full-time, seasonal	$15–$20/hr	1 year-Working Holiday permit – Visitor visa – 1-year Young Professional permit – Planning to apply for permanent residence either via Express Entry or spousal sponsorship at time of interview
Jusa	Winnipeg	Czech Republic	High School Diploma	Unemployed	n/a	n/a	1-year Working Holiday permit – Planning to apply for permanent residence via a PNP at time of interview
Mila	Toronto	Germany	College diploma and vocational training as a media assistant	Hospitality (housekeeper and supervisor); food service (hostess)	Hourly, fixed term; Part-time, casual	$15/hr	1-year Working Holiday permit – 9-month young professional permit – Visitor visa – planning to apply for permanent residence via spousal sponsorship at time of interview
Maya	Banff	Australia	Not disclosed	Food service (cashier); Sports (basketball coach); legal (administrator); retail (skin consultant); informal (underground club bouncer)	Part-time, casual; part-time, seasonal	$15–$17/hr	Academic exchange program – 2-year Working Holiday Permit – Visitor Visa

(Continued)

(Continued)

Pseudonym	Location of Interviewee	Country of Origin	Education (at time of interview)	Industry and Position during Permit	Contract Type	Income	Trajectory
Clara	Toronto	United Kingdom	Not disclosed	Electrical (event and networking coordinator)	Permanent	$26/hr	2-year Working Holiday Permit – Planning to apply for permanent residence via Canadian Experience Class at time of interview
Samuel	Toronto	Ireland	Not disclosed	Tech (software developer)	Permanent	$100,000/yr	Tourist visa – 2-year Working Holiday Permit – Planning to apply for permanent residence via spousal sponsorship at time of interview
Reiko	Victoria	Japan	Master's degree	Unemployed	n/a	n/a	1-year Working Holiday permit
So-hyun	Vancouver	South Korea	Master's degree	Food service (cashier; kitchen); informal (babysitter; photographer)	Part-time, ongoing; full-time; ongoing	Minimum wage	1-year Working Holiday permit

Post-graduation Permitholders

Pseudonym	Location of Interviewee	Country of Origin	Education (at time of interview)	Industry and Position during Permit	Contract Type	Income	Trajectory
Leela	Edmonton	India	In India: bachelor's degree in nursing; In Canada: 2-year diploma in gerontology and palliative care	Food service (crew member; supervisor)	Full-time, regular over time	$16.15/hr	Study permit – 3-year Post-graduation permit – Planning to apply for permanent residence via Canadian Experience Class
Nita	Brampton	India	In Canada: master's degree in gender, feminist, and women studies	Executive search firm (consultant); university (teaching assistant)	Full-time, ongoing	$55,000/yr	Study permit – 1-year Post-graduation permit – Planning to apply for permanent residence via Ontario PNP at time of interview
Reshma	Windsor	India	In Canada: 2 postgraduate nursing diplomas. First in critical care nursing, second in palliative nursing	Food service (cook; supervisor; assistant manager)	Full-time, ongoing	$14–$17/hr	Study permit – 3-year Post-graduation permit – Obtained permanent residency via Canadian Experience Class
Sadia	Kingston	Bangladesh	In Canada: bachelor's degree in development studies	Fashion/apparel (accounting)	Full-time, fixed term; through an agency	$16.50/hr	Study permit – 3-year Post-graduation permit – Obtained permanent residency via Canadian Experience Class

(Continued)

(Continued)

Pseudonym	Location of Interviewee	Country of Origin	Education (at time of interview)	Industry and Position during Permit	Contract Type	Income	Trajectory
Rezwan	Oakville	Bangladesh	In Canada: bachelor's degree in mechanical engineering	Finance (data Scientist)	Full-time, ongoing	$65,000–$80,000/yr	Study permit/Co-op Permit – 3-year Post-graduation permit – Planning to apply for permanent residency via Ontario PNP
Bhavnish	Windsor	India	In Canada: master's degree in engineering	Rental vehicles (customer service); software development (developer)	Part-time, temporary; full-time ongoing	$14–$45/hr	Study permit – 3-year Post-graduation permit – Applied for permanent residency via Ontario PNP at time of interview
Sharhriar	Winnipeg	Bangladesh	In Canada: bachelor's degree in economics and political science	Retail (logistics and fulfilment associate); e-commerce (support adviser)	Full-time, ongoing	$42,000/hr	Study permit – 3-year Post-graduation permit – Planning to apply for permanent residence at time of interview
Shushma	Victoria	Bangladesh	In Canada: master's degree in art history and visual studies	Fine arts (gallery operations manager)	Full-time, permanent	$40,000/yr	Study permit/Co-op permit – 3-year Post-graduation permit – Planning to apply for permanent residence via Canadian Experience Class at time of interview
Rahee	Vancouver	South Korea	In Canada: diploma in international transportation and customs	Logistics and transportation (sales; logistics coordinator)	Full-time, permanent	$53,000/yr	Study permit – 3-year Post-graduation permit – Planning to apply for permanent residence via Canadian Experience Class or spousal sponsorship at time of interview

Name	Location	Country	Education	Industry (role)	Employment	Wage/Salary	Immigration status
Nuri	Okanagan Valley	South Korea	In Canada: 2 1-year postgraduate diplomas. First in marketing management and second in content strategy	Programmatic advertising (intern; associate; background actor)	Part-time, casual; full-time, permanent	$15/hr $58,000/yr	Study permit – 3-year Post-graduation permit – Obtained permanent residence via Ontario PNP as dependant applicant
Jia	Ottawa	South Korea	In United States: bachelor's degree in marketing In Canada: advanced diploma in HR	Insulation (office manager); facilities management (receptionist; finance administrator; accounts payable; projects administrator)	Full-time, permanent	$35,000 – $52,000/yr	Visitor visa – Spousal permit – Study permit – 3-year Post-graduation permit – 1.5-year Post-graduation permit extension – Planning to apply for permanent residence at time of interview
Ai	Toronto	China	In Canada: bachelor's degree in science	Food manufacturing (quality assurance technician)	Full-time, permanent	$20/hr	Study permit – 3-year Post-graduation permit – Obtained permanent residence via Alberta PNP

Spousal Permitholders

Pseudonym	Location of Interviewee	Country of Origin	Spouse of Skilled Worker or Full-Time Student?	Industry and Position during Permit	Contract Type	Income	Trajectory
Valdir	Toronto	Brazil	Full-time student	Non-governmental organization (researcher) – located in source country	n/a	n/a	Spousal permit (student) – Unsure about applying for permanent residence at time of interview
Sonali	Winnipeg	Nepal	Full-time student and skilled worker	Retail; florist shop (bouquet maker); salon (personal care services)	Part-time, permanent; full-time, fixed term	$13.90–$15/hr	Spousal permit (student) – Spousal permit (skilled worker) – Applied for permanent residence via temporary residency to permanent residency as dependant applicant
Chun-hua	Toronto	Hong Kong	Skilled worker	Data management and logistics (supply chain specialist)	Full-time, fixed term	$35.70/hr	Spousal permit (skilled worker) – Planning to apply for permanent residency at time of interview
Mason	Trois-Rivières	United States	Skilled worker	Architecture and design (business owner)	Self-employed	$375/hr	Spousal permit (skilled worker) – Obtained permanent residency via Quebec PNP – Applying for citizenship at time of interview
Kaleb	Toronto	Costa Rica	Full-time student	Food services (busboy); tech (customer service; quality assurance)	Full-time, permanent	$60,000/yr	Spousal permit (student) – Obtained permanent residency via Express Entry as dependant applicant

Davina	Halifax	Colombia	Full-time student	Unemployed	n/a	n/a	Spousal permit (student) – Planning to apply for permanent residency via Atlantic Immigration Pilot, PNP or Express Entry at time of interview
Abel	Toronto	South Africa	Full-time student	Retail (warehouse packaging); electrician	Full-time, casual; full-time, informal	$11–$15/hr	Spousal permit (student) – Planning to apply for permanent residency as dependant applicant at time of interview
Wesley	Toronto	United States	Full Time Student	Construction (labourer)	Full-time, permanent	$13/hr	Spousal permit (student) – Planning to apply for permanent residency as dependant applicant at time of interview
Marcus	Regina	South Africa	Full-time student	Warehouse (packaging); food services (waiter)	Full-time, ongoing	$10–$15/hr	Spousal permit (student) – Planning to apply for permanent residence at time of interview
Evelyn	Toronto	Uganda	Full-time student	Food services (chef)	Part-time, ongoing	n/a	Spousal permit (student)
Jia (see also above)	Ottawa	South Korea	Full-time student & skilled worker	Retail (customer service); administrative (receptionist)	Part-time, fixed term; full time, ongoing	Minimum wage; $40,000/yr	Spousal permit (student) – Spousal permit (skilled worker) – (see above)

Appendix 2

Appendix Tables

Table A.1 List of Exemptions from Labour Market Impact Assessment, 2024

	2024						
R204: International Agreements	R205: Canadian Interests	R206: No other means of support	R207: Permanent Residence Applicants	R207.1: Vulnerable Workers	R208: Humanitarian Reasons	A25.2: Public Policies
• Canada-International	• Significant Benefit	• Refugee claimants*	• Live-in caregiver class*	• Vulnerable workers	• Destitute students*	• Special measures to support Hong Kong residents to come to Canada
o CUSMA/NAFTA (business visitor; trader; investor; professional; intra-company transfer-executive/ senior manager; intra-company transfer-specialized knowledge)*	o Unique work situations	• Persons under an unenforceable removal order*	• Spouse or common-law partner class*	• Family member of vulnerable worker	• Holders of a Temporary Resident Permit of minimum 6 months*	• OWP for applicants under the TR to PR pathway
o Canada-Chile FTA (business visitor; trader; investor; professional; intra-company transfer-executive/ senior manager; intra-company transfer-specialized knowledge)*	o Entrepreneurs*		• Protected persons under A95(2)*			

- o Canada-Peru FTA (business visitor; trader; investor; professional; intra-company transfer-executive/ senior manager; intra-company transfer-specialized knowledge; management trainees)**

- o Canada-Colombia FTA (business visitor; trader; investor; professional; intra-company transfer-executive/ senior manager; intra-company transfer-specialized knowledge; spouse) **

- o Canada-Korea fta (business visitor; trader; investor; professional; intra-company transfer-executive/ senior manager; intra-company transfer-specialized knowledge; management trainees; spouse)

- o CETA (investors; professionals; engineering/ scientific technologist; intra-company transfers)

- o CPTPP (investors; professionals and technicians; intra-company transfers; spouse)

- o UK (Independent professionals, Intra-company transfers, spouses, investors, contractual service providers, engineering and scientific technologists

---

- o Provincial business candidates

- o Intra-company transfers*

- o Emergency Repairs*

- o TV/film production

- o Live-in caregivers with submitted PR applications

- o Spouses and dependants of Live-in caregivers with submitted PR applications

---

- • Section A(25) exemption*

- • Family members of above*

(Continued)

Table A.1 (Continued)

	2024					
R204: International Agreements	R205: Canadian Interests	R206: No other means of support	R207: Permanent Residence Applicants	R207.1: Vulnerable Workers	R208: Humanitarian Reasons	A25.2: Public Policies
o *GATS Professional** • *Provincial/territorial-international (none currently in effect)* • *Canada-provincial/territorial* o Nominated by a province for PR o Significant Investment Projects o Exceptional/unforeseen events o Atlantic Immigration Program	o Bridging Open Work Permits o Start-up business class PR applicants o PR applicants in spouse in Canada stream o Quebec Selection Certificate holders • **Reciprocal employment** o **Unique work situations** o **Camp counsellors** o **International Experience Canada*** o **Exchange Professors*** o **Visiting lecturers*** o **Performing arts** • Designated by minister o Research, educational or training					

- Post-secondary co-op
- Secondary co-op
  - o Competitiveness and Public Policy
    - Spouses of skilled workers*
    - Spouses of students*
    - Post-graduate work permit program*
    - Post-doctoral fellows and award recipients*
    - Off-campus employment*
    - Medical residents and fellows**
    - Spouse of low-skilled worker
    - Family members of economic PR applicants
  - o Charitable/religious work*

LEGEND:

* = Stream present in 2004 Foreign Worker Manual

** = Stream present in 2013 Foreign Worker Manual

International streams are in bold.

Transnational streams are in italic.

National streams are underlined.

Table A.2 Industrial Distribution of Permitholders, Select International Mobility Program Categories and Streams, 2021

	Agreements	Canadian Interests (CI)	CI – Significant Benefit	CI – Reciprocal Employment	CI – Competitiveness and Public Policy
Agriculture and mining or utilities	6%	1%	1%	2%	1%
Construction	5%	3%	3%	5%	3%
Manufacturing	11%	7%	7%	6%	8%
Whole-sale trade	5%	3%	5%	3%	4%
Retail trade	6%	12%	5%	8%	12%
Transport and warehouse	6%	6%	4%	2%	7%
Information and cultural industry	7%	3%	6%	4%	2%
Finance and insurance	3%	4%	5%	2%	4%
Real estate; rental and leasing	1%	1%	1%	2%	1%
Professional, scientific, and technical services	13%	12%	39%	15%	10%
Management of companies and enterprises	4%	5%	4%	5%	5%
Administrative and support services	4%	13%	4%	8%	14%
Educational services	5%	5%	2%	3%	5%
Health care and social assistance	5%	5%	3%	4%	5%
Arts, entertainment, and recreation	1%	1%	1%	8%	1%
Accommodation and food services	15%	16%	7%	19%	15%
Other services	3%	3%	2%	3%	2%
Public administration	2%	1%	1%	1%	1%

Source: Statistics Canada (2023).
Note: Agriculture, forestry, fishing and hunting, mining, quarrying, and oil and gas extraction, and utilities are combined into one to ensure minimum cell counts were achieved for each IMP category and stream.

Table A.3 Post-graduation Work Permit holders, Top 10 Countries of Origin, 2002–...

	2002	2003	2004	2005	2006	2007	2008	2009	2010	2011
1	China (325)	China (545)	China (1,175)	China (2,065)	China (2,990)	China (3,995)	China (6,730)	China (5,300)	China (5,530)	China (6,715)
2	India (180)	India (280)	India (510)	India (800)	India (1,005)	India (1,120)	India (1,660)	India (1,580)	India (2,515)	India (4,995)
3	France (145)	UK (145)	Korea (225)	Korea (320)	Korea (345)	Korea (390)	Korea (740)	Korea (740)	Korea (885)	Korea (950)
4	UK (145)	Korea (140)	France (170)	UK (185)	USA (235)	USA (290)	USA (670)	USA (665)	France (685)	France (865)
5	Japan (120)	France (125)	UK (165)	France (180)	UK (210)	Japan (245)	France (450)	France (660)	USA (685)	USA (805)
6	USA (120)	Japan (120)	USA (140)	USA (180)	Japan (200)	France (240)	Japan (390)	Japan (385)	Pakistan (355)	Morocco (425)
7	Korea (115)	USA (115)	Pakistan (100)	Bangladesh (150)	France (185)	Bangladesh (205)	UK (355)	Pakistan (295)	Morocco (340)	Nigeria (340)
8	Pakistan (65)	Pakistan (80)	Bangladesh (70)	Pakistan (130)	Bangladesh (175)	Nigeria (155)	Pakistan (305)	UK (285)	Mexico (270)	Japan (335)
9	Taiwan (60)	Bangladesh (50)	Taiwan (70)	Mexico (85)	Pakistan (125)	Pakistan (135)	Bangladesh (295)	Morocco (275)	Nigeria (255)	Mexico (330)
10	Mexico (40)	Taiwan (40)	Mexico (65)	Taiwan (75)	Mexico (100)	Indonesia (130)	Taiwan (255)	Taiwan (260)	UK (245)	Iran (330)

	2012	2013	2014	2015	2016	2017	2018	2019	2020	2021
1	India (7,895)	India (9,740)	India (10,950)	China (9,955)	India (16,540)	India (18,770)	India (33,070)	India (52,980)	India (70,515)	India (79,205)
2	China (7,070)	China (9,175)	China (10,305)	India (9,000)	China (14,430)	China (13,890)	China (14,445)	China (13,900)	China (13,905)	China (10,530)
3	Korea (1,120)	France (1,345)	France (1,470)	France (1,500)	France (2,285)	France (2,385)	France (2,430)	France (2,565)	Vietnam (2,885)	Iran (2,855)
4	France (945)	Korea (1,275)	Korea (1,350)	Korea (1,180)	Nigeria (1,970)	Korea (2,050)	Korea (2,095)	Brazil (2,405)	Brazil (2,620)	Vietnam (2,855)
5	USA (840)	USA (850)	Nigeria (1,015)	Nigeria (1,105)	Korea (1,915)	Nigeria (1,730)	Brazil (1,960)	Korea (2,160)	France (2,550)	France (2,780)
6	Pakistan (560)	Iran (740)	Pakistan (785)	Pakistan (775)	Pakistan (1,050)	Brazil (1,190)	Nigeria (1,850)	Vietnam (1,915)	Korea (2,115)	Philippines (2,300)

(Continued)

Table A.3 (Continued)

	2012	2013	2014	2015	2016	2017	2018	2019	2020	2021
7	Nigeria (485)	Pakistan (730)	USA (755)	USA (655)	USA (880)	USA (840)	Iran (1,020)	Iran (1,260)	Nigeria (2,085)	Brazil (2,160)
8	Morocco (470)	Nigeria (725)	Iran (745)	Iran (540)	Iran (880)	Pakistan (810)	Vietnam (965)	Philippines (1,120)	Iran (2,055)	Nigeria (2,000)
9	Iran (460)	Morocco (520)	Russia (480)	Morocco (490)	Brazil (775)	Iran (725)	USA (850)	Morocco (850)	Philippines (1,850)	Korea (1,995)
10	Bangladesh (360)	Mexico (385)	Morocco (450)	Russia (430)	Vietnam (635)	Jamaica (590)	Pakistan (820)	Pakistan (770)	Bangladesh (1,140)	Morocco (1,450)

	2022	2023
1	India (76,155)	India (145,820)
2	China (12,870)	China (17,115)
3	Iran (3,405)	Philippines (10,150)
4	Philippines (2,990)	Nigeria (5,670)
5	France (2,920)	Iran (4,905)
6	Vietnam (2,775)	France (3,925)
7	Nigeria (2,550)	Vietnam (3,740)
8	Korea (1,960)	Brazil (3,430)
9	Bangladesh (1,865)	Colombia (3,260)
10	Colombia (1,300)	Bangladesh (2,995)

Sources: Data from IRCC (2021a, 2023a, 2024a).
Note: Values between 0 and 5 are suppressed; all values are rounded to the nearest 5 to maintain anonymity.

Table A.4 Number of Study Permits Issued by Year and Country of Origin, 2016–20

Country of Citizenship	Level of Study	2016	2016%	2017	2017%	2018	2018%	2019	2019%	2020	2020%
1. India	CEGEPs, colleges, and PTC/TCST/DVS/AVS	29,708	73.7%	47,091	71.0%	55,251	67.6%	70,778	68.8%	20,854	77.3%
	ESL/FSL college and university programs	54	0.1%	116	0.2%	145	0.2%	57	0.1%	7	0.0%
	Other studies and post-secondary > than 1 year	3,527	8.8%	5,731	8.6%	7,389	9.0%	8,691	8.4%	2,471	9.2%
	University – BA	2,049	5.1%	4,307	6.5%	6,865	8.4%	9,575	9.3%	1,128	4.2%
	University – MA	3,462	8.6%	5,394	8.1%	7,461	9.1%	8,864	8.6%	1,478	5.5%
	University – PhD	185	0.5%	267	0.4%	299	0.4%	318	0.3%	57	0.2%
	University – other	1,314	3.3%	3,449	5.2%	4,311	5.3%	4,614	4.5%	971	3.6%
	Unspecified and not applicable	1	0.0%	2	0.0%	5	0.0%	6	0.0%	5	0.0%
	Total # of issued permits	40,300	100%	66,357	100.0%	81,726	100.0%	102,903	100%	26,971	100.0%
2. China	CEGEPs, colleges, and PTC/TCST/DVS/AVS	2,354	12.5%	1,500	7.5%	1,269	6.4%	1,340	7.4%	185	16.7%
	ESL/FSL college and university programs	3,511	18.7%	6,727	33.7%	6,839	34.8%	6,030	33.3%	275	24.8%
	Other studies and post-secondary > than 1 year	802	4.3%	2,071	10.4%	2,033	10.3%	1,047	5.8%	70	6.3%
	University – BA	8,160	43.4%	5,888	29.5%	5,574	28.3%	5,523	30.5%	168	15.1%
	University – MA	2,754	14.7%	2,525	12.6%	2,650	13.5%	2,871	15.9%	257	23.2%
	University – PhD	624	3.3%	750	3.8%	735	3.7%	825	4.6%	107	9.6%
	University – other	573	3.1%	522	2.6%	575	2.9%	463	2.6%	44	4.0%
	Unspecified and not applicable	8	0.0%	2	0.0%	1	0.0%	1	0.0%	3	0.3%
	Total # of issued permits	18,786	100.0%	19,985	100.0%	19,676	100.0%	18,100	100.0%	1,109	100.0%

(Continued)

Table A.4. (Continued)

Country of Citizenship	Level of Study	2016	2016%	2017	2017%	2018	2018%	2019	2019%	2020	2020%
3. France	CEGEPs, colleges, and PTC/TCST/DVS/AVS	1,485	21.0%	1,905	22.9%	2,542	25.4%	2,738	28.0%	1,060	42.0%
	ESL/FSL college and university programs	32	0.5%	84	1.0%	67	0.7%	34	0.3%	6	0.2%
	Other studies and post-secondary > than 1 year	236	3.3%	256	3.1%	257	2.6%	278	2.8%	93	3.7%
	University – BA	3,028	42.8%	3,325	40.0%	4,219	42.2%	3,939	40.2%	662	26.3%
	University – MA	1,503	21.2%	1,619	19.5%	1,947	19.5%	1,871	19.1%	414	16.4%
	University – PhD	277	3.9%	301	3.6%	332	3.3%	356	3.6%	141	5.6%
	University – other	501	7.1%	805	9.7%	622	6.2%	566	5.8%	144	5.7%
	Unspecified and not applicable	15	0.2%	12	0.1%	19	0.2%	10	0.1%	1	0.0%
	Total # of issued permits	7,077	100.0%	8,307	100.0%	10,005	100.0%	9,792	100.0%	2,521	100.0%
4. Korea	CEGEPs, colleges, and PTC/TCST/DVS/AVS	1,506	25.4%	1,831	27.5%	2,156	30.8%	2,228	33.5%	581	30.3%
	ESL/FSL college and university programs	3,634	61.3%	3,863	58.0%	3,778	54.0%	3,341	50.2%	1,116	58.1%
	Other studies and post-secondary > than 1 year	69	1.2%	99	1.5%	124	1.8%	117	1.8%	38	2.0%
	University – BA	494	8.3%	584	8.8%	647	9.2%	683	10.3%	85	4.4%
	University – MA	134	2.3%	158	2.4%	156	2.2%	158	2.4%	50	2.6%
	University – PhD	50	0.8%	53	0.8%	74	1.1%	68	1.0%	24	1.3%
	University – other	38	0.6%	74	1.1%	63	0.9%	56	0.8%	24	1.3%
	Unspecified and not applicable	3	0.1%	1	0.0%	2	0.0%	1	0.0%	2	0.1%
	Total # of issued permits	5,928	100.0%	6,663	100.0%	7,000	100.0%	6,652	100.0%	1,920	100.0%

5. Nigeria

CEGEPs, Colleges, and PTC/TCST/DVS/AVS	481	28.2%	418	27.0%	507	25.6%	630	26.5%	253	29.4%
ESL/FSL College and University programs	2	0.1%	2	0.1%	4	0.2%	1	0.0%	1	0.1%
Other Studies and Post-secondary > than 1 yr	36	2.1%	24	1.5%	26	1.3%	38	1.6%	16	1.9%
University – BA	565	33.2%	596	38.5%	729	36.8%	967	40.8%	324	37.6%
University – MA	491	28.8%	400	25.8%	567	28.6%	587	24.7%	224	26.0%
University – PhD	52	3.1%	59	3.8%	73	3.7%	70	2.9%	18	2.1%
University – other	77	4.5%	51	3.3%	75	3.8%	80	3.4%	25	2.9%
Unspecified and ot applicable	0	0.0%	0	0.0%	0	0.0%	0	0.0%	1	0.1%
Total # of issued permits	1,704	100.0%	1,550	100.0%	1,981	100.0%	2,373	100.0%	862	100.0%

6. Brazil

CEGEPs, colleges, and PTC/TCST/DVS/AVS	1,807	46.1%	2,199	50.7%	2,668	53.0%	2,720	58.1%	514	56.9%
ESL/FSL college and university programs	1,147	29.3%	1,070	24.7%	1,227	24.4%	1,039	22.2%	249	27.6%
Other studies and post-secondary > than 1 year	265	6.8%	289	6.7%	228	4.5%	84	1.8%	10	1.1%
University – BA	144	3.7%	217	5.0%	264	5.2%	227	4.9%	21	2.3%
University – MA	262	6.7%	280	6.5%	318	6.3%	267	5.7%	51	5.6%
University – PhD	118	3.0%	135	3.1%	211	4.2%	220	4.7%	34	3.8%
University – other	168	4.3%	144	3.3%	112	2.2%	106	2.3%	20	2.2%
Unspecified and Not Applicable	8	0.2%	5	0.1%	5	0.1%	15	0.3%	4	0.4%
Total # of ssued permits	3,919	100.0%	4,339	100.0%	5,033	100.0%	4,678	100.0%	903	100.0%

(Continued)

Table A.4. (Continued)

Country of Citizenship	Level of Study	2016	2016%	2017	2017%	2018	2018%	2019	2019%	2020	2020%
7. Pakistan	CEGEPs, colleges, and PTC/TCST/DVS/AVS	138	14.9%	122	16.0%	135	14.1%	157	16.0%	83	26.8%
	ESL/FSL college and university programs	3	0.3%	5	0.7%	9	0.9%	14	1.4%	2	0.6%
	Other studies and post-secondary > than 1 year	11	1.2%	15	2.0%	7	0.7%	11	1.1%	9	2.9%
	University – BA	453	48.9%	375	49.3%	468	49.0%	457	46.7%	103	33.2%
	University – MA	284	30.7%	188	24.7%	265	27.7%	279	28.5%	75	24.2%
	University – PhD	27	2.9%	44	5.8%	61	6.4%	47	4.8%	32	10.3%
	University – other	9	1.0%	12	1.6%	10	1.0%	14	1.4%	6	1.9%
	Unspecified and not applicable	1	0.1%	0	0.0%	1	0.1%	0	0.0%	0	0.0%
	Total # of issued permits	926	100.0%	761	100.0%	956	100.0%	979	100.0%	310	100.0%
8. Iran	CEGEPs, colleges, and PTC/TCST/DVS/AVS	95	7.7%	310	13.6%	537	15.2%	889	17.4%	211	14.2%
	ESL/FSL college and university programs	51	4.1%	112	4.9%	423	12.0%	581	11.4%	109	7.4%
	Other studies and post-secondary > than 1 year	15	1.2%	28	1.2%	41	1.2%	35	0.7%	6	0.4%
	University – BA	99	8.0%	235	10.3%	351	9.9%	390	7.6%	79	5.3%
	University – MA	514	41.7%	859	37.7%	1,289	36.5%	2,102	41.1%	704	47.5%
	University – PhD	424	34.4%	660	28.9%	768	21.8%	1,002	19.6%	338	22.8%
	University – other	35	2.8%	73	3.2%	119	3.4%	112	-2.2%	34	2.3%
	Unspecified and not applicable	1	0.1%	4	0.2%	1	0.0%	1	0.0%	0	0.0%
	Total # of issued permits	1,234	100.0%	2,281	100.0%	3,529	100.0%	5,112	100.0%	1,481	100.0%

9. United States	CEGEPs, colleges, and PTC/TCST/DVS/AVS	695	16.3%	801	17.1%	758	16.7%	809	16.9%	370	22.7%
	ESL/FSL college and university programs	13	0.3%	10	0.2%	12	0.3%	11	0.2%	1	0.1%
	Other studies and post-secondary > than 1 year	157	3.7%	93	2.0%	80	1.8%	102	2.1%	45	2.8%
	University – BA	2,211	51.9%	2,377	50.8%	2,371	52.1%	2,402	50.1%	764	46.8%
	University – MA	734	17.2%	867	18.5%	829	18.2%	913	19.1%	246	15.1%
	University – PhD	337	7.9%	432	9.2%	406	8.9%	451	9.4%	168	10.3%
	University – other	107	2.5%	92	2.0%	89	2.0%	95	2.0%	35	2.1%
	Unspecified and not applicable	7	0.2%	6	0.1%	4	0.1%	7	0.1%	2	0.1%
	Total # of issued permits	4,261	100.0%	4,678	100.0%	4,549	100.0%	4,790	100.0%	1,631	100%
10. Vietnam	CEGEPs, colleges, and PTC/TCST/DVS/AVS	693	29.7%	1,763	32.9%	1,637	29.6%	1,131	39.6%	180	31.0%
	ESL/FSL college and university programs	1,094	46.9%	2,553	47.7%	2,789	50.4%	772	27.0%	232	39.9%
	Other Studies and Post-secondary > than 1 yr	76	3.3%	261	4.9%	311	5.6%	121	4.2%	32	5.5%
	University – BA	275	11.8%	433	8.1%	542	9.8%	567	19.9%	64	11.0%
	University – MA	114	4.9%	182	3.4%	152	2.7%	184	6.4%	50	8.6%
	University – PhD	34	1.5%	58	1.1%	38	0.7%	23	0.8%	11	1.9%
	University – other	48	2.1%	105	2.0%	65	1.2%	56	2.0%	12	2.1%
	Unspecified and not applicable	0	0.0%	0	0.0%	2	0.0%	0	0.0%	0	0.0%
	Total # of issued permits	2,334	100.0%	5,355	100.0%	5,536	100.0%	2,854	100.0%	581	100%

Source: GCMS & COGNOS (MBR) extracted as of 6 May 2021 (data compiled by OPP-DART-2021-12416).
Notes: The category CEGEP includes both pre-university and technical CEGEP. The college category encompasses technical and applied degrees, certificates, and diplomas.

Notes

1. Introduction

1 In announcing a major overhaul in 2014, the federal government (ESDC 2014, 10–11) noted that "the TFWP is no longer being used as it was intended to be used – as a last and limited resort to allow employers to bring foreign workers to Canada on a temporary basis to fill jobs for which qualified Canadians are not available. Reforms are needed to end the growing practice of employers building their business model on access to the TFWP." It justified these reforms as a means of "driv[ing] down the overall number of low-wage temporary foreign workers in Canada and end[ing] the distortion in the labour market caused by their prevalence in some sectors and regions". In the process, policymakers emphasized how such distortion was creating problems for young people: "for many youth, these jobs are their first opportunity to participate in the labour market and each time an employer hires a temporary foreign worker in one of these jobs it potentially deprives a Canadian from that all-important first job."

2 This "new International Mobility Program (IMP)," it asserted "will include those [TFWP and other] streams in which foreign nationals are not subject to an LMIA [i.e., a labour market test] whose primary objective is to advance Canada's broad economic and cultural national interest, rather than filling particular jobs" (ESDC 2014, 1).

3 Although Canadian government policy uses the term "temporary foreign workers" (or TFWs) to describe this group, I reject this term as it denies workers' agency and reproduces a problematic distinction between "foreigners" and "nationals," and because TFWP participants fall along a complex permanent/temporary divide. I thereby characterize this group as "migrant workers" or "TFWP participants."

4 The three largest freestanding IMP subprograms collectively represented fully 62 per cent of permitholders in 2023. I use the term "freestanding" here to contrast these programs to time-limited programs, such as those devoted to Ukrainians, many of whom migrated for employment under the auspices of the IMP in the early 2020s due to war.

The in-depth analysis relying on administrative data (i.e., linked databases) pursued in this book take 2018 or 2019 as reference year for working holiday work permitholders because border closures led their numbers to ebb considerably during the COVID-19 pandemic. As such, these years represent the closest proxy for permitholders present-day situation and the most recent years available prior to the pandemic for which extensive data are available. In the cases of Post-graduation and Spousal permitholders, it uses 2021 as a reference year as this was the most recent and reliable year available in this database at time of publication.

5 In this book, I use the term "transnational workers" to refer to all workers migrating to Canada for employment on a temporary basis (i.e., regardless of the umbrella program in which they are enrolled). I adopt this terminology to encompass work permitholders on both sides of the "mobility/migration" policy construct to avoid reifying particular categories and understandings.

6 As economic imperatives came to hold sway, as Abu-Laban, Tungohan and Gabriel (2022, 105) illustrate, "Canada's family reunification imperatives and its humanitarian obligations [became] secondary and tertiary considerations."

7 Under these programs, eligible workers enter Canada with sectoral permits that permit them to leave abusive situations, have family members accompany them and obtain open work and study permits, and be provided with a direct route to permanent residency once they obtain 24 months of qualifying employment in Canada (IRCC 2019b).

8 Drawing on records from the House of Commons Human Resources Committee, Dobrowolsky (2017, 207) aptly characterizes overall growth in the IMP as emanating from the then Liberal government's efforts to "speed up the processing of work permits" for "high-skilled" labour alongside initiating improvements in protection for "lower-skilled, lower-waged workers."

9 For example, as studies of the Canadian case show, workers, many of whom migrated under the TFWP until the late 2010s, holding varied residency statuses involving gradations of temporariness, often occupy the spatial domain of the receiving state (Hennebry 2012; Rajkumar et al. 2012; Goldring & Landolt 2013).

10 Building on my previous research critiquing the notion (Vosko 2010a, 2012), informed by the work of Wimmer & Schiller (2002, 301), I view

"methodological nationalism" as the tendency to take "the nation/state/ society [a]s the natural social political form of the modern world" or to equate society and the nation-state. Scholars analysing its prevalence in academic inquiry point to two intersecting modes of methodological nationalism in particular: first, naturalization, that is, taking national discourses, agendas, and logics for granted, contributing to a "container model of society that encompasses a culture, a polity, an economy, and a bounded social group" (Wimmer & Schiller 2003, 579), and, second, territorial limitation (or what some label the territorialization of the imaginary) (Wimmer & Schiller 2003, 581; see also Wimmer & Schiller 2002), that is, the reduction of analytic focus to boundaries of nation-states, with the effect of making a category of practice (the nation-state) the category of analysis, leading to the treatment of nation-states as domains of identity in which "the people" share common origins and of states as sovereign systems of government identified with particular territories (Beck & Sznaider 2006, 3–4).

11 In this book, I use "social reproduction" to refer, broadly, to processes, and the institutions through which they take shape, devoted to nurturing and sustaining people, communities, and societies that are vital to making and maintaining working populations. However, in the tradition of feminist political economy, I view production (for the market) and social reproduction (i.e., the production of people) as intimately intertwined (Picchio 1992) as well as connected to relations of distribution (Acker 1988).

12 For example, as Chartrand and I (Chartrand & Vosko 2021) demonstrate, drawing on the work of André (1990), who shows how the Caribbean Seasonal Agricultural Worker Program originated partly from the considerable Canadian ownership of resources in the region, Calliste (1991, 144), who links Caribbean domestic worker programs with the "near monopoly" that Canadian banks held over Caribbean banking and debt, and Smith (2015), who likewise characterizes Canada as an imperialist state in its relationship to the Caribbean, broad expropriative processes that remove resources from Latin America and the Caribbean and reallocate them to Canada play a role in shaping the actions of transnational workers following the same trajectory.

13 As Ray, Herd, & Moynihan (2023, 140) note, "white-dominated [institutions, such as (im)migration policy, and] organizations are also racialized."

14 While Canada is often cited as officially ending explicit racial discrimination in the admission of immigrants by way of regulation in 1962, via an analysis of various decisions, evaluations, and experiences characterizing selection and employment of migrant workers of Caribbean

origin, Satzewich (1989) establishes that immigration policy remained steeped in racializing discourses and practices thereafter.

15 As illustrated by Abu-Laban (2024, 1807–8), even as the point system ostensibly represented a universal, and thus neutral and objective, method of evaluating newcomers, on the basis of socially constructed notion of what constitutes "skills," this system and skills discourse worked to effectively limit immigration from countries in the global south. On the gendered character of the social construction of skill informing the formal recognition of prior education and learning within the points system, see also Abu-Laban & Gabriel (2002, 49–50).

16 In elevating country of citizenship, I do not aim to falsely separate nationality from other axes of social difference, or to subordinate one axis to another. Rather, I seek to further analyses of country of origin towards deeper investigation of the intersecting axes of differentiation shaping processes of migrantization.

17 Several studies focusing on Australia, for example, illustrate working holidaymakers' precariousness in employment and link it to their ambiguous status as both overseas travellers seeking extended cultural experiences and workers engaged in industries identified with high levels of precariousness, such as agriculture and food and accommodation services (Reilly 2015; Robertson 2014; Tham & Fudge 2019). Studies on Canada taking this focus are few, although emerging examinations of the experiences of youth engaged in cultural exchange programs point to the precariousness of their jobs (on youth mobility programs under International Experience Canada, see Coderre & Nakache 2021).

18 In 2023, there were 764,770 permitholders under the IMP as a whole, 241,815 of whom were enrolled in the Post-graduation Work Permit program (IRCC 2024a).

19 From 2015 to 2023, there was a threefold increase in annual permits issued to international students (reaching 683,235 in 2023) (IRCC 2024c).

20 The latter category also includes spouses of Bridging Open Work permitholders (workers granted an open work permit while they await approval of their permanent residency applications). Effectively this category allows the spouses of principal applicants to access open work permits while the principal applicant is in a permanent residency pipeline but has yet to be granted this status.

21 ATIPs under the *Access to Information Act* (1985) aim "to enhance the accountability and transparency of federal institutions in order to promote an open and democratic society and to enable public debate on the conduct of those institutions" (s. 2(1)). They are a neglected means of data collection and analysis in the social sciences (Walby & Larsen 2011), but nonetheless instructive in accessing two key sources of records

produced by policy actors: namely, data produced for use internally otherwise outside of public view and data produced for official purposes/records. As Moffette (2021, 277, citing Marx 1984) helpfully notes, while the former might be characterized as "dirty" data and the latter is, in contrast "polished," ATIPs can in no way replace detailed empirical research; however, they can assist researchers in filling in or bridging gaps in knowledge about the rationale behind particular policies and processes (e.g., policy administration/implementation and enforcement) that analysis of qualitative and administrative data is ill-equipped to uncover.

22 That is, as the CEEDD database is a set of linkable files organized by Statistics Canada as "vintages" updated every three years for customized releases, the analysis undertaken utilizing this source takes 2018 and 2019 as its final years for working holiday work permitholders due to data availability and the duration of the global COVID-19 pandemic, whose effects on migration policy were most pronounced on this group between early 2020 and early 2022, during which time Canada largely put a pause on the admission of new permitholders (i.e., entrants). However, it uses 2021 as its final year for Post-graduation and Spousal permitholders as their numbers had rebounded by that year and as many such permitholders who entered Canada before 2020 still held valid permits during the pandemic.

23 In contrast to other databases, like Statistics Canada's Longitudinal Immigration Database (which does not capture temporary residents that do not become permanent residents), CEEDD provides information on temporary migrant workers who do not necessarily transition to permanency and allows for analysis of their employment experiences. Given that a Labour Market Impact Assessment (LMIA) (Canada's variant of a labour market test), otherwise providing vital information on conditions of work and employment among workers migrating internationally for employment on a temporary basis, is not required for participation in IMP subprograms, administrative data collected via the CEEDD also help compensate for the dearth of data on work permitholders under its auspices, especially open work permitholders.

24 Due to the ongoing and uncertain nature of the COVID-19 pandemic, most interviews were conducted via Zoom, utilizing audio-only recordings for transcription.

25 The coding of interviews utilized Taguette, an open-source qualitative research tool.

26 In conformance with the Canadian Tri-Council Research Ethics guidelines, this research received ethics approval by the Human Participants Review Sub-Committee of York University's Ethics Review Board (certificate number 2021-231).

27 Using pseudonyms for research participants is a conventional and widely accepted means of achieving this balance in social science research. Despite the ubiquity of this practice, there is a dearth of scholarly discussion of why, when, and especially how best to confer anonymity in this manner (van den Hoonaard 2003; Guenther 2009, 412; Lahman et al. 2015, 445; Allen & Wiles 2016, 150). This lacuna reflects, in part, the assumption that assigning pseudonyms is largely a technical exercise. As scholars of the *social*, it is, however, important that social scientists lend greater attention to conventional naming practices and their identity-shaping and positioning effects (Heaton 2022, 130).

A small but growing body of literature addressing approaches to anonymity yields a series of pros and cons for attaching names to interview participants. On the plus side, some scholars argue that assigning pseudonyms is a "tenet of good research practice" as it holds "researchers ... accountable for maintaining anonymity and confidentiality" (Allen & Wiles, 2016, 151). As Lahman et al. (2023, 679) suggest, using pseudonyms can be vital to protecting participants social-emotional health, safety (e.g., security of presence), and/or job security while giving voice to their experiences. At the same time, some research on the impact of seeing one's words in publications reveals certain participants' dislike of the use of pseudonyms because "using made-up names ... [is] simply false" or potentially misleading since "whatever pretend names [a]re chosen [a]re likely to be real names of other people ... [which] could lead to wrong identifications or assumptions among readers" (Corden & Sainsbury 2006, 105). Unless it is undertaken with care, that is, with the aim of capturing "the richness of, and thickly describ[ing], participants' lived experiences and social worlds" (Heaton 2022, 127), selecting pseudonyms may also run the risk of contributing to harmful forms of racialized labelling. For example, as Brear (2018, 724, citing Foster 2006) argues, in contexts subject to historical and ongoing legacies of colonialism, people have often been compelled to adopt colonial-language names; in such cases, "not using Indigenous-language names [in research publications] might represent, or be interpreted as, a subtle form of racism or white supremacy."

In light of these dilemmas, I pursue a middle ground. On the one hand, I seek to recognize that "oronyms have personal, social, and symbolic meanings: they are markers of, and convey ideas about, ethnicity, age, gender, religion, and other identity characteristics" – social markers with which I grapple, and aim to centre, by invoking the voices of research participants in context sensitive ways (Heaton 2022, 127–8; see also Seidman 2019, 131). On the other hand, I am mindful that, albeit necessary in research involving people with precarious residency status, exchanging the real names of people with pseudonyms can contribute to removing participant identities. Attending to these tensions, I adopt pseudonyms drawing on common names in countries of origin that use participants' first initials to give voice to their distinct identities while preserving anonymity. I also introduce each research participant, by way of their pseudonym, at first reference, in a manner illustrative of their social location (e.g., age, self-identified gender, country of origin, family status) and context (e.g., industry and geography).

28 Before 1951, official immigration policy barred non-immigrant (i.e., temporary) visitors from working while in Canada (unless they were in-demand workers approved by the National Employment Service) (IRCC 2019b, 10).

29 I first developed and advanced the notion of "probationary precarity" in an article devoted principally to policy analysis utilizing descriptive data outside the CEEDD and a small number of in-depth interviews (Vosko 2023). This chapter refines and extends this concept, drawing on this novel administrative data and both a greater number of open-ended interviews and utilizing a more expansive interview schedule.

2. Querying the Migration/Mobility Program Policy Construct

1 For example, in the agreements with Costa Rica in 2002, the European Free Trade Agreement region in 2009, Colombia and Peru in 2008, Panama in 2013, Honduras in 2014, and South Korea in 2015, the Government of Canada used positive lists of professions, cast by Pellerin (2017, 359) as lists that authorize mobility solely for professional categories cited explicitly, indicating its capacity to negotiate the mobility of persons as a recruitment tool for specific professions. This gesture, which may, on the surface, indicate closure on the part of Canada to nationals from signatory countries, is more accurately interpreted as willingness to establish specific conditions for the mobility of professionals, beyond the simple reciprocity requirements that apply to trade agreements (Pellerin 2017, 359).

2 In Canada, the United States, Australia, and Aotearoa New Zealand, the circulation of policy categories and ideas, integral to international migration for employment on a temporary basis and to (re)producing the migration/mobility policy construct itself, by a wide range of governmental and non-governmental actors has long been fundamental to the establishment of both seasonal and human capital migration regimes, with policy innovation often followed by circulation and adaptation in other contexts (Bedford & Spoonley 2014; Bedford et al. 2017). For example, as recently as 2021/2, the US-based Migration Policy Institute called for the simultaneous expansion of the US H-2A temporary work

visa to migrants from El Salvador, Guatemala, and Honduras alongside the expansion of neighbouring countries' model managed migration programs, including Canada's Seasonal Agricultural Worker Program, designed to facilitate access to often low-waged deportable labour (Vosko 2019), to these same regions (Ramón 2021, 2022). This contemporaneous push to expand regularized migration programs to specific Central American countries – namely, the predominant countries of origin of undocumented migrants, often linked by imperial/neo-colonial relations with the United States and Canada – is often cast as a collaborative solution to chronic labour shortages in essential industries in higher-income countries in the Americas, while also curbing high levels of irregular migration at the US-Mexico border.

3 In moving towards this overhaul of the TFWP, in 2013 the federal government introduced reforms, including an immediate suspension of the program that permitted employers to pay foreign workers up to 15 per cent less, and halted the provision of accelerated Labour Market Opinions, the precursor to the contemporary LMIAs. Later that year, as Marsden, Tucker, & Vosko (2021b) document in chronicling events spurring action at the federal level, it promulgated a regulation (*RAIRP Regulations* 2013) implementing other policy changes aimed to protect the integrity of the Canadian labour market by providing enhanced authority to verify employer compliance with TFWP requirements (such as efforts to hire Canadians) and to apply penalties for non-compliance as well as to protect so-named TFWP participants from abuse. Other changes introduced during this period directed specifically to the TFWP included a switch from high/low skill levels to high/low wage levels to classify job categories, a 10 per cent cap on the percentage of low-wage TFWP participants an employer could hire, limiting access to low-wage TFWP participants to areas of high unemployment, and limiting the duration of stays. Also at this time, the federal government announced reforms to the caregiver program under the TFWP. Framing these October 2014 changes as addressing concerns about mistreatment, they included ending the live-in requirement, clearing the backlog of applications for permanent residency made by caregivers who had satisfied the work requirement, and new criteria for the permanent residency pathway itself (Government of Canada 2014).

Pertinent to the exclusion of open work permits from increased protection, subsequently the federal government stepped up enforcement efforts by increasing the number and scope of inspections so that one in four businesses employing TFWP participants were inspected annually; increasing the number of program requirements that inspectors could review from three to twenty-one; expanding the TFWP Tip Line and creating a new "Complaints" website; augmenting publicity of employers suspended and/or under investigation under the TFWP, and those who have had an LMIA revoked and are banned from participation; providing greater funding for the Canadian Border Services Agency to increase the number of criminal investigations of employers/recruiters; improving information-sharing among departments and agencies involved in overseeing the TFWP, including provincial and territorial governments; and introducing significant monetary fines, of up to $100,000 (Marsden, Tucker, Vosko 2021a, 2021b).

4 Simultaneously, utilizing previous administrative data on "temporary foreign workers," government officials also retroactively split program/entry categories into either the new TFWPs or IMPs (Chartrand & Vosko 2021).

5 The remaining five categories likewise emanating from LMIA exemption codes include "public policies," a narrow grouping encompassing generally temporary policy measures to facilitate entry for particular groups – i.e., temporary and permanent residence measures for Hong Kong youth, family reunification for residents of Hong Kong with relatives in Canada (the Temporary Resident to Permanent Resident (TRPR) pathway was also processed under this category); "no other means of support" (R206), a small grouping comprised of refugee claimants awaiting determination on their status and persons that are under an unenforceable removal order; "PR applicants to Canada" (R207), determined eligible as members of certain in-Canada permanent residence classes, including protected persons, whether or not they have applied for permanent resident status, and the live-in caregiver class; "vulnerable workers" (R207.1), a category for TFWP participants in Canada on valid employer-specific work permits deemed to be experiencing abuse, or are at risk of abuse, in the context of their employment; and "humanitarian reasons," a small subcategory with two substreams which allow for the issuance of work permits to foreign nationals who cannot support themselves without working, and who are study permitholders that have become temporarily destitute through circumstances beyond their control, or temporary resident permitholders who have a permit of at least six months (IRCC 2024e).

Among these categories, "vulnerable workers" accounted for just under 0.3 per cent of total IMP permitholders in 2023 and "other IMP participants" comprised 30 per cent of permitholders in 2023, a percentage which includes, for instance, temporary programs such as those for Ukrainians fleeing conflict. As these categories emanate from exemptions rationalized on bases distinct from the twin notions of "reciprocity" and "competitiveness" (e.g., humanitarianism) forming the policy rationale for IMP, they are not a focus in the analysis to follow.

6 Except for those deemed ineligible for failing to comply with conditions or involved in procuring certain services, open work permitholders are allowed to work for virtually any employer in the country (IRCC 2023c). They are not required to have job offers from prospective employers in order to come to Canada to work on a temporary basis. Nor are they mandated to work in specified occupations, industries, or regions upon arrival.

In contrast, closed work permitholders normally require such job offers (unless they receive a sectoral permit), which typically tie them to a particular occupation, industry, and/or region upon arrival.

7 In 2023, IRCC created a pilot program to extend the possibility of holding open work permits to spouses of other permitholders proceeding in three phases, documented in Chapter 5.

8 Although during the research undertaken for Chapter 5, spouses of full-time students was an expansive category, as I completed this book, the Government of Canada took a decision to limit spousal accompaniment to students enrolled in graduate programs exclusively.

9 During the COVID-19 pandemic, each of the foregoing routes of entry were modified temporarily as Canada introduced travel restrictions, effectively closing the border to overseas permanent residency applicants. To meet immigration targets, IRCC boosted Canadian Experience Class invitations for eligible candidates already resident in the country and introduced the Temporary Resident to Permanent Resident Pathway for "essential workers and international graduates" already in the country on temporary work permits (IRCC 2021b, 2021c). The Temporary Resident to Permanent Resident Pathway encompassed six streams, three for English and French speakers, with caps, and three for French speakers, without caps. The stream devoted to recruiting international graduates of Canadian institutions was the largest among TRPR streams (i.e., it was created to offer as many as 40,000 spaces between 6 May and 5 November 2021 (IRCC 2021c). In 2021, 2,125 former spouses of students or spouses of skilled worker permitholders attained permanent residency through this stream.

10 Before they can apply for permanent residency under the Federal Skilled Worker Program, applicants must demonstrate language proficiency (i.e., they must meet a minimum score of 7 in all four categories of the English Canadian Language Benchmark or the French Niveau de compétence linguistique Canadian (IRCC 2024f)), meet stringent occupational requirements (i.e., they must demonstrate that they have worked in a TEER 0, 1, 2, or 3 category, and performed the duties set out in the lead statement regarding the occupation, including all essential duties and most main duties listed, in the last ten years, and offer proof of experience in the same type

of job they are using for immigration purposes (IRCC 2024g)), demonstrate employment experience (i.e., they must show that they have worked for pay and have had at least one year of continuous full-time employment (i.e., full-time at 30 hours/week for 12 months (1,560)) or an equal amount of part-time employment (e.g., 15 hours/week for 24 months), provide proof of funds, be admissible to Canada, and plan to live outside Quebec.

11 As of November 2022, Canada shifted from the 2016 to the 2021 version of the NOC. Whereas the 2016 version defined skilled employment for immigration purposes as those falling under codes A (professional), B (technical/skilled trade), and 0 (managerial), the 2021 version establishes TEERs 0 through 3 as the equivalent codes.

12 Both the Federal Skilled Worker and the Federal Skilled Trades Programs require proof of sufficient funds to support applicants and their families (if applicable). The amount required is determined based on family size, including the applicant themselves, their spouse or common-law partner, their dependent children, and their spouse or common-law partner's children. As of 2024, the funds required range from $13,757 for a single applicant, to $36,407 for a family of seven. Applicants in either stream do not need to demonstrate sufficient funds if they are able to legally work in Canada at the time they apply for PR and have a valid job offer from a Canadian employer (IRCC 2024h).

13 In the CEEDD, the indicator for unionization (i.e., the variable labelled "union dues") is defined broadly to encompass those that paid annual dues for membership in a trade union or an association of public servants, and/or professional board dues required under provincial or territorial law and/or professional or malpractice liability insurance premiums or professional membership dues required to keep a professional status recognized by law and/or parity or advisory committee (or similar body) dues required under provincial or territorial law (Statistics Canada 2018). I thereby label this indicator "unionization/professionalization." While recognizing that "unionization," narrowly defined, is a more precise indicator of control in the form of worker power, mediated typically by the presence of a collective agreement, professional associations tend to promote adherence to guidelines/regulations regarding professional conduct and provide supports to their members to enable them to exercise their professional judgment etc.; they thus give their members greater control over the labour process than those professionals devoid of such representation.

14 Annual employment income is the measure used in this analysis as income; it is only reported on this basis in the CEEDD and the number of hours work is not included in the dataset, making it impossible to measure

hourly wages. This indicator nevertheless helps reveal transnational workers' level of dependency on paid employment.

15 In utilizing this index, I recognize the limitations of the professionalization/unionization variable, as indicated in note 13. Specifically, these shortcomings may result in an underestimation of precariousness among permitholders in the Reciprocal Employment stream of the Canadian Interests category in which Working Holiday permitholders are located (For further discussion, see also Chapter 3). But, while in-depth exploration of the case studies of working holiday, Post-graduation, and Spousal permitholders' employment experiences, pursued through multiple methods in Chapters 3 to 5, offer more nuanced insights into precariousness among specific IMP permit holders, arguably this measure is sufficiently supple to utilize in the analysis of the large umbrella categories of focus in the present chapter.

16 In 2018, intra-company transferees accounted for a considerable proportion of permitholders under the Significant Benefit stream (14,555 out of 26,265 (55 per cent); notably, their numbers in, and percentage share of, this stream grew substantially between 2018 and 2023 such that 18,335 out of 43,165 (42 per cent) of Significant Benefit permitholders were intra-company transferees in 2023). As Tucker (2020) shows, fissuring can profoundly affect this group, including in firms employing large numbers of people holding different citizenship and employment statuses. Indeed, in Tucker's assessment, based on a novel case study, intra-company transferees can face fissuring along two dimensions: first, the "fissuring of employer responsibility because of a blurring of the lines of legal responsibility between the parent firm and the sending and receiving subsidiaries" (Tucker 2020, 373), and, second, at the level of the workforce in a given firm, whereby workers with several different immigration statuses and types of employment contracts are part of the same workforce producing "organized disorganization" (Tucker 2020, 373; see also Costello & Freedland, 2016). As such, even though intra-company transferees are often destined for relatively more secure industries and occupations than other groups falling within this substream, access to collective representation (i.e., unionization) can be challenging.

17 This lower rate of non-unionization/professionalization among Reciprocal Employment permitholders must be read with caution; as explained above, a higher level of unionization among this group does not indicate a true sense of control over the labour process associated with unionization/professionalization, insofar as a collective agreement may be absent among professionals. Moreover, this employer-reported measure may be unreliable

for the case of Reciprocal Employment, given that Working Holiday permitholders, a significant proportion of whom make up this stream, appear to be overrepresented in unionized/professionalized jobs. See Chapter 3 for a more in-depth analysis of this apparent overrepresentation of Working Holiday permitholders in unionized/professionalized jobs.

3. Cultural Exchange Precarity

1 This growth was continuous until program numbers dipped significantly during the COVID-19 pandemic, rebounding in 2022.
2 While dominant language appears to be a key characteristic segmenting Working Holiday permitholders, it is difficult to separate this variable from the ways in which countries of origin are racialized. Specifically, the prevalence of one of Canada's official languages seems to have a strong association with the countries of origin of permitholders closely approximating "cultural sojourners" with greatest access to permanent residency. Yet this axis of differentiation is integral to the ways in which these largely affluent countries of origin, whose Working Holiday quotas, permit length, etc. tend to be relatively more generous than those accorded to less affluent countries, are racialized as white.
3 See Oommen (2021) for a complementary example of a study of polarization among Working Holiday permitholders on the basis of race in the context of the UK labour market with attention to colonial relations.
4 Illustrating how some permitholders engage in multiple jobs, during this time, So-hyun also worked for cash as a babysitter and a photographer.
5 National Archive of Canada Photos 7527, 7530, 7531–4, 7535–6, 7537–40, 7541, 7572–3, 5459–62, on file with the author.
6 Citing the restrictions placed on Brazilians from applying for a Canadian working holiday visa, Davi, who holds a doctorate, initially came to Canada from Brazil through the young professionals stream of International Experience Canada rather than through the working holiday program, and subsequently shifted to the latter.
7 Portugal also signed a Youth Mobility Agreement with Canada providing for 24-month terms starting in 2019.
8 As yet, no administative data sources allow researchers to discern the precise proportion of Working Holiday permitholders that *desire* permanent residency. One small-sample qualitative study found that a majority of permitholders enrolled in programs under the International Experience Canada umbrella sought permanent residency. This study also revealed that, among those surveyed, permitholders from countries of origin with shorter work permit lengths employ a range of strategies

to extend their stay, including prevailing upon their employers to hire them under another program or to sponsor them independently, often risky ventures, which can lead to participants' extreme dependence on employers solely because access to permanent residency is conditioned by the length of stay (Coderre & Nakache 2021, 12–13).

9 However, certain recognized organizations may be geared to assisting Working Holiday permitholders find work in sectors where they have expertise (e.g., International Rural Exchange) or may offer placement services at an additional cost in industries such as hospitality (e.g., GO International).

10 In the absence of direct pathways to permanent residency via any subprogram, 39,085 former International Experience Canada permitholders transitioned to permanent residency between 2002 and 2023 (IRCC 2023u; IRCC 2024z).

11 In contrast, co-op participants are excluded from applying under Canadian Experience Class as the work experience they gain while students does not count towards permanent residency requirements, even if they are on a co-op work term, because work experience can only be attained by working in Canada under temporary resident status with authorization to work for pay.

12 Illustrating how this permitholder was able to navigate Canada's doors of entry, upon the expiration of her working holiday visa, Mila applied and received a nine-month young professionals work permit so she could stay in Canada and continue her full-time work as a supervisor in hospitality services.

13 At the time of her interview, Sophia was working as a manager for a recognized organization.

14 Another Working Holiday permitholder, Lilly, explained her strategy to navigate International Experience Canada in order to secure permanent residency: "My idea was to use the young professional first and then if that didn't get me PR, then I could still apply for the Working Holiday open work permit, allowing me to look for work more broadly." Lilly first came to Canada from Germany on a university cultural exchange/co-op program, and then returned to Canada through the young professionals subset of International Experience Canada. During this time, she worked full-time in manufacturing as a project coordinator.

15 In calling on Canada to enter into more reciprocal agreements with countries in the Global South, Fabrício, introduced below, offered the following justification: "I think that they should open [agreements] up to other countries, like Brazil. We have ... a lot of people who are eligible, who have the knowledge needed to work here. And Canada needs people ... I don't know why it restricts ... some countries, like Brazil maybe, are too

risky, but at the same time we have like people like me ... that can work and can contribute to Canada's workforce."

16 CEEDD data for 2018, based on data drawn from tax files (T1s and T4s) show a lower (76 per cent) employment rate among Working Holiday permitholders. However, the percentage of those that are employed is likely higher for at least three reasons: first, not all Working Holiday permitholders submit T1s due to the short duration of their work permits (i.e., 12 months); second, employer's issuance of T4s is subject to an earnings threshold of $500 (Government of Canada 2023), which Working Holiday permitholding employees working in short-term jobs may not meet; and, third, there can be a time delay for employers to issue T4s (IRCC 2019b).

17 Of those reporting employment, most permitholders surveyed for this evaluation (82 per cent) report receiving financial compensation, although a larger percentage of respondents employed as young professional permitholders (90 per cent) than Working Holiday permitholders (84 per cent) received financial compensation for their work (IRCC 2019b, 24).

18 A caveat must be offered here: earnings data are only available for 62 per cent of the more than 85,000 Working Holiday permitholders who were employed in 2018 – that is, data associated with T1s submitted by employees.

19 Contrary to the experiences of the permitholders interviewed, and the scholarly literature illustrating their precariousness overall, analysis of the CEEDD indicates that Working Holiday permitholders are overrepresented in unionized/professionalized jobs. As discussed in Chapter 2, part of the explanation for this finding is the way in which the indicator for "unionization" is operationalized in this administrative dataset; that is, it covers unionized and professionalized workers. However, in the case of Working Holiday permitholders, another explanation is seemingly at play: compared to Post-Graduation and Spousal permitholders, a relatively low proportion of Working Holiday permitholders file taxes, presumably due to the short-term nature of the jobs they hold given their short work permits, jobs which neither trigger employers to issue T4s nor compel permitholders to file T1s because they yield low levels of income from employment, making it appear that a greater proportion hold unionized/ professionalized positions. Moreover, because CEEDD's harmonized sex variable is based on data from the T1 Public Master File, gender and its relationship to employer provided indicators of precariousness, such as non-unionization/non-professionalization, is less reliable for this group. (Note: the relationship between country of origin and indicators of precariousness is, in contrast, reliable insofar as country of origin variables are derived from the Longitudinal Immigration Database (IMDB)). For

these reasons, this chapter neither utilizes an index of precariousness nor examines gender in relation to indicators of precariousness.

20 On her two-year Working Holiday permit, Maya worked multiple jobs to make ends meet: for cash as an underground club bouncer, part-time in the food services sector as a cashier, part-time as a basketball coach, full-time as an administrator in the legal sector, and part-time as a consultant in beauty products in the retail sector.

4. Probationary Precarity

1 From 2015 to 2023, there was a threefold increase in annual permits issued to international students (reaching 683,235 in 2023) (IRCC 2024c).

2 Excluding those funded though Canadian Commonwealth Scholarship Programs or Government of Canada awards programs funded by Foreign Affairs Canada or the Canadian International Development Agency.

3 Eligible learning institutions include public post-secondary institutions, such as colleges, trade/technical schools, universities or CEGEP, private post-secondary schools (in Quebec) that operate under the same rules as public schools in that province; private secondary or post-secondary schools (in Quebec) that offer qualifying programs of 900 hours or longer that leads to a diplôme d'études professionnelles (DEP) or an attestation de spécialisation professionnelle (ASP); or Canadian private schools that can award degrees under provincial law, if international students are enrolled in a study program that leads to a degree as authorized by the province (IRCC 2024p).

4 This requirement does not apply to the final semester of the program, which can be part-time, or if the applicant took an approved leave from their studies for the following reasons: their school has authorized a leave from their program of study for medical reasons or pregnancy, family emergency, death or serious illness of a family member, any other type of leave that the school in question authorizes; their school has closed permanently or temporarily because of a strike; the student changed schools; the student (or their school) deferred their program start date (IRCC 2024q).

5 These include the Government of Canada Awards Program funded by Global Affairs Canada (GAC), other GAC-funded scholarship programs, the Canada-Chile Equal Opportunity Scholarship, the Canada-China Scholars' Exchange Program, and the Organization of American States Fellowships Program (IRCC 2024q).

6 In 2016, the last year for which IRCC data on level of study completed in Canada are publicly available, of the 53,848 Post-graduation permitholders admitted, 18,673 were college-educated, followed by 13,195 with BA, 10,565 with MA, and 8,568 with CEGEP degrees; the remainder held PhDs (1,636) or other university degrees (1,211) (IRCC 2018).

Among incoming international students (i.e., as an entry category), level of study varies notably by country of origin: for example in 2019, nearly 68.8 per cent of incoming international students from India were bound for college or CEGEP-level study, a much higher proportion compared to other leading source countries including the US (16.9 per cent) and France (28 per cent) (See Appendix Table A.4; ATIP 2A-2021-44358 on file with author).

7 At that time, Post-graduation permitholders whose work permits had already expired in 2023 and those who were eligible for the foregoing facilitative measure had the opportunity to apply for an additional 18-month work permit. And those with expired work permits were able to restore their status, even if they were beyond the 90-day restoration period, and received an interim work authorization while awaiting processing of their new work permit application.

8 This requirement amounts to full-time work of 30 hours/week for 12 months or an equal amount of part-time work over 24 months maximum. Weekly hours exceeding 30 are not counted such that applicants cannot qualify without performing eligible work for at least a year.

9 Despite only being open for part of 2021, on account of its accessibility, the Temporary Resident to Permanent Resident Pathway became one of the top five admission categories for former Post-graduation permitholders over the 2010–23 period (Table 4.1).

10 The relatively low rate of reporting taxable earnings among Post-graduation permitholders from China is notable insofar as China was the second-largest country of origin for the Post-graduation Work Permit program that year. Yet it may also signal that large numbers of educational migrants from China are struggling to find employment required to qualify for permanent residency, pursuing permanent residency through another pathway, or planning not to remain in Canada (Crossman, Lu, & Hou 2022). Moreover, this finding suggests that not controlling for country of origin could skew analyses of earnings from employment.

11 This high proportion of Post-graduation permitholders working in small firms is consistent with Yoon's (2014, 587) qualitative study of Korean Working Holiday permitholders in Canada, finding that those located in Kelowna, a small city in British Columbia with a "dominantly white population," versus Toronto, Canada's "largest multi-ethnic city," often resorted to working in Korean-owned small businesses and/or using connections to the Korean diaspora to secure employment in the face of racialized discrimination in the local labour market.

12 Jia first came to Canada from South Korea with her husband and held a Spousal permit, tied to her husband's student permit and then his Post-graduation permit. After the spousal relationship dissolved, Jia decided to

pursue a diploma in Canada and obtained a student visa and then a Post-graduation permit to stay in Canada with her son.

13 On this note, Sadia speaks about pursuing permanent residency and then citizenship as soon as possible to enable her to sponsor parents: "I am talking specifically about [sponsoring my] parents ... that went into my decision in pursuing citizenship ... The reason I decided to stay here ... is that the [immigration] pathway [under the Post-graduation program] would eventually allow me to sponsor my family." Relating this potential to bring parents to Canada to the precariousness she otherwise grudgingly endures on the job, Sadia notes further, "If that's not the case then I am not sure if I would have stayed here."

5. Relational Precarity

1 In this analysis, I adopt the terms "dependant" and "principal" as they are utilized in the policies under study (see, for example, IRCC 2024d); while critiquing both concepts and their effects throughout, I remove quotations after they are introduced formally.

2 Family migration, conceived broadly by the OECD (2017, 110) to include "natives of OECD countries bringing spouses from abroad, but also immigrants arriving with accompanying family, or sponsoring their reunification," represents the main channel of migration to OECD countries. In 2008/9, almost 1.8 million migrants moved to OECD countries on the basis of residence permits for family migrants (OECD 2017). While this number declined slightly from that year to 2014/15, in 2021, as the global health pandemic began to ebb, family migration increased by fully 39 per cent in the OECD and remained the largest category of inflows, accounting for more than a third of total permanent-type migration (OECD 2022).

3 I place the terms "full-time students" and "skilled-workers" in quotations at first usage as they refer to designated entry categories.

4 Recall that under the IMP, in 2023, in numeric terms, spousal programs were second only to the burgeoning Post-graduation Work Permit program.

5 Alongside this shift, it has also sought to bolster the efficacy of laws extending rights to migrant workers, particularly those falling under the TFWP (or subject to LMIAs) through the IRPA (2002).

6 While the Spousal permitholders of focus in this chapter typically hold open work permits, relational precarity can also affect closed (or employer-tied) work permitholders seeking to pursue permanent residency via a partner or principal applicant. In such instances, in which the closed work permitholder's security of presence is conditioned on maintaining a good

relationship with the employer, the de facto spouse can face amplified precarity.

7 The latter category also includes spouses of bridging open work permitholders (workers granted an open work permit while they wait for their permanent residency application to be approved – including those in Provincial and Territorial Nominee Programs or the Atlantic Immigration Pilot). Effectively, this category allows the spouses of principal applicants to access open work permits while the so-named principal applicant is in a permanent residency pipeline but has yet to be granted this status.

8 In recent years, some free trade agreements have also specifically provided for spousal entry with open work permits for certain workers entering pursuant to those agreements. Spouses tied to principal applicants for permanent residency, issued "Bridging Open Work Permits" because the principal previous work permits are expiring and they are waiting for a decision to be made on their applications, are also eligible for open work permits. However, the numbers of such entries are small.

9 Please see note 3 of Chapter 4 for a definition of approved educational institutions.

10 Eligible programs include the Agri-Food Pilot, the Atlantic Immigration Program, Canadian Experience Class, Federal Skilled Trades, Federal Skilled Worker, the Quebec Selection Certificate (encompassing those who apply for permanent residency while their certificate is still valid), Home Child-Care Provider Pilot, Home Support Worker Pilot, Provincial Nominee Programs, Quebec Skilled Trades Class, Quebec Skilled Worker Class, Rural and Northern Immigration Pilot Program, and the Start-up Business Class (IRCC 2024v).

11 If the principal holds an open work permit, they may be required to provide additional documentary evidence to demonstrate eligibility on this criterion in order to secure a work permit for their spouse (IRCC 2024v).

12 As noted in Chapters 2 and 4, during the COVID-19 pandemic, each of the three foregoing routes of entry were modified temporarily as Canada introduced travel restrictions effectively closing the border to overseas permanent residency applicants. To meet immigration targets, IRCC boosted Canadian Experience Class invitations for eligible candidates already resident in the country and introduced the Temporary Resident to Permanent Resident Pathway for "essential workers and international graduates" already in the country on temporary work permits (IRCC 2021b and 2021c). Accordingly, between 2021 and 2023, a total of 9,055 former spouses of students or spouses of skilled worker permitholders attained permanent residency through this stream (IRCC 2024x).

13 In addition to the skilled work requirement, Canadian work experience points for Spousal permitholders must involve full-time (or equivalent)

work experience, acquired within the preceding 10 years prior to the allocation of points, experience that must be remunerated by wages or commission. Points range from 0 for no or less than one year of Canadian work experience, 5 points for one year, 7 points for two years, 8 points for three years, 9 points for four years, and 10 points for five years of Canadian work experience. Language points are allocated on the basis of benchmarks set out in *Canadian Language Benchmarks* for listening, reading, speaking, and writing in either of Canada's official languages. Spousal permitholders can earn up to 5 points in each category (for an overall total of 20 possible points). Spousal permitholders earn 0 points for being assessed at level 4 or lower, 1 point for being assessed at level 5 or 6, 3 points for being assessed at levels 7 or 8, or 5 points for being assessed at level 9 or higher. Applicants earn educational points for spouses where a spouse's credentials are either Canadian educational credentials or equivalent foreign educational credentials earned at a designated institution. Spousal permitholders earn 0 points for less than a secondary school credential, 2 points for a secondary school credential, 6 points for a one-year secondary school credential, 7 points for a two-year post-secondary school credential, 8 points for a post-secondary school credential of 3 or more years, 9 points for two post-secondary credentials where at least one of them was issued at the completion of a post-secondary program of three or more years, and 10 points for a master's, doctoral, or entry-to-practice professional degree for a TEER 1 occupation for which licensing by a provincial/territorial regulatory body is required (IRCC 2023q).

14 The proportion of women Spousal permitholders in precarious jobs may be underestimated as "multiple jobholding" is a limited indicator insofar as its uptake can be gendered. Many workers with socially ascribed caregiving responsibilities constraining their ability to take on multiple jobs are women.

15 This trend is amplified among spouses of students, where 18 per cent of employed women spouses of students work in retail compared to 11 per cent of their counterparts who are men.

16 Twenty-four per cent of employed Spousal permitholders from Iran hold a primary job in retail, compared to 13 per cent of those from all other source countries.

17 Education is the main industry wherein jobs tend to be less precarious in which women Spousal permitholders' shares are larger than those of men; however, those from India and the Philippines are underrepresented in education (in contrast to those from the United States and Iran, who are overrepresented). Finally, the scientific and professional industry, the fifth-largest industry of employment among Spousal permitholders, is

characterized by gender parity among this group, although those from India and the Philippines are underrepresented whereas those from the United States and Iran are overrepresented, patterns resembling those in education.

18 As Abel noted, "my wife, she knows some people, and she knows a guy that works at Walmart, and he got me a job at Walmart."

6. Conclusion

1 Both interview participants' self-reports and a review of organizing initiatives attest to these patterns and tendencies; for example, when asked about organizing efforts, few Working Holiday and Spousal permitholders interviewed spoke of formal initiatives or campaigns while most indicated that they were connected to grassroots/informal social media support groups. Frequently, as Post-graduation permitholders Rahee and Ai, Spousal permitholders Sonali and Chun-hua, and Working Holiday permitholders Clara, Mila, and Samuel, whose experiences are described in the foregoing chapters, further indicated, such groups are either organized around participants' countries of origin (i.e., IMP participants from the same country of origin find each other and share resources) or by IMP program, where potential permitholders exchange information and strategies for applying to work in Canada, an avenue common especially among Spousal permitholders. While the latter initiatives do not represent a direct space for political organizing, they do important work in connecting permitholders that might otherwise be isolated from one another and offer venues for mobilizing around shared issues.

2 In 2024, as this book was nearing completion, in an effort to address the "unsustainable growth" of the international student program and "set students up for success," IRCC announced it would cap the issuance of international study permits, resulting in a 35 per cent decrease of new study permitholders compared with 2023 (IRCC 2024u). A further announcement in September 2024 indicated that the government would reduce the cap on study permits by another 10 per cent in 2025 (IRCC 2024y).

3 This proposal emanates partly from recommendations of permitholders' themselves, such as Leela, who was working as a manager at a fast food restaurant. She notes that "I think if there were no manager position restriction, right now I would be in the nursing profession … I wouldn't have to waste these three or four years in a profession that I am not going to continue with for my future." The proposal falls in line with campaigns by university-based international students' organizations and

their allies calling for all employment, regardless of NOC, to be counted towards permanent residency, and for all NOC 0/A/B work experience accumulated by Post-graduation Work Permit program participants while holding study permits, including during co-ops, to count towards the Express Entry and Canadian Experience Class criteria (Simon Fraser University Graduate Student Society 2020).

Bibliography

Abu-Laban, Y. (2024). Middle class nation building through a tenacious discourse on skills: Immigration and Canada. *Journal of Ethnic and Migration Studies, 50*(7), 1803–1821. https://doi.org/10.1080/1369183X.2024.2315357

Abu-Laban, Y., & Gabriel, C. (2002). *Selling diversity: Immigration, multiculturalism, employment equity, and globalization.* University of Toronto Press.

Abu-Laban, Y., Tungohan, E., & Gabriel, C. (2022). *Containing Diversity: Canada and the Politics of Immigration in the 21st Century* (1st ed.). Toronto: University of Toronto Press.

Access to Information Act, RSC 1985, c A-1.

Acker, J. (1988). Class, gender, and the relations of distribution. *Signs: Journal of Women in Culture and Society, 13*(3), 473–497. https://doi.org/10.1086/494429

Allen, R.E.S., & Wiles, J.L. (2016). A rose by any other name: Participants choosing research pseudonyms. *Qualitative Research in Psychology, 13*(2), 149–165. https://doi.org/10.1080/14780887.2015.1133746

Anderson, B. (2019). New directions in migration studies: Towards methodological de-nationalism. *Comparative Migration Studies, 7*(1), 36. https://doi.org/10.1186/s40878-019-0140-8

André, I. (1990). The genesis and persistence of the Commonwealth Caribbean Seasonal Agricultural Workers Program in Canada. *Osgoode Hall Law Journal, 28*(2), 243–301. https://doi.org/10.60082/2817-5069.1770

Arat-Koç, S. (1992). Immigration policies, migrant domestic workers and the definition of citizenship in Canada. In V. Satzewich (Ed.), *Deconstructing a nation: Immigration, multiculturalism and racism in 90's Canada* (pp. 229–242). Halifax: Fernwood Publishing.

Arat-Koç, S. (2006). Whose social reproduction? Transnational motherhood and challenges to feminist political economy. In K. Bezanson & M. Luxton (Eds.), *Social reproduction: Feminist political economy challenges neo-liberalism* (pp. 75–92). Montreal and Kingston: McGill-Queen's University Press.

Arat-Koç, S. (2018). Culturalizing politics, hyper-politicizing "culture": "White" vs. "Black Turks" and the making of authoritarian populism in Turkey. *Dialectical Anthropology*, *42*(4), 391–408. https://doi.org/10.1007/s10624-018-9500-2

Atanackovic, J., & Bourgeault, I.L. (2014). Economic and social integration of immigrant live-in caregivers in Canada. *Institute for Research on Public Policy*, *46*.

Auditor General. (2017). *Annual Report 2017 of the Office of the Auditor General of Ontario*. Office of the Auditor General of Ontario.

Bakan, A.B., & Stasiulis, D. (2012). The Political economy of migrant live-in caregivers: A case of unfree labour? In P.T. Lenard & C. Straehle (Eds.), *Legislated inequality: Temporary labour migration in Canada* (pp. 202–226). Montreal and Kingston: McGill-Queen's University Press. https://doi.org/10.1515/9780773586932-012

Banerjee, R., & Lam, L. (2024). Paths to permanence: Permit categories and earnings trajectories of workers in Canada's International Mobility Program. *Canadian Public Policy*, *50*(1), 143–160. https://doi.org/10.3138/cpp.2023-062

Barnetson, B. (2015). "Fortis Et Liber" unless you are a farm worker: Workers' Compensation exceptionalism in Alberta, Canada. *Sage Open*, *5*(2). https://doi.org/10.1177/2158244015575632

Basok, T. (2002). *Tortillas and tomatoes: Transmigrant Mexican harvesters in Canada*. Montreal and Kingston: McGill-Queen's University Press.

Basok, T., Bélanger, D., & Rivas, E. (2014). "Reproducing deportability: Migrant agricultural workers in south-western Ontario." *Journal of Ethnic and Migration Studies*, *40*(9), 1394–1413. https://doi.org/10.1080/1369183X.2013.849566

Beck, U., & Sznaider, N. (2006). Unpacking cosmopolitanism for the social sciences, a research agenda: Cosmopolitan sociology. *British Journal of Sociology*, *57*(1), 1–23. https://doi.org/10.1111/j.1468-4446.2006.00091.x.

Bedford, R., & Spoonley, P. (2014). Competing for talent: diffusion of an innovation in New Zealand's immigration policy. *International Migration Review*, *48*(3), 891–911. https://doi.org/10.1111/imre.12123

Bedford, R., Bedford, C., Wall, J., & Young, M. (2017). Managed temporary labour migration of Pacific Islanders to Australia and New Zealand in the early twenty-first century. *Australian Geographer*, *48*(1), 37–57. https://doi.org/10.1080/00049182.2016.1266629

Bélanger, D., Ouellet, M., Coustere, C., & Fleury, C. (2023). Staggered inclusion: Between temporary and permanent immigration status in Quebec, Canada. *Nationalism and Ethnic Politics*, *29*(4), 412–425. https://doi.org/10.1080/13537113.2023.2174667

Beneria, L. (2008). The crisis of care, international migration, and public policy. *Feminist Economics*, *14*(3): 1–21. https://doi.org/10.1080/13545700802081984

Bhuyan, R., Korteweg, A., & Baqi, K. (2018). Regulating spousal migration through Canada's multiple border strategy: The gendered and racialized effects of structurally embedded borders: "Marriage fraud" at multiple borders. *Law & Policy, 40.* https://doi.org/10.1111/lapo.12111

Block, S., & Galabuzi, G.-E. (2018). Persistent inequality: Ontario's colour-coded labour market. In *Policy File.* Ottawa: Canadian Centre for Policy Alternatives.

Bonjour, S., & Kraler, A. (2015). Introduction: Family migration as an integration Issue? Policy perspectives and academic insights. *Journal of Family Issues, 36*(11), 1407–1432. https://doi.org/10.1177/0192513X14557490

Bosniak, L. (2006). *The Citizen and the Alien: Dilemmas of Contemporary Membership.*

Princeton, NJ: Princeton University Press.

Bowman, C., & Bair, J. (2017). From cultural sojourner to guestworker? The historical transformation and contemporary significance of the J-1 visa Summer Work Travel Program. *Labor History, 58*(1), 1–25. https://doi.org/10.1080/0023656X.2017.1239889

Boyd, M., Taylor, C., & Delaney, P. (1986). Temporary workers in Canada: A multifaceted program. *International Migration Review, 20*(4), 929–950. https://doi.org/10.2307/2545743

Brear, M. (2018). Swazi co-researcher participants' dynamic preferences, and motivations for, representation with real names and (English-language) pseudonyms – an ethnography. *Qualitative Research, 18*(6), 722–740. https://doi.org/10.1177/1468794117743467

Calliste, A. (1991). Canada's immigration policy and domestics from the Caribbean: The second domestic scheme. In J. Vorst (Ed.), Race, class gender: Bonds and barriers Toronto: Garamond Press.http://www.migrantworkersrights.net/en/resources/canada-s-immigration-policy-and-domestics-from-the-

Canada. (2015). *Evaluation of the Canadian Experience Class.* Ottawa: Immigration, Refugees and Citizenship Canada. https://www.canada.ca/content/dam/ircc/migration/ircc/english/pdf/pub/e1-2013-cec-e.pdf

Canadian Council for Refugees. (n.d.) "Take action to make family reunification for all!" Last accessed 31 January 2024. https://ccrweb.ca/en/family-reunification/action

Canadian Federation of Students. (n.d.). "Fairness for International Students." Last accessed 31 January 2024. https://www.cfs-fcee.ca/campaigns/fairness-for-international-students

Canmac Economics Ltd. (2020), Economic impact of international education in Canada – 2020 update: Final report. Report presented to International Affairs Canada. https://www.international.gc.ca/education/assets/pdfs/economic_impact_international_education_canada_2017_2018.pdf

Casas-Cortes, M., Cobarrubias, S., & Pickles, J. (2015). Riding routes and itinerant borders: Autonomy of migration and border externalization. *Antipode, 47*(4), 894–914. https://doi.org/10.1111/anti.12148

Castles, S. (2004). Why migration policies fail. *Ethnic and Racial Studies, 27*(2), 205–227. https://doi.org/10.1080/0141987042000177306

Castles, S. (2006). Guestworkers in Europe: A resurrection? *International Migration Review, 40*(4), 741–766. https://doi.org/10.1111/j.1747-7379 .2006.00042.x

Chartrand, T., & Vosko, L.F. (2021). Canada's Temporary Foreign Worker and International Mobility Programs: Charting change and continuity among source countries. *International Migration, 59*(2), 89–109. https://doi.org/10.1111/imig.12762

Chiose, S. (2016, 31 March). International student work program creating low -wage work force: Report. *Globe and Mail.* https://www.theglobeandmail .com/news/national/international-student-work-program-needs-overhaul -report-says/article29463566/

Cho, L. (2002). Rereading Chinese head tax racism: Redress, stereotype, and antiracist critical practice. *Essays on Canadian Writing, 75*(62).

Choudry, A., & Smith, A.A. (Eds.). (2016). *Unfree labour?:Sstruggles of migrant and immigrant workers in Canada.* Binghamton, NY: PM Press.

Choudry, A.A., Hanley, J., & Shragge, E. (2012). *Organize!:Bbuilding from the local for global justice.* Binghamton, NY: PM Press.

CIC News. (2014, 14 May) Temporary moratorium on certain work permit issuances. *CIC News.* www.cicnews.com/2014/05/temporary-moratorium -work-permit-issuances-053419.html#gs.5inhim.

Citizenship and Immigration Canada. (2004). *FW 1: Foreign Worker Manual.* https://publications.gc.ca/site/eng/9.815040/publication.html

Citizenship and Immigration Canada. (2013). *FW 1: Foreign Worker Manual.* https://publications.gc.ca/collections/collection_2013/cic/Ci63-27-2013 -eng.pdf

Coderre, M., & Nakache, D. (2021). From working tourists to permanent residents: Experiences of migrant workers with youth mobility schemes in Canada. *Journal of International Migration and Integration, 23*(3), 971–988. https://doi.org/10.1007/s12134-021-00873-7

Cohen, E.F. (2015). The political economy of immigrant time: Rights, citizenship, and temporariness in the post-1965 era. *Polity, 47*(3), 337–351. https://doi.org/10.1057/pol.2015.15

Corden, A., & Sainsbury, R. (2006). Exploring "quality": Research participants' perspectives on verbatim quotations. *International Journal of Social Research Methodology, 9*(2), 97–110. https://doi.org/10.1080/13645570600595264

Costello, C., & Freedland, M. (2016). Seasonal workers and intra-corporate transferees in EU law: Capital's handmaidens? In J. Howe & R. Owens (Eds.), *Temporary labour migration in the global era: The regulatory challenges.*

London: Bloomsbury Academic. https://www.rsc.ox.ac.uk/publications /seasonal-workers-and-intra-corporate-transferees-in-eu-law-capital2019s -handmaidens

Coulthard, G.S. (2014). *Red skin, white masks: Rejecting the colonial politics of recognition.* Minneapolis: University of Minnesota Press. https://www.jstor .org/stable/10.5749/j.ctt9qh3cv

Cranford, C.J., & Vosko, L.F. (2006). Conceptualizing precarious employment: Mapping wage work across social location and occupational context. In L. Vosko (Ed.) *Precarious Employment* (pp. 43–66). Montreal and Kingston: McGill-Queen's University Press. https://doi.org/10.1515/9780773585195-003

Crenshaw, K. (1990). Mapping the margins: Intersectionality, identity politics, and violence against women of color. *Stanford Law Review, 43*(6), 1241–1299. https://doi.org/10.2307/1229039

Crossman, E., Lu, Y., & Hou, F. (2022). *International students as a source of labour supply: Engagement in the labour market after graduation.* Ottawa: Statistics Canada: Economic and Social Reports. https://www150.statcan.gc.ca/n1 /pub/36-28-0001/2021012/article/00002-eng.htm

Daenzer, P.M. (1993). *Regulating class privilege: Immigrant servants in Canada, 1940s–1990s.* Toronto: Canadian Scholars' Press.

Das Gupta, T. (1994). Multiculturalism policy: A terrain of struggle for immigrant women. *Canadian Woman Studies, 14*(2), 72–75.

De Genova, N. (2002). "Migrant 'illegality' and deportability in everyday life" *Annual Review of Anthropology, 31*(1), 419–447. https://doi.org/10.1146 /annurev.anthro.31.040402.085432

De Genova, N. (2013). Spectacles of migrant "illegality:: The scene of exclusion, the obscene of inclusion. *Ethnic and Racial Studies, 36*(7), 1180–1198. https://doi.org/10.1080/01419870.2013.783710

Dobrowolsky, A. (2017). Bad versus Big Canada: State imaginaries of immigration and citizenship. *Studies in Political Economy, 98*(2), 197–222. https://doi.org/10.1080/07078552.2017.1343001

Dua, E. (1992). Racism or gender: Understanding gender oppression of South-Asian Canadian women. *Canadian Women's Studies, 13*(1), 6–10.

ESDC (Employment and Social Development Canada). (2014). *Overhauling the Temporary Foreign Worker Program.* Ottawa: Author. https://www.canada .ca/en/employment-social-development/services/foreign-workers/reports /overhaul.html

Fraser, N., & Gordon, L. (1994). A Genealogy of dependency: Tracing a keyword of the U.S. welfare state. *Signs: Journal of Women in Culture and Society, 19*(2), 309–336. https://doi.org/10.1086/494886

Fudge, J., & Tham, J.C. (2017). *Dishing up migrant workers for the Canadian food services sector: Labor law and the demand for migrant workers. Comparative Labor Law & Policy Journal.* https://papers.ssrn.com/abstract=3216971

Gabriel, R. (2008). Changing statuses: Freedom of movement, locality and transnationality of irregular Romanian migrants in Milan. *Journal of Ethnic and Migration Studies, 34*(5), 787–802. https://doi.org/10.1080/13691830802106069

Gabriel, R. (2011). From irregular migrants to fellow Europeans: Changes in Romanian migratory flows. *Foggy Social Structures, 23.*

Gaucher, M. (2018). *A family matter: Citizenship, conjugal relationships, and Canadian immigration policy.* Vancouver: UBC Press.

Go International. (2021). Application Process. *Go International.* https://gointernational.ca/faq/application-process/

Goldring, L. (2014). Resituating temporariness as the precarity and conditionality of non-citizenship. In L. Vosko, V. Preston, & R. Latham (Eds.), *Liberating temporariness? Migration, work and citizenship in an age of insecurity* (pp. 218–254). Montreal and Kingston: McGill-Queen's University Press.

Goldring, L., & Landolt, P. (2013). *Producing and negotiating non-citizenship: Precarious Legal Status in Canada.* Toronto: University of Toronto Press. https://www.jstor.org/stable/10.3138/j.ctt2ttkpx

Goldring, L., & Landolt, P. (2021). From illegalized migrant toward permanent resident: Assembling precarious legal status trajectories and differential inclusion in Canada. *Journal of Ethnic and Migration Studies.* https://doi.org/10.1080/1369183X.2020.1866978.

Government of Canada. (2005). *More reasons for international students to choose Canada* [News release]. https://www.canada.ca/en/news/archive/2005/04/more-reasons-international-students-choose-canada.html

Government of Canada. (2023). T4 slip – Information for Employers. https://www.canada.ca/en/revenue-agency/services/tax/businesses/topics/payroll/completing-filing-information-returns/t4-information-employers/t4-slip.html

Government of Ontario. (2024). *Ontario Immigrant Nominee Program Streams.* https://www.ontario.ca/page/ontario-immigrant-nominee-program-streams.

Graduate Student Society at Simon Fraser University. (2020, 23 December). Addressing precarious status of international students." Last accessed 31 January 2024. https://sfugradsociety.ca/addressing-the-precarious-status-of-international-students/.

Graefe, P. (2007). Political economy and Canadian public policy. In M. Orsini & M. Smith (Eds.), *Critical policy studies* (pp. 19–40). Vancouver: UBC Press.

Grimm, A. (2019). Studying to stay: Understanding graduate visa policy content and context in the United States and Australia. *International Migration, 57*(5), 235–251. https://doi.org/10.1111/imig.12561

Guenther, K.M. (2009). The politics of names: Rethinking the methodological and ethical significance of naming people, organizations, and places. *Qualitative Research, 9*(4), 411–421. https://doi.org/10.1177/1468794109337872

Hage, G. (2000). *White nation: Fantasies of white supremacy in a multicultural society*. Hove, UK: Psychology Press.

Hall, S. (1986). Gramsci's relevance for the study of race and ethnicity. *Journal of Communication Inquiry, 10*(2), 5–27. https://doi.org/10.1177/019685998601000202

Hanley, J., Larios, L., & Koo, J.-H. (2017). Does Canada "care" about migrant caregivers?: Implications under the reformed caregiver program. *Canadian Ethnic Studies, 49*(2), 121–139.

Haque, E. (2014). Language training and labour market integration for newcomers to Canada. In *Liberating temporariness?: Migration, work, and citizenship in an age of insecurity* (pp. 201–217). Montreal and Kingston: McGill-Queen's University Press. https://doi.org/10.1515/9780773592223-010

Hari, A. (2018). Putting "Canadians first": Problematizing the crisis of "foreign" workers in Canadian media and policy responses. *International Migration, 56*(6), 191–206. https://doi.org/10.1111/imig.12453

Hari, A., & Ahmed, S. (2023). Invisibility while under scrutiny: Media portrayals of white temporary foreign workers. *Canadian Journal of Communication, 48*(1), 1–24. https://doi.org/10.3138/cjc.2022-0018

Heaton, J. (2022). "*Pseudonyms are used throughout": A footnote, unpacked. *Qualitative Inquiry, 28*(1), 123–132. https://doi.org/10.1177/10778004211048379

Helleiner, J. (2017). Recruiting the "culturally compatible" migrant: Irish Working Holiday migration and white settler Canadianness. *Ethnicities, 17*(3), 299–319. https://doi.org/10.1177/1468796815610354

Hennebry, J. (2012). Permanently temporary? Agricultural migrant workers and their integration in Canada. *Institute for Research on Public Policy, 6*. https://policycommons.net/artifacts/1186251/permanently-temporary/1739376/

Hou, F. & Picot, G. (2023). *Earnings of one-step and two-step economic immigrants: Comparisons from the arrival year*. Ottawa: Statistics Canada, Economic and Social Reports. https://doi.org/10.25318/36280001202400100006-eng

Howe, J., Charlesworth, S., & Brennan, D. (2020). Migration pathways for frontline care workers in Australia and New Zealand: Front doors, side doors, back doors and trapdoors. *University of New South Wales Law Journal, 42*(1), 211–241. https://doi.org/10.3316/ielapa.276332668575692

Hune-Brown, N. (2021, 18 August). The shadowy business of international education. *The Walrus*. https://thewalrus.ca/the-shadowy-business-of-international-education/.

IEC Working Holiday Forum – Moving2Canada. (n.d.) Last accessed 31 January 2024. https://www.facebook.com/groups/Moving2Canada.IEC.Forum

Immigration and Refugee Protection Act. S.C. 2001, c. 27. https://laws-lois.justice.gc.ca/eng/acts/I-2.5/

Immigration and Refugee Protection Regulations (SOR/2002-227). https://laws
-lois.justice.gc.ca/eng/regulations/SOR-2002-227/page-26.html#docCont

IRCC. (2014, 6 June). *Recognized organizations for foreign youth – IEC [R205(b) –
C21] – Reciprocity – International Mobility Program* [Program descriptions].
https://www.canada.ca/en/immigration-refugees-citizenship/corporate
/publications-manuals/operational-bulletins-manuals/temporary
-residents/foreign-workers/exemption-codes/international-experience
/canadian-interests-reciprocal-employment-international-experience-canada
-recognized-organizations-foreign-youth.html

IRCC. (2015). *Evaluation of the Canadian Experience Class.* Ref. No.: E1-2013.
https://www.canada.ca/content/dam/ircc/migration/ircc/english/pdf
/pub/e1-2013-cec-e.pdf.

IRCC. (2018). *Post-Graduation Work Permit Program: Presentation to provinces and
territories.* [Internal Document]. Accessed via ATIP Request A-2018-37539.

IRCC. (2019a). *Launching 2 new pilots: Home Child Care Provider and Home
Support Worker* [News releases]. https://www.canada.ca/en/immigration
-refugees-citizenship/news/2019/06/canada-caring-for-caregivers.html

IRCC. (2019b). *Evaluation of the International Experience Canada Program.*
https://www.canada.ca/content/dam/ircc/documents/pdf/english
/evaluation/e2-2017-iec-en.pdf

IRCC. (2021a). *CR-21-0358: Canada – Work permit holders by program, country of
citizenship and year in which permit(s) became effective, 2002.* Customized data
request.

IRCC. (2021b, 13 February). *Thousands of skilled workers in Canada invited to stay
permanently.* News release. https://www.canada.ca/en/immigration
-refugees-citizenship/news/notices/skilled-workers-in-canada.html

IRCC. (2021c). *New pathway to permanent residency for over 90,000 essential
temporary workers and international graduates.* https://www.canada.ca
/en/immigration-refugees-citizenship/news/2021/04/new-pathway-to
-permanent-residency-for-over-90000-essential-temporary-workers-and
-international-graduates.html

IRCC. (2022a) *Immigrate as a provincial nominee through Express Entry.* https://
www.canada.ca/en/immigration-refugees-citizenship/services/immigrate
-canada/provincial-nominees.html

IRCC. (2022b). *New measures to address Canada's labour shortage.* News
release. https://www.canada.ca/en/immigration-refugees-citizenship
/news/2022/04/new-measures-to-address-canadas-labour-shortage.html

IRCC. (2022c). *Employers and temporary workers to benefit from family work
permits to address labour shortages.* News release. https://www.canada.ca
/en/immigration-refugees-citizenship/news/2022/12/employers-and
-temporary-workers-to-benefit-from-family-work-permits-to-address
-labour-shortages.html

IRCC. (2022d). *Help Centre: I have an open work permit because my spouse is working/studying in Canada. For how long is my permit valid?*. https://www
.cic.gc.ca/english/helpcentre/answer.asp?qnum=1522&top=17

IRCC. (2023a). *CR-23-0177: Canada – Work permit holders by permit holder type and year in which permit(s) became effective, 2021–2022*. Customized data request.

IRCC. (2023b) *CR-23-0635: Canada-International Experience Canada (IEC) working holiday work permit holders by program and year in which permit(s) became effective, 2002 – September 2023*. Customized data request.

IRCC. (2023c). *Glossary: Open Work Permit*. https://www.canada.ca/en
/services/immigration-citizenship/helpcentre/glossary.html#o

IRCC. (2023d). *Significant benefit to Canada [R205(a) – C10] – Canadian Interests – International Mobility Program* [Program descriptions]. https://www.canada
.ca/en/immigration-refugees-citizenship/corporate/publications-manuals
/operational-bulletins-manuals/temporary-residents/foreign-workers
/exemption-codes/canadian-interests-significant-benefit-general-guidelines
-r205-c10.html

IRCC. (2023e). *International Mobility Program (IMP): Canadian Interests – Reciprocal Employment General Guidelines R205(b), C20* [Program descriptions].
https://www.canada.ca/en/immigration-refugees-citizenship/corporate
/publications-manuals/operational-bulletins-manuals/temporary-residents
/foreign-workers/exemption-codes/canadian-interests-reciprocal
-employment-general-guidelines-r205-b-c20.html

IRCC. (2023f). *Overview of work designated by the Minister [R205(c)(ii) – C41, C42, C44, C45, C46, C47, C48, C49, C52] – Canadian Interest – International Mobility Program*. https://www.canada.ca/en/immigration-refugees
-citizenship/corporate/publications-manuals/operational-bulletins
-manuals/temporary-residents/foreign-workers/exemption-codes/public
-policy-competitiveness-economy.html

IRCC. (2023g). *CR-23-0635: Canada – International Experience Canada (IEC) work permit holders by gender and year in which permit(s) became effective, 2002 – September 2023*.Customized sata eequest.

IRCC. (2023h). *CR-23-0635: Canada – International Experience Canada (IEC) work permit holders by age and year in which permit(s) became effective, 2002 – September 2023*.Customized data request.

IRCC. (2023i). *Rounds of invitations*. https://ircc.canada.ca/english/work/iec
/selections.asp

IRCC. (2023j). *Find out if you're eligible – International Experience Canada: Who can apply*. https://www.canada.ca/en/immigration-refugees-citizenship
/services/work-canada/iec/eligibility.html.

IRCC. (2023k). *Rounds of invitations – International Experience Canada: France – Working Holiday*. https://www.cic.gc.ca/english/work/iec/selections
.asp?country=fr&cat=wh

IRCC. (2023l). *Rounds of invitations – International Experience Canada: Ireland – Working Holiday.* https://www.cic.gc.ca/english/work/iec/selections .asp?country=ie&cat=wh

IRCC. (2023m). *Rounds of invitations – International Experience Canada: Australia – Working Holiday.* https://www.cic.gc.ca/english/work/iec/selections .asp?country=au&cat=wh

IRCC. (2023n, 9 January). *"International Experience Canada program is now open to welcome international youth to Canada."* News release. https:// www.canada.ca/en/immigration-refugees-citizenship/news/2023/01 /international-experience-canada-program-is-now-open-to-welcome -international-youth-to-canada.html

IRCC. (2023o) *Canada announces extension of post-graduation work permits for up to 18 months to retain high-skilled talent.* News release. https://www.canada .ca/en/immigration-refugees-citizenship/news/2023/03/canada -announces-extension-of-post-graduation-work-permits-for-up-to-18 -months-to-retain-high-skilled-talent.html.

IRCC. (2023p, 8 My). *Canada announces extension to the Agri-Food Pilot, facilitating access to permanent residence for workers and their families.* News release 2023. https://www.canada.ca/en/immigration-refugees -citizenship/news/2023/05/canada-announces-extension-to-the-agri-food -pilot-facilitating-access-to-permanent-residence-for-workers-and-their -families.html

IRCC. (2023q). *Ministerial instructions respecting the Express Entry system – Current.* https://www.canada.ca/en/immigration-refugees-citizenship /corporate/mandate/policies-operational-instructions-agreements /ministerial-instructions/express-entry-application-management-system /current.html

IRCC. (2023r). *CR-23-0293: Canada – –Admissions of permanent residents with prior work permit holder status under the International Mobility Program (IMP) by Family Status, 2010–2022.*

IRCC. (2023s). *CR-23-0218: Admissions of permanent residents with prior work permit holder status under spouses of students and spouses of skilled workers by family status and age group, 2002–2022.* Customized sata eequest

IRCC. (2023t). *CR-23-0177: Canada – International Mobility Program (IMP) work permit holders under spouses of skilled workers and spouses of students by gender and year in which permit(s) became effective, 2021 – 2022.* Customized data request.

IRCC. (2023u) *CR-23-0635: Canada – Admissions of Permanent Residents with Prior International Experience Canada (IEC) Work Permit by Immigration Category, 2002–September 2023.* Customized data request.

IRCC. (2024a) *CR 24-0318: Canada – Work permit holders by program, country of citizenship and year in which permit(s) became effective, 2023.* Customized data request.

IRCC. (2024b) *CR 24-0318: Canada – International Experience Canada (IEC) working holiday work permit holders by program and year in which permit(s) became effective, 2023.* Customized data request.

IRCC. (2024c) *Canada – Study permit holders by country of citizenship and year in which permit(s) became effective, January 2015 – February 2024.* Open dataset. https://open.canada.ca/data/en/dataset/90115b00-f9b8-49e8-afa3 -b4cff8facaee/resource/b505b9bc-d375-4525-af39-afdf25639acf

IRCC. (2024d). *Spouses and common-law partners of study permit holders – [R205(c)(ii) – C42]– Canadian interest – International Mobility Program.* https://www.canada.ca/en/immigration-refugees-citizenship/corporate /publications-manuals/operational-bulletins-manuals/temporary -residents/foreign-workers/public-policy-competitiveness-economy /c42.html

IRCC. (2024e). *Labour market impact assessment (LMIA) exemption codes – International Mobility Program.* https://www.canada.ca/en/immigration -refugees-citizenship/corporate/publications-manuals/operational -bulletins-manuals/temporary-residents/foreign-workers/exemption -codes.html

IRCC. (2024f). *Language requirements – Skilled immigrants (Express Entry).* https://www.canada.ca/en/immigration-refugees-citizenship/services /immigrate-canada/express-entry/documents/language-requirements .html

IRCC. (2024g). *Eligibility to apply as a Federal Skilled Worker (Express Entry),* https://www.canada.ca/en/immigration-refugees-citizenship/services /immigrate-canada/express-entry/eligibility/federal-skilled-workers .html#proof

IRCC. (2024h) *Proof of funds – Skilled immigrants (Express Entry).* https://www .canada.ca/en/immigration-refugees-citizenship/services/immigrate -canada/express-entry/documents/proof-funds.html

IRCC. (2024i). *Compare all Express Entry programs.* https://www.canada.ca /en/immigration-refugees-citizenship/services/immigrate-canada/express -entry/eligibility/compare.html

IRCC. (2024j). *Reasons you may be inadmissible to Canada.* https://www.canada .ca/en/immigration-refugees-citizenship/services/immigrate-canada /inadmissibility/reasons.html

IRCC. (2024k). *Express Entry: Express Entry via the Provincial Nominee Program.* https://www.canada.ca/en/immigration-refugees-citizenship/corporate /publications-manuals/operational-bulletins-manuals/permanent -residence/express-entry/provincial-nominee-program.html.

IRCC. (2024l). *CR-24-0318. Canada – International Experience Canada (IEC) work permit holders by age and year in which permit(s) became effective, 2023.* Customized data request.

IRCC. (2024m). *Work and travel in Canada using a recognized organization.* https://www.canada.ca/en/immigration-refugees-citizenship/services/work-canada/iec/recognized-organizations.html.

IRCC. (2024n). *CR-23-0752: Canada – Admissions of permanent residents with prior post-graduate work permit (PGWP) holder status by immigration category, 2008–23.* Customized data request.

IRCC. (2024o). *CR-24-0318: Canada – Admissions of permanent residents with prior work permit holder status under the International Mobility Program (IMP) by family status, 2023.* Customized data request.

IRCC. (2024p). *Designated learning institutions list.* https://www.canada.ca/en/immigration-refugees-citizenship/services/study-canada/study-permit/prepare/designated-learning-institutions-list.html

IRCC. (2024q). *Post-graduation work permit (PGWP) [R205(c) – C43] – International Mobility Program.* https://www.canada.ca/en/immigration-refugees-citizenship/corporate/publications-manuals/operational-bulletins-manuals/temporary-residents/study-permits/post-graduation-work-permit-program.html#s13

IRCC. (2024r). *CR-24-0195. Canada – Post-graduate work permit holders by age, and year in which permit(s) became effective, 2008–23.* Customized data request.

IRCC. (2024s). *CR-24-0195. Canada – Post-graduate work permit holders by country of citizenship, gender, and year in which permit(s) became effective, 2022–2023.* Customized data request.

IRCC. (2024t). *CR-23-0752: Canada – Admissions of permanent residents with prior post-graduate work permit (pgwp) holder status by age and gender, 2008–23.* Customized data request.

IRCC. (2024u). *Canada to stabilize growth and decrease number of new international student permits issued to approximately 360,000 for 2024.* News release. https://www.canada.ca/en/immigration-refugees-citizenship/news/2024/01/canada-to-stabilize-growth-and-decrease-number-of-new-international-student-permits-issued-to-approximately-360000-for-2024.html

IRCC. (2024v). *Open work permits for family members of foreign workers: Who can apply?* https://www.canada.ca/en/immigration-refugees-citizenship/services/work-canada/permit/temporary/open-work-permit-spouses-dependent-children/eligibility.html#economicwp

IRCC. (2024w). *Family members of WP holders who are Economic Class PR applicants or chosen by a province [R205(c)(ii) – C49] – Canadian interest – IMP.* https://www.canada.ca/en/immigration-refugees-citizenship/corporate/publications-manuals/operational-bulletins-manuals/temporary-residents/foreign-workers/public-policy-competitiveness-economy/c49.html

IRCC. (2024x). *CR-23-0779: Canada – Admissions of permanent residents with prior work permit holder status under spouses of students or spouses of skilled worker by family status and gender, 2002–23.* Customized data request.

IRCC. (2024y). *Strengthening temporary residence programs for sustainable volumes.* https://www.canada.ca/en/immigration-refugees-citizenship /news/2024/09/strengthening-temporary-residence-programs-for -sustainable-volumes.html

IRCC. (2024z) CR-24-0550: *Canada – Admissions of Permanent Residents with Prior International Experience Canada Work Permit Holder Status by Immigration Category, 2023.* Customized data request.

IRCC. (2025). *Changes to open work permits for family members of temporary residents. Government of Canada.* https://www.canada.ca/en/immigration -refugees-citizenship/news/notices/changes-open-work-permits-family -members-temporary-residents.html#:~:text=Effective%20January%20 21%2C%202025%2C%20only,apply%20for%20a%20family%20 OWP.&text=These%20include%20occupations%20in%20the, education%2C%20sports%20and%20military%20sectors.

Jayasuriya-Illesinghe, V. (2018). Immigration policies and immigrant women's vulnerability to intimate partner violence in Canada. *Journal of International Migration and Integration, 19*(2), 339–348. https://doi.org/10.1007/s12134 -018-0545-5

Kaushal, A. (2019). Do the means change the ends: Express entry and economic immigration in Canada. *Dalhousie Law Journal, 42 ,* 83.

Kelley, N., & Trebilcock, M.J. (2014). *The making of the mosaic: A history of Canadian immigration policy.* Toronto: University of Toronto Press.

Kernerman, G.P. (2005). *Multicultural nationalism: Civilizing difference, constituting community.* Vancouver: UBC Press.

Kim, A., Buckner, E., & Montsion, J.M. (2024). *International students from Asia in Canadian universities: Institutional challenges at the intersection of internationalization, racialization and inclusion.* Milton Park, UK: Taylor & Francis.

Kofman, E. (2018). Family migration as a class matter. *International Migration, 56*(4), 33–46. https://doi.org/10.1111/imig.12433

Lahman, M.K.E., Rodriguez, K.L., Moses, L., Griffin, K.M., Mendoza, B.M., & Yacoub, W. (2015). A rose by any other name is still a rose? Problematizing pseudonyms in research. *Qualitative Inquiry, 21*(5), 445–453. https://doi.org /10.1177/1077800415572391

Lahman, M.K.E., Thomas, R., & Teman, E.D. (2023). A good name: Pseudonyms in research. *Qualitative Inquiry, 29*(6), 678–685. https://doi.org/10.1177/10778004 221134088

Landolt, P., Goldring, L. & Pritchard, P. (2022). Decentering methodological nationalism to survey precarious legal status trajectories. *International Journal of Social Research Methodology, 25*(2), 183–195. https://doi.org/10.108 0/13645579.2020.1866339.

Latham, R., Preston, V., & Vosko, L.F. (2014). *Liberating temporariness?: Migration, work, and citizenship in an age of insecurity.* Montreal and Kingston: McGill-Queen's Press.

Leckenby, D., & Hesse-Biber, S.N. (2007). *Feminist research practice*. Thousand Oaks, CA: Sage. https://doi.org/10.4135/9781412984270

Lo, L., Li, W. & Yu, W. (2017). Highly-skilled migration from China and India to Canada and the United States. *International Migration, 57*(3), 317–333. https://doi.org/10.1111/imig.12388

Lu, Y. & Hou, F. (2019). Temporary foreign workers in the Canadian labour force: Open versus employer-specific work permits. *Statistics Canada: Economic Insights*. https://www150.statcan.gc.ca/n1/en/pub/11-626-x /11-626-x2019016-eng.pdf?st=unmHN97x

Marsden, S., Tucker, E., & Vosko, L.F. (2021a). The trilemma of Canadian migrant worker policy: Facilitating employer access while protecting the Canadian labour market and addressing migrant worker exploitation. In C. Dauvergne (Ed.), *Research handbook on the law and politics of migration* (pp. 63–81). Cheltenham, UK: Edward Elgar Publishing. https://www .elgaronline.com/display/edcoll/9781789902259/9781789902259.00014.xml

Marsden, S., Tucker, E., & Vosko, L. (2021b). Flawed by design?: A case study of federal enforcement of migrant workers' labour rights in Canada. *Canadian Labour and Employment Law Journal 23*(1): 71–102. https:// digitalcommons.osgoode.yorku.ca/scholarly_works/2932

Mathew, Minu. (2022, 25 April). "'Minister Sean Fraser, why exclude us from the post-graduate work permit extension?'" *New Canadian Media*. Last accessed 31 January 2024. https://www.newcanadianmedia.ca/minister -sean-fraser-why-exclude-us-from-the-post-graduate-work-permit -extensionask-excluded-international-students-pgwp/

McBride, S. (2004). Towards perfect flexibility: Youth as an industrial reserve army for the new economy. In J. Stanford. & L.F. Vosko (Eds.), *Challenging the market: The struggle to regulate work and income*. Montreal and Kingston, ON: McGill-Queen's University Press.

McCall, L. (2005). The complexity of intersectionality. *Signs: Journal of Women in Culture and Society, 30*(3), 1771–1800. https://doi.org/10.1086/426800

McLaughlin, J., & Hennebry, J. (2013). Pathways to precarity: Structural vulnerabilities and lived consequences for migrant farmworkers in Canada. In L. Goldring and P. Landolt (Eds.), *Producing and negotiating non-citizenship: Precarious legal status in Canada* (pp. 175–194). Toronto: University of Toronto Press.

Meldrum-Hanna, C., Russell, A., & Christodoulo, M. (2015, 5 July). Slave-like conditions found on farms supplying big supermarkets. https://www.abc .net.au/news/2015-05-04/supermarkets-food-outlets-exploit-black-market -migrant-workers/6441496

Miles, R., & Brown, M. (2003). *Racism*. Hove, UK: Psychology Press.

Mirchandani, K. (2007). *Criminalizing race, criminalizing poverty: Welfare fraud enforcement in Canada*. Halifax: Fernwood .

Mirchandani, K., & Chan, W. (2007). *Criminalizing race, criminalizing poverty: Welfare fraud enforcement in Canada*. Halifax: Fernwood.

Mirchandani, K., Vosko, L.F., Soni-Sinha, U., Perry, J.A., Noack, A.M., Hall, R.J., & Gellatly, M. (2018). Methodological k/nots: Designing research on the enforcement of labor standards. *Journal of Mixed Methods Research*, 12(2), 133–147. https://doi.org/10.1177/1558689816651793

Moffette, D. (2021). Immigration status and policing in Canada: Current problems, activist strategies and abolitionist visions. *Citizenship Studies*, 25(2), 273–291. https://doi.org/10.1080/13621025.2020.1859194

Mongia, R.V. (1999). Race, nationality, mobility: A history of the passport. *Public Culture*, 11(3), 527–555. https://doi.org/10.1215/08992363-11-3-527

Mongia, R.V. (2018). *Indian migration and empire: A colonial genealogy of the modern state*. Durham, NC: Duke University Press.

NAFTA. (1994). *NAFTA Chapter 16: Temporary entry for business persons*. Foreign Trade Information System. http://www.sice.oas.org/trade/nafta/chap-161. asp

Nakache, D., & Kinoshita, P. J. (2010). *The Canadian Temporary Foreign Worker Program: Do short-term economic needs prevail over human rights concerns?* (SSRN Scholarly Paper 1617255). https://papers.ssrn.com/abstract=1617255

Nyers, P. (2019). *Irregular citizenship, immigration, and deportation*. London: Routledge.

OCASI. (2011, 25 April). *Community groups and women's organizations oppose conditional visa for sponsored spouses*. Last accessed 31 January 2024. https://ocasi.org/community-groups-and-women%E2%80%99s-organizations-oppose-conditional-visa-sponsored-spouses

OECD. (2014). *Recruiting immigrant workers: New Zealand 2014*. Paris: Author. https://www.oecd.org/newzealand/recruiting-immigrant-workers-nz-2014.htm

OECD. (2017). *International migration outlook 2017 – Chapter 3: A portrait of family migration in OECD countries*. https://www.oecd.org/els/mig/IMO-2017-chap3.pdf

OECD. (2019). *International Migration Outlook 2019*. Paris: Author.

OECD. (2022). *International migration outlook 2022 – Chapter 1: Recent developments in international migration movements and labour market inclusion of immigrants*. Paris: Author. https://www.oecd-ilibrary.org/sites/30fe16d2-en/1/3/1/index.html?itemId=/content/publication/30fe16d2-en&_csp_=97175d429ae5e4e04cd3cccbbfc84945&itemIGO=oecd&itemContentType=book

Oommen, E.T. (2021). Privilege and youth migration: Polarised employment patterns of youth mobility workers in London. *Journal of Ethnic and Migration Studies*, 47(5), 1119–1135. https://doi.org/10.1080/1369183X.2019.1583094

Pearson, R. (2004) The social is political: Towards the re-politicization of feminist analysis of the global economy. *International Feminist Journal of Politics* 6(4): 603–22. https://doi.org/10.1080/1461674042000283381

Pellerin, H. (2008). Governing labour migration in the era of GATS: The growing influence of *lex mercatoria*. In H. Pellerin & C. Gabriel (Eds.), *Governing international labour migration: Current issues, challenges and dilemmas*. London: Routledge. https://doi.org/10.4324/9780203564479

Pellerin, H. (2017). States and the management of the international mobility of highly skilled labour in the age of neoliberalism. *International Journal of Migration and Border Studies*, 3(4), 352–367. https://doi.org/10.1504/IJMBS.2017.086979

Picchio, A. (1992). *Social reproduction: The political economy of the labour market* (pp. 1–29, 30–56). Cambridge: Cambridge University Press.

Plewa, P., & Miller, M. (2005). Postwar and post-cold war generations of European temporary foreign worker policies: Implications from Spain. *Migraciones Internacionales*, 3(2), 58–83.

Portes, A. (1997). Immigration theory for a new century: Some problems and opportunities. *International Migration Review*, 31(4), 799–825. https://doi.org/10.2307/2547415

Pringle, S. (2020). The "threat" of marriage fraud: A story of precarity, exclusion, and belonging. *Canadian Journal of Family Law*, 33(1), 1.

Rajkumar, D., Berkowitz, L., Vosko, L.F., Preston, V., & Latham, R. (2012). At the temporary–permanent divide: How Canada produces temporariness and makes citizens through its security, work, and settlement policies. *Citizenship Studies*, 16(3–4), 483–510. https://doi.org/10.1080/13621025.2012.683262

Ramón, C. (2021). *Investing in alternatives to irregular migration from Central America: Options to expand U.S. employment pathways*. Washington, DC: Migration Policy Institute. https://www.migrationpolicy.org/sites/default/files/publications/labor-pathways-central-america_eng_final.pdf

Ramón, C., Ruiz Soto, A.G., Mora, M.J., & Gil, A.M. (2022). *Temporary worker programs in Canada, Mexico, and Costa Rica: Promising pathways for managing Central American migration?* Washington DC: Migration Policy Institute. https://www.migrationpolicy.org/sites/default/files/publications/mpi-temp-work-pathways-ca-mx-cr_eng-final.pdf

Ray, V., Herd, P. & Moynihan, D. (2023). Racialized burdens: Applying racialized organization theory to the administrative state. *Journal of Public Administration Research and Theory*, 33(1), 139–152. https://doi.org/10.1093/jopart/muac001

Regulations Amending the Immigration and Refugee Protection Regulations 2013. Government of Canada, Public Works and Government Services Canada,

Integrated Services Branch, Canada Gazette. https://gazette.gc.ca/rp-pr/p2/2014/2014-01-01/html/sor-dors245-eng.html

Reilly, A. (2015). *Low-cost labour or cultural exchange? Reforming the working holiday visa programme.* Last accessed 27 August 2023. https://journals.sagepub.com/doi/10.1177/1035304615598160

Robertson, S. (2014). Time and temporary migration: The case of temporary graduate workers and working holiday makers in Australia. *Journal of Ethnic and Migration Studies, 40*(12), 1915–1933. https://doi.org/10.1080/1369183X.2013.876896

Sassen, S. (1981). Towards a conceptualization of immigrant labor. *Social Problems, 29*(1), 65–85. https://doi.org/10.2307/800079

Satzewich, V. (1989). Racism and Canadian immigration policy: The government's view of Caribbean migration, 1962–1966. *Canadian Ethnic Studies = Études Ethniques au Canada, 21*(1), 77–97.

Satzewich, V. (1991). *Racism and the incorporation of foreign labour: Farm labour migration to Canada since 1945.* London: Routledge.

Satzewich, V. (2014). Visa officers as gatekeepers of a state's borders: The social determinants of discretion in spousal sponsorship cases in Canada. *Journal of Ethnic and Migration Studies, 40*(9), 1450–1469. https://doi.org/10.1080/1369183X.2013.854162

Seccombe, W. (1974). The housewife and her labour under capitalism. *New Left Review, 83* (Jan./Feb.).

Seidman, I. (2019). Interviewing as qualitative research: A guide for researchers in education and the social sciences. New York: Teachers College Press. http://ebookcentral.proquest.com/lib/york/detail.action?docID=5790771

Sharma, N. (2006). *Home economics: Nationalism and the making of "migrant workers" in Canada.* Toronto: University of Toronto Press.https://www.jstor.org/stable/10.3138/9781442675810

Sharma, N. (2007). Freedom to Discriminate: A national state sovereignty and temporary migrant workers in Canada. In G. Yurdakul and Y.M. Bodemann (Eds.), *Citizenship and immigrant incorporation* (pp. 163–183). New York: Palgrave Macmillan. https://doi.org/10.1007/978-1-137-07379-2_9

Sharma, N. (2019). Citizenship/borders. In D. Brock, A. Martin, R. Raby, & M.P. Thomas (Eds.), *Power and everyday practices* (2nd ed.). Toronto: University of Toronto Press.

She, Q., & Wotherspoon, T. (2013). International student mobility and highly skilled migration: A comparative study of Canada, the United States, and the United Kingdom. *SpringerPlus, 2*(1), 132. https://doi.org/10.1186/2193-1801-2-132

Smith, A., & Staveley, J. (2014). Toward an ethnography of mobile tourism industry workers in Banff National Park. *Anthropologica, 56*(2), 435–447.

Smith, A.A. (2015). Troubling "Project Canada": The Caribbean and the making of "unfree migrant labor." *Canadian Journal of Latin American and Caribbean Studies / Revue Canadienne des Études Latino-Américaines et Caraïbes, 40*(2), 274–293. https://doi.org/10.1080/08263663.2015.1054682

Smith, A.A. (2019). Toward a critique of political economy of "sociolegality" in settler capitalist Canada. In M.P. Thomas, L.F. Vosko, C. Fanelli, & O. Lyubchenko (Eds.), *Change and continuity: Canadian political economy in the new millennium*. Montreal and Kingston: McGill-Queen's University Press.

Spring, C. & Vosko, L. (under review with *Canadian Public Policy*). The price of activation: The relationship between international students' employment experiences and transitions to permanent residency in Canada.

Stasiulis, D., & Bakan, A.B. (1997). Negotiating citizenship: The case of foreign domestic workers in Canada. *Feminist Review, 57*(1), 112–139. https://doi .org/10.1080/014177897339687

Statistics Canada. (2020). *Canadian employer-employee dynamics database: 2020 vintage*. Toronto: Statistics Canada Research Data Centre, York University. Contract number: 1-MAPA-YRK-7112.

Statistics Canada (2023). *Canadian employer-employee dynamics database: 2023 vintage*. Statistics Canada Research Data Centre, York University. Contract number: 1-MAPA-YRK-7112

Stepwest. (2019). *Recognized Organization – International Experience Canada FAQs 2019*. Stepwest. https://www.stepwest.com/blog/recognized-organization -ro/recognized-organization-international-experience-canada-faqs-2019/

Stringer, C., & Michailova, S. (2019). *Understanding the exploitation of temporary migrant workers: A comparison of Australia, Canada, New Zealand and the United Kingdom*. Report prepared for Ministry of Business, Innovation and Employment. Auckland: University of Auckland Business School.

Suwandi, I. (2019). Labor-value commodity chains: The hidden abode of global production. *Monthly Review, 71*(3), 46–69.

Tham, J.-C., & Fudge, J. (2019). Unsavoury employer practices: Understanding temporary migrant work in the Australian food services sector. *International Journal of Comparative Labour Law and Industrial Relations, 35*(1). https:// kluwerlawonline.com/api/Product/CitationPDFURL?file=Journals\IJCL \IJCL2019002.pdf

Trumper, R., & Wong, L.L. (2007). Canada's guest workers: Racialized, gendered and flexible. In B.S. Bolaria & S.P. Hier (Eds.), *Race and racism in 21st-century Canada: Continuity, complexity, and change*. Guelph, ON: Broadview Press.

Tucker, E. (2020). Migrant workers and fissured workforces: CS Wind and the dilemmas of organizing intra-company transfers in Canada. *Economic and Industrial Democracy, 41*(2), 372–396. https://doi.org/10.1177 /0143831X17707822

Tucker, E.M., Marsden, S., & Vosko, L.F. (2020). Federal enforcement of migrant workers' labour rights in Canada: A research report. *Articles & Book Chapters*. https://digitalcommons.osgoode.yorku.ca/scholarly_works/2795

Tungohan, E. (2023) *Care activism: Migrant domestic workers, movement-building, and communities of care*. Champaign: University of Illinois Press.

Tungohan, E., Banerjee, R., Chu, W., Cleto, P., Leon, C., Garcia, M., Kelly, P., Luciano, M., Palmaria, C., & Sorio, C. (2015). After the live-in caregiver program: Filipina caregivers' experiences of graduated and uneven citizenship. *Canadian Ethnic Studies*, *47*, 87–105. https://doi.org/10.1353/ces.2015.0008

van den Hoonaard, W.C. (2003). Is anonymity an artifact in ethnographic research? *Journal of Academic Ethics*, *1*(2), 141–151. https://doi.org/10.1023/B:JAET.0000006919.58804.4c

Vosko, L.F. (2006). *Precarious employment: Understanding labour market insecurity in Canada*. Montreal and Kingston: McGill-Queen's Press.

Vosko, L.F. (2010). *Managing the margins: Gender, citizenship, and the international regulation of precarious employment*. Oxford: Oxford University Press.

Vosko, L.F. (2011). Out of the shadows? The non-binding multilateral framework on migration (2006) and prospects for using international labour regulation to forge global labour market membership. In G. Davidov and B. Langille, *The Idea of Labour Law* (pp. 365–384). Oxford: Oxford University Press.

Vosko, L.F. (2012). The Challenge of Expanding EI Coverage. In K. Banting & J. Medow (Eds.), *Making EI work: Research from the Mowat Centre Employment Insurance Task Force*. Montreal and Kingston: McGill Queen's University Press.

Vosko, L.F. (2018). "Legal but deportable: Institutionalized deportability and the limits of collective bargaining among participants in Canada's Seasonal Agricultural Workers Program." *ILR Review Special Issue on the Impact of Immigrant Legalization Initiatives: International Perspectives*. 71(4): 882–907. https://doi.org/10.1177/0019793918756055

Vosko, L.F. (2019). *Disrupting deportability: Transnational workers organize*. Ithaca, NY: Cornell University Press.

Vosko, L.F., et al. (2020). *Closing the enforcement gap: Improving employment standards protections for people in precarious jobs*. Toronto: University of Toronto Press.

Vosko, L.F. (2022). Through the back-door: How Australia and Canada use working holiday programs to fulfill demands for migrant work via cultural exchange. *Journal of Industrial Relations*, *65*(1), 88–111. https://doi.org/10.1177/00221856221131579

Vosko, L.F. (2023). Probationary precarity? Differential inclusion among post-graduation work permit-holders in Canada. *International Migration*. https://doi.org/10.1111/imig.13152

Vosko, L.F., Basok, T., & Spring, C. (2023). *Transnational employment strain in a global health pandemic: Migrant farmworkers in Canada*. Berlin: Springer Nature.

Vosko, L.F., & Spring. C. (2021). COVID-19 outbreaks in Canada and the crisis of migrant farmworkers' social reproduction: Transnational labor and the need for greater accountability among receiving states. *Journal of International Migration and Integration*: 1–27. https://doi.org/10.1007/s12134-021-00905-2

Walby, K., & Larsen, M. (2011). Getting at the live archive: On access to information research in Canada. *Canadian Journal of Law and Society, 26*, 623–633. https://doi.org/10.3138/cjls.26.3.623

Walters, W. (2015). Reflections on migration and governmentality. *Movements: Journal for Critical Migration and Border Regime Studies, 1*(1). http://movements-journal.org/issues/01.grenzregime/04.walters--migration.governmentality.html

Wimmer, A., & Glick Schiller, N. (2002). Methodological nationalism and beyond: Nation-state building, migration and the social sciences. *Global Networks (Oxford), 2*(4), 301–334. https://doi.org/10.1111/1471-0374.00043

Wimmer, A., & Schiller, N.G. (2002). Methodological nationalism, the social sciences, and the study of migration: An essay in historical epistemology. *International Migration Review, 37*(3), 576–610.

Wray, H. (2011). Regulating Marriage Migration into the UK: A stranger in the home. Farnham, UK: Ashgate. https://www.book2look.com/book/f5XdXeHgaR

Wray, H. (2022). What do states regulate when they regulate spousal migration? A study of France, the United Kingdom, the United States, and Denmark. In A-M d'Aoust (Ed.), *Transnational Marriage and Partner Migration: Constellation of Security, Citizenship, and Rights*. New Brunswick, NJ: Rutgers University Press. https://scholar.google.com/scholar?cluster=15679472226101017774&hl=en&oi=scholarr

Wright, C.F., & Clibborn, S. (2017). Back door, side door, or front door: An emerging de-factor low-skilled immigration policy in Australia. *Comparative Labor Law and Policy Journal, 39*, 165.

Yin, R.K. (2006). Mixed methods research: Are the methods genuinely integrated or merely parallel? *Spring, 13*(1), 41–47.

Yoon, K. (2014a). The racialised mobility of transnational working holidays. *Identities, 21*(5), 586–603. https://doi.org/10.1080/1070289X.2014.909815

Yoon, K. (2014b). Transnational youth mobility in the neoliberal economy of experience. *Journal of Youth Studies, 17*(8), 1014–1028. https://doi.org/10.1080/13676261.2013.878791

Yoon, K. (2015). A national construction of transnational mobility in the
   "overseas working holiday phenomenon: in Korea. *Journal of Intercultural
   Studies, 36*(1), 71–87. https://doi.org/10.1080/07256868.2014.990361
Zolberg, A.R. (1989). The next waves: Migration theory for a changing world.
   International Migration Review, 23(3), 403–430. https://doi.org/10.2307/2546422

Index

Page references in *italics* indicate tables and figures.

Studies in Comparative Political Economy and Public Policy